BOOK 2

SAFFRON SWORDS

52 Episodes of Sanatani Valor against Invaders

ॐ
Vande Mataram

Manoshi Sinha Rawal

गरुड

Published by
Garuda Prakashan Private Limited
Gurugram, India

www.garudabooks.com

First published in India 2022

ISBN: 979-8-8857-5023-3

Cover Design: Rakesh Chaudhary

Illustrations by: Hitharth S Bhatt

Printed in India

ॐ

ॐ श्रीसरस्वतयैनमः।।

शुक्लांब्रह्मविचारसारपरमांद्यांजगद्व्यापिनीं
वीणा-पुस्तक-धारिणीमभयदांजाड्यांधकारपहाम्।
हस्तेस्फाटिकमालिकांविदधतींपद्मासनेसंस्थिताम्
वन्देतांपरमेश्वरींभगवतींबुद्धिप्रदांशारदाम्।।

सत्यमेव जयते

भारत के उपराष्ट्रपति

VICE-PRESIDENT OF INDIA

MESSAGE

I am happy to know that a chronicle of the brave exploits of 52 warriors in defending the motherland against invaders is being published under the title 'Saffron Swords'. This is a sequel to an earlier book with the same title containing 52 episodes of valour of Indian men and women.

I have always maintained that the brave tales of all Indians, including many unsung heroes, who had fought against foreign invaders and the oppressive British rule, should be published in various Indian languages.

My compliments to the author, Smt Manoshi Sinha Rawal for writing this book and including stiores of women warriors like Velu Nachiyar, Kurma Devi and Rani Durgavati in the book.

Naidu.

(M. Venkaiah Naidu)

New Delhi
06th April, 2022.

Dedicated to

Mahendra Sinha, my father,

who instilled in me the love for History by narrating to me, since childhood, stories from the epics and scriptures, and inspiring tales of valor of our warrior ancestors.

Anupoma Sinha, my mother,

who taught me to love my thousands of years old Vedic and Sanatani culture, to believe in Krishna, to have faith in our pantheon of deities, and for teaching me persistence and of facing challenges with ease.

I am who I am because of them, my first Gurus in life and my inspiration.

Contents

Preface

History is like Hollywood and Bollywood. Every film has a story, so does History. Almost every film, irrespective of what the theme is, projects and portrays equally both, heroes and villains, so does History. But does Indian History follow this justification of equal portrayal of both sides? No! It is only a one-sided and biased narrative supplemented with distortions. Even that one-sided narrative portrays only one aspect. If we consider Indian History from the eighth century till 1947 in our academic books, it is a portrayal of only the invaders, looters, and plunderers projected in detail in good light. Where are the heroes and heroines of the soil in the textbooks? Only a counted, select few warriors, find a place in the textbooks.

Were we always defeated? Were we on the losing side always? Did our warrior ancestors easily surrender? Didn't our warrior ancestors offer resistance? These questions often lurk in lakhs of *Bharatiya* (Indian) minds because we have been projected as losers and as always having been defeated. A sense of inferiority complex and avoiding remembrance of the past thousand years prevail in our minds. This is a result of the one-sided, biased, and distorted historical narrative fed to us for decades. And this happens to such an extent that one robotically tends to think that all that is from foreign lands is better than what we have here.

But the truth is different. There are lakhs of warriors from the east to west, north to south–warriors who put up a brave resistance against Muslim invaders, rulers, and plunderers in battle and against British oppression. But their stories are missing in our history textbooks. When our history books blank the exploits of the warriors of the soil and when we read only about defeats, and no resistance by our ancestors, we end up alienating ourselves from a sense of belongingness for the nation. We do not know about our own historical roots. Hence, History needs to be retold.

We are the oldest surviving civilization in the world. Despite 1,300-plus years of loot, plunder, genocide, and atrocities, our civilization is still in existence. Many civilizations perished as a result of invasions. This is clear evidence of how over a period of 1,300-plus years, our warrior ancestors from all walks of life consistently resisted and sacrificed their lives to defend *Dharma* and the motherland. Marcus Garvey, a Jamaican-born political leader, and social activist rightly said: "A people without knowledge of their past history, origin, and culture is like a tree without roots." The objective behind writing *Saffron Swords* is to present to the citizens of the country and the world our past history, our roots–about the brave exploits of our warriors of the last 1,300 plus years. This book is an effort to bring to the readers, the centuries of Indic resistance to invaders–tales of valor which we should feel proud of.

Yogaditya Singh Rawal, research partner, especially on visits to historical sites across the country, and co-author of *Saffron Swords* Part I, says: "Let us trace the path of finding and knowing about the valor which we seldom or have never read before, about heroes we never knew existed. Let us read about the stratagems, the pure valor, and the strength of our brave warriors who decimated the invaders."

There are 52 episodes of Indian valor in this book. Many of these warriors are unheard of. Few names are Dantidurga II, Rani Durgavati, Rani Bhavashankari, Samgramaraja, Chennabhairadevi, Sangoli Rayanna, Bhoja Paramara, Pratapaditya, Krishnadevaraya, Kurma Devi, Dhan Singh Gurjar, U. Kiang Nangbah, Chhatrasal, Birsa Munda, and Prafulla Kumari Devi. All of these warriors put up a brave resistance against Muslim rulers and British supremacy. Few of these warriors won battles against Mughals, Turks, Lodhis, Sultanates, and the British.

This is Volume II of *Saffron Swords*. Through Volume I of the book, comprising of 52 episodes of valor, we have been able to kindle thousands of minds of all age groups to relive the glory of our past 1,300-plus years. There will be several volumes in this series with each volume portraying 52 episodes of valor of our warrior ancestors.

Saffron Swords is based on years of research that include visits to historical sites, meeting freedom fighters, descendants of freedom fighters and warrior ancestors, interpretations based on epigraphs and inscriptions, available historical records in the form of gazettes, and books written by both Indian and foreign historians over a period of several centuries. Few stories of valor, besides being based on one or more of the above research criteria, are also anchored in historical and cultural folklore from various regions. This statement: "Without adequate exploration of folk culture, rewriting of people's histories will always be incomplete"–quoted by Badri Narayan in the article *'Popular Culture and 1857: A Memory against Forgetting'* in *Social Scientist* journal, citing from two reference books on History, holds ground on the folklore aspect. The book has a reference section, in the end, wherein all literary sources for each episode of heroism are mentioned.

A rich heritage and culture identify India. Let's bask in the glory, the valor of our ancestors.

–Manoshi Sinha Rawal

1

Kurma Devi

Chittor Rani Who Defeated and Wounded Qutb al-Din Aibak

Kurma Devi! Very few from Rajasthan and almost none from the rest of India know her!!! This Queen Regent of Chittorgarh defeated Qutb al-Din Aibak and wounded him in a battle near Amber. Since ancient times, Indian women not only proved themselves as leaders and administrators but also exhibited great courage on the battlefield. When Chittorgarh faced an emergency, Kurma Devi played the role of Shakti, saving her kingdom from Islamic invaders. According to the book *Annals and Antiquities of Rajasthan*, Vol. I by Lt. Col. James Tod, nine neighboring kings, and 11 chiefs extended their help to the Rani in that battle. The victorious battle of the Hindus against foreign invaders debunks the fake narrative that Indian kings were not united in battle against enemies.

In the early medieval period, Chittorgarh was a principality of the Mewar kingdom. Udaipur, Pirawa, Neemuch, Bhilwara, Rajsamand, including parts of Madhya Pradesh (Mandsaur), and parts of Gujarat were also parts of Mewar. Chittorgarh was the main base. Mewar's defense was the formidable and well-fortified Chittor Fort, built during the seventh century. This fort, spread across 700 acres, had stood robust against the tides of time and attacks! This region carries a legacy of valor and bravery right from the time of Bappa Rawal, who decimated the Arabs in battle during the eighth century.

During the latter half of the 12th century, Samar Singh was the ruler of Mewar with the capital at Chittorgarh. Samar Singh was a descendent of Bappa Rawal. He married Kurma Devi in 1170 CE and Prithi Bai, the sister of Raja Prithviraj Chauhan in 1171 CE.

Written historical records mention the valor of Kurma Devi (also spelled Kurmadevi, Kormatdevi, Korma Devi), but do not mention her parents or childhood. According to historical folklore, she is described as the daughter of Naiki Devi, the Chalukyan queen of Gujarat. Lt. Col. James Tod's book *Annals and Antiquities of Rajasthan: The Central and Western Rajpoot States of India*–Vol. I mentions Kurma Devi as the princess of Putun (Patan in Gujarat, the capital of the Chalukyan kingdom). This reference also suggests her as a Chalukyan princess and thus the daughter of Naiki Devi. Among Samar Singh's sons were Kalyan Rai from Prithi Bai and Karna Singh from Kurma Devi.

Samar Singh's contemporary was Raja Prithviraj Chauhan (Prithviraj III), also known as Rai Pithora. We have read about the several battles between Mohd Ghori and Prithviraj Chauhan, and how the latter pardoned the former every time he was defeated. In the final battle–the Battle of Tarain in 1192 CE against Mohd Ghori, Prithviraj Chauhan sought the alliance of several neighboring Hindu kings. Raja Samar Singh along with his elder son Kalyan Rai not only extended military support to Prithviraj Chauhan with an army but also themselves participated in the battle.

Muhammad Ghori, the co-Sultan of the Ghurid Empire of Afghanistan led the first Indian expedition against Mularaja II, the Chalukyan ruler of Gujarat in 1178. As Mularaja II was a minor, his mother Rani Naiki Devi was then the Queen Regent. In the fierce battle that took place between the two forces, Rani Naiki Devi defeated Mohd Ghori and his forces at the Battle of Kayadara. The Queen had the military support of numerous neighboring Hindu feudatory chiefs. So devastating was his defeat and so heavy were the casualties on his side that Muhammad Ghori retreated to Afghanistan and avoided the idea of attacking India for the next several years. In the final Battle of Tarain in 1192 CE and all of Ghori's military exploits, Qutb al-Din Aibak steered the forces as the chief general.

Raja Samar Singh and Kalyan Rai attained *Veergati* on the battlefield in the Battle of Tarain. Prithviraj Chauhan was taken prisoner. One of the key reasons why Prithviraj Chauhan lost was the surprise attack by Ghori at night before dawn. Since time immemorial, the Hindu army always followed rules of Dharma in warfare wherein battles were fought only between sunrise and sunset. Treachery was a part of the strategy of Islamic invaders, hence, Ghori's attack at night when the city was asleep. Besides, not all Hindu allies with their army reached the battlefield and many of the allied forces were on their way towards Chauhan's kingdom when Ghori attacked. The available Hindu army immediately made formations and offered resistance but in vain.

The news of the defeat of Prithviraj Chauhan and martyrdom of Raja Samar Singh and Kalyan Rai reached Mewar. Prithi Bai, due to her triple loss–defeat of her brother, death of her husband and son, no longer desired to live. She jumped into the funeral pyre of her husband. Karna Singh was then a minor, aged 12 years. Kurma Devi became the Queen Regent of her kingdom and pledged to attack Ghori.

Meanwhile, Muhammad Ghori had retreated to Multan, leaving Qutb al-Din Aibak in-charge of Delhi and Ajmer. Qutb al-Din Aibak was a native of Turkistan. During his childhood, he was sold as a slave to a Qazi at Nishapur in Persia. Under the Qazi, Aibak learned the art of warfare including horse-riding and archery. The Qazi then sold him

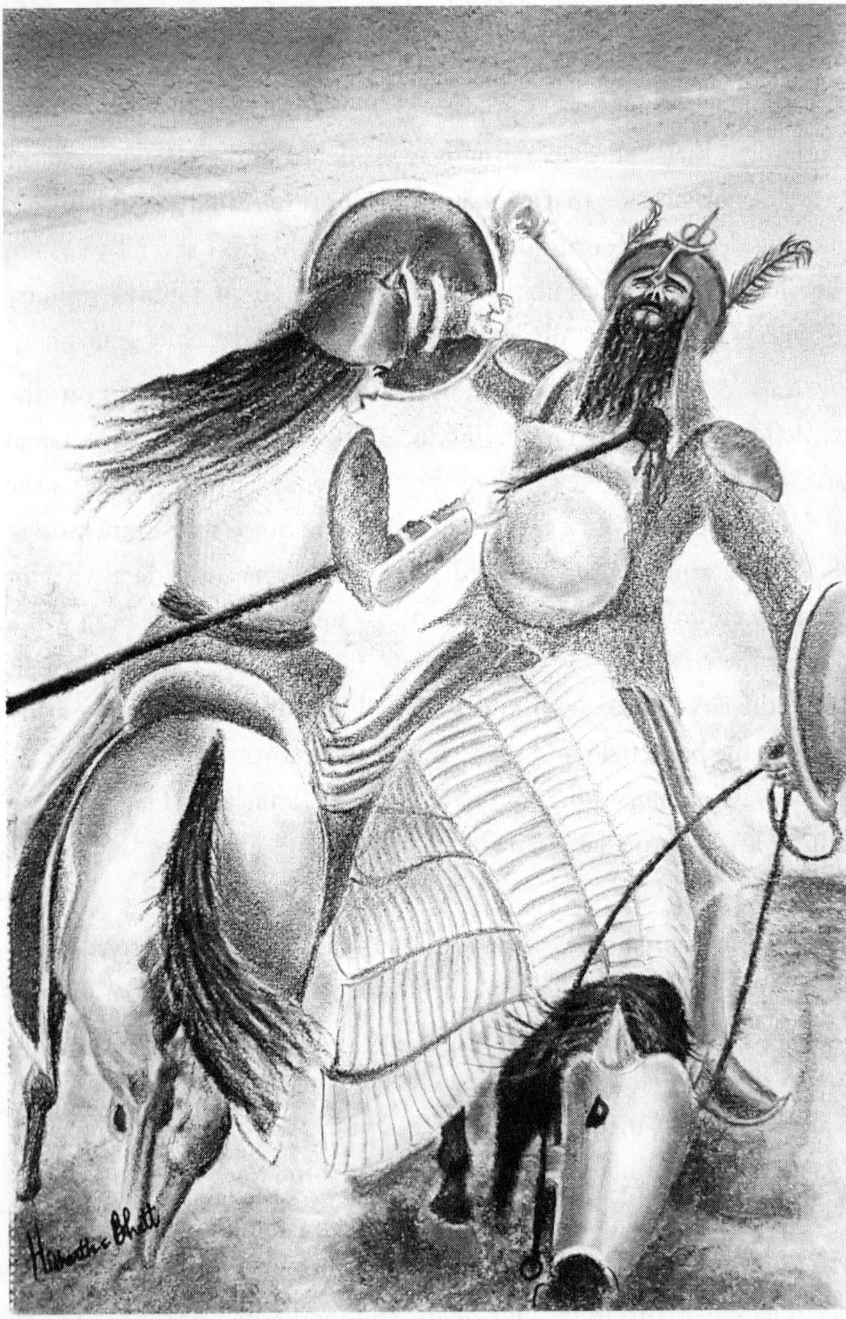

Kurma Devi attacking and injuring Qutb al-Din Aibak in battle

to Muhammad Ghori in Ghazni. Soon he rose to the position of a general from a mere officer at the stables by dint of his skills and dedication. He became a favorite of Ghori. After the death of Ghori, Aibak declared himself the Sultan of Delhi. As he was a slave, his dynasty came to be known as the Slave Dynasty.

Kurma Devi decided to attack Qutb al-Din Aibak. Her mother Naiki Devi too had become a widow and as her son, the heir to the throne was a minor, she undertook the responsibilities of her kingdom and led from the front in battles. Drawing inspiration from her mother's brave exploits, Kurma Devi built her forces, garnering support from neighboring Hindu rulers. Mewar had lost a huge force in the 2nd Battle of Tarain. Kurma Devi re-strengthened the Mewari forces in no time.

In 1193, with the support of nine kings from neighboring kingdoms and eleven feudatory chiefs, Rani Kurma Devi marched towards Delhi, leading from the front. Meanwhile, during the same time, Aibak and his army were advancing towards Mewar. Both the forces met at Amber, today's Jaipur. *Annals and Antiquities of Rajasthan*, Vol. I by Lt. Col. James Tod describes how both the armies met near Amber. According to this book, Kurma Devi entered the battlefield after her general fell wounded.

Kurma Devi motivated her forces like never before. She addressed the soldiers and hailed their bravery and together pledged to fight and die for the motherland. Stimulated, the Hindu army fell upon the enemy forces like lions on their prey. With sword swinging high, killing the Ghurid soldiers as fast as the lightning's stroke, Kurma Devi drove deep into the ranks of Aibak's army. She marched towards Qutb al-Din Aibak. She soon confronted Aibak and challenged him to a personal duel. In the fight that followed, Kurma Devi wounded Aibak so severely that the latter fell from his horse on the battlefield. His forces started dispersing seeing his fall. Surmising him to be dead, a victorious Kurma Devi left the battlefield and marched towards Chittorgarh. But the heavily wounded Aibak was not dead. His followers managed to take him out of the battlefield to safety and provided him medical care.

Back at Chittorgarh, Kurma Devi installed her 13-year-old son Karna Singh to the throne of Mewar. According to historical folklore, she lit a pyre and immolated herself, as she desired no longer to live without her husband. She considered it equivalent to burning herself at the funeral pyre of her husband.

Qutb al-Din Aibak recovered and had declared himself as the Sultan of Delhi. He destroyed the ancient Vishnu temple and Nakshatra temples and renamed the site with the tower as Qutub Minar. After a few years, he marched towards Mewar with a huge army to avenge his defeat at the hands of a woman warrior. He plundered the city and looted its wealth. He took Karna Singh prisoner along with the king's ornamented horse Subhrak to Lahore. Karna Singh tried to escape but in vain.

In 1210, Aibak ordered the beheading of Karna Singh in Lahore at a polo match ground. He decided to play the polo match with Karna's head. As decided, he arrived at the venue riding on Subhrak. Karna Singh was in chains. Subhrak instantaneously recognized his master. When the Hindu king was released from his chains for the execution, Subhrak suddenly turned violent and uncontrollable. Qutb al-Din Aibak fell to the ground and Subhrak attacked the enemy Sultan several times. Aibak died on the spot. Before Aibak's army realized what happened, Subhrak ran towards his master. In seconds, Karna Singh mounted his horse and soon vanished. It was only after Subhrak reached safely the boundary of the Mewari kingdom that he fell dead. Karna Singh mourned aloud the loss of his loyal horse.

2

Rani Durgavati

Resisted Malwa Sultan and Mughals

A warrior, an expert in the art of warfare, and an ace hunter since childhood, married at age 18, became mother at 21, was widowed at 26, ruler of the Gondwana kingdom at 26, and attained *Veergati* (martyrdom) at 40! She is Rani Durgavati. Her chronicle is a saga of valor, romance, versatility, gallantry, and preserving womanly honor! Rani Durgavati truly personifies the warrior Goddess! She led many battles to victory including one against Baz Bahadur, the Sultan of Malwa, and two against Mughals, herself commanding her army. It was in the third battle that Rani Durgavati lost against Akbar's Mughal forces where she attained *Veergati.*

Rani Durgavati was born on 5th October 1524 at Kalinjar Fort in the Chandela royal family of Bundelkhand. Her father Keerat Rai was the ruler of Mahoba. This region is well-known for the heroic exploits of Alha-Udal, two brave commanders of the then Chandela king Paramardideva, a contemporary of Prithviraj Chauhan. Kalinjar was a hill fortress city, now located in the Banda district of Uttar Pradesh (UP). The fortress, which originally existed since the Gupta period with several temples, had been the center of attraction for possession for many neighboring rulers including Islamic invaders. A Chandela king, whose base was at Kalinjar Fort, stopped the advances of Mahmud of Ghazni from destroying the Khajuraho groups of temples by paying a huge ransom. Khajuraho temples were built by the Chandelas. Both Kalinjar Fort and the kingdom of Mahoba carry a legacy of protecting Dharma. Rani Durgavati, who belonged to this kingdom, carried forward this legacy with her heroic exploits.

As Durgavati grew up, her beauty and exceptional intelligence were the talk of Mahoba and nearby kingdoms. Keerat Rai wanted his daughter to learn all the arts and skills required of a future ruler. He provided her all the facilities in the royal household. Soon, Durgavati became an expert in the sciences, politics, administration, art of warfare including the use of guns, archery, sword-fight, horse-riding, and hunting. Both father and daughter loved hunting and the duo often went together to the jungles to pursue their favorite pastime. When her father would not be accompanying, Durgavati, at times, would go hunting all alone.

Durgavati's fame as an expert hunter, especially of tigers, spread far and wide. Abu'l-Fazl ibn Mubarak, the author of *Akbarnamah*, the grand vizier and one of the nine jewels at Mughal ruler Akbar's court, wrote about Durgavati thus quoted in the book *Ideals, Images, and Real Lives: Women in Literature and History*, edited by Alice Thorner and Maithreyi Krishna Raj: "She was a good shot with gun and arrow, and continually went hunting and shot animals of the chase with her gun. It was her custom that whenever she heard that a tiger had made his appearance she did not drink water till she had shot him."

During a hunting expedition in the jungles of the Vindhya hills, Durgavati chanced to meet Dalpat Shah, the eldest son of Sangram Shah, the ruler of Garh Mandla kingdom of Gondwana. Sangram Shah, who was the 48th ruler of the Gond dynasty of tribal origin, was known far and wide for conquering 52 forts and never losing a battle in his life. He constructed the Chauragarh Fort, commemorating his victories. A Sanskrit scholar, he wrote a book in Sanskrit titled *Rasratnamala* and patronized education in his kingdom.

Durgavati met Dalpat Shah as strangers but both started appreciating each other at the very first meeting. The very sight of the beautiful Durgavati riding her horse and aiming at the target with her bows and arrows in precision stole Dalpat Shah's heart. Durgavati, at the same time, admired the handsome young prince for his invincible traits. Both happened to rest for some time at the same spot. The accidental meeting soon ended up with an exchange of words. They spoke little but when they parted both longed for each other at heart.

Both Durgavati and Dalpat Shah were of marriageable age. Meanwhile, Raja Keerat Rai had been looking for a suitable groom for his daughter. The Chandelas being Rajputs, Keerat Rai was looking for an able Rajput prince. Finally, he found a groom and gave word to the groom's father. During the same time, Raja Sangram Shah sent a messenger to the court of Raja Keerat Rai seeking Durgavati's hand as a bride for his son Dalpat Shah. It was quite probable that Dalpat Shah confessed to his father about his love for the Chandela princess. Keerat Rai had already pledged to give his daughter in marriage to a Rajput prince. Hence, he expressed his regret rejecting the proposal. Durgavati came to know about it. She would not let that happen, as she loved Dalpat Shah too. An idea struck her mind and she immediately wrote a letter, addressed to Dalpat Shah. She was just on time to give the letter to the Gondwana messenger and asked him to deliver it to the eldest Gondwana prince. In that letter, Durgavati confessed her love for Dalpat Shah at the same time inviting him against her father's wishes and pledge, to take her away by any means and make her his queen.

Dalpat Shah was thrilled upon receiving Durgavati's letter. He expressed his interest to his father Sangram Shah in bringing and marrying the Chandela princess even at the cost of war if Raja Keerat Rai rejected a second time. Raja Sangram Shah agreed. Dalpat Shah reached Mahoba with a huge army. He again sent word to the Chandela king, asking his daughter's hand in marriage. The Chandela king rejected the marriage proposal once again as he would not break his pledge. Dalpat Shah besieged Mahoba, defeated Raja Keerat Rai, and carried away Durgavati to the Garh Mandla kingdom. Their marriage was consummated soon after in 1542. Raja Keerat Rai and Raja Sangram Singh became friends soon after. The alliance proved to be a boon for Raja Keerat Rai. He was able to successfully resist the advances of Sher Shah Suri with military support from the Gond ruler in 1545. Meanwhile, in 1545, Rani Durgavati gave birth to a son named Vir Narayan.

Four years later, Raja Sangram Shah died and Dalpat Shah succeeded him as the king of the Garh Mandla kingdom around 1548. Soon after ascending the throne, Raja Dalpat Shah often toured his kingdom to closely study the needs of his people. In 1550, during one of these tours, Dalpat Shah's horse suddenly went berserk and the king fell from his horse down a rough gorge. He was heavily injured. He died soon after he returned home.

As Vir Narayan, the heir to the throne was only five years old, Durgavati took charge of the Garh Mandla kingdom as Queen Regent. In no time, she undertook a number of developmental works for the welfare and prosperity of her subjects. She strengthened her military base and infrastructure. She herself looked after the military unit and ensured maintaining strict discipline required of soldiers. According to an account by Abu'l-Fazl, Rani Durgavati had 20,000 good cavalry and 1,000 famous elephants. The region was also known for wild elephants. She shifted her capital base to the strategically located Chauragarh Fort from Singaurgarh Fort. To avert possible drought situations, she dug up several large reservoirs across her kingdom so that enough water was stored. Rani Tal near Jabalpur is the existing reservoir built by the queen. In areas where wild beasts were more in number, which affected the safety of residents, she cleared the area and facilitated cultivation. Rani Durgavati personally looked after the revenue and ensured prompt payments. This made the people as well as the kingdom wealthier. She enacted numerous reforms to the advantage of her subjects.

The prosperity of the Garh Mandla kingdom soon invited invasions from neighboring regions as well as Islamic rulers. Rani Durgavati defeated them all, she led the armies on the battlefield. Amongst the Islamic invaders, she defeated Baz Bahadur, the Sultan of Malwa, and the Mughals twice. Many historians including Akbar's Navaratna Abu'l-Fazl ibn Mubarak sang praises about the queen's victories in battle in their writings. To quote from *Ideals, Images, and Real Lives: Women in Literature and History*, Rani Durgavati "inflicted two defeats on the Mughal invaders". To quote Abu'l-Fazl ibn Mubarak as depicted in *Mughal Empire in India: 1526-1761, Part I*, by S.R. Sharma, Rani Durgavati "had great contests with Baz Bahadur and the Miahs, and was always victorious". The Miahs refer to the Islamic soldiers. There are no detailed descriptions but only mentions about Rani Durgavati's battle victories against the foreigners.

Rani Durgavati inflicted a crushing defeat on Miyan Bayezid Baz Bahadur Khan (more popular as Baz Bahadur), the Sultan of Malwa when the latter attacked her kingdom in 1557. Baz Bahadur came with a large force. The battle took place on the plains of the Narmada. Rani Durgavati herself led the battle. The Gonds, in no time, outflanked the Muslim army. Baz Bahadur could not withstand the furious charge of

Rani Durgavati's forces and his army experienced major casualties. He fled with his surviving forces. Baz Bahadur was so badly defeated that he never dared to attack the Gondwana kingdom again. *Tarikh-i Alfi* written by Akbar's court historians as quoted in *Mughal Empire in India: 1526-1761, Part I* described Gondwana as a region 'which had never been conquered by any ruler of Hindustan since the rise of the faith of Islam'.

The year 1564 proved a turning point for Rani Durgavati and the Gondwana kingdom. She was then aged 40. Meanwhile, Vir Narayan, then aged 19, became an expert in the art of warfare. During this time the Malwa kingdom had already fallen in the hands of the Mughals. Akbar was then the Mughal ruler. In 1561, Mughal forces captured Malwa and Baz Bahadur fled to Khandesh; the latter regained his kingdom for a brief period. Mughals attacked Malwa again and the region was finally annexed to the Mughal dominion after Baz Bahadur died in 1562. Akbar entrusted Asaf Khan to look after this part of the Mughal dominion. Malwa geographically touched one part of the borders of the Gondwana boundaries. Asaf Khan heard a lot about the wealth of Gondwana. Akbar allowed Asaf Khan to attack Gondwana in 1564.

The Mughals under the commandment of Asaf Khan attacked Gondwana. Given the might of the Mughal army, Durgavati's courtiers advised the Rani to avoid resistance. But the Rani would neither surrender nor flee. She was resolute to offer resistance and save her kingdom. Rani Durgavati herself commanded her forces along with her son Vir Narayan with an army of 20,000 men defended by an array of 1,000 elephants. The Mughals were outnumbered and were armed with ammunition, which the Gondwana army lacked. Sounds of war drums, conch shells, and war cries echoed in the air as the battle began. Three battles took place between Rani Durgavati's forces and the Mughals near the fort of Singorgarh. According to the book *Ideals, Images, and Real Lives: Women in Literature and History:* "Cloaked in armour, mounted on an elephant, with her bow and quiver lying by her side and with a burnished lance in her hand, the Rani herself led the troops, even in opposition to the advice of her officers." The Rani defeated the Mughals twice.

In the third battle against the Mughals, Durgavati took up a strong position in a narrow mountain pass. As the battle began, the Gonds were resisting bravely. The Mughals' use of guns proved advantageous, which injured the elephants, which in turn ran berserk, harming the Gonds. And then Vir Narayan fell wounded and taken prisoner by the enemy forces. That demoralized the Gonds and many retreated from the battlefield, leaving Rani Durgavati with only a faithful band of soldiers. The Rani, positioned on her elephant, continued her resistance, killing the Mughal soldiers one after another with her bows and arrows. Her faithful followers begged her to retreat. But she continued to fight. A stray arrow struck her eye, yet she refused to leave despite being requested again to retreat. And she continued to fight. Meanwhile, her small group of soldiers dwindled fast in front of her eyes as the enemy bullets hit them. Yet, undeterred, she continued shooting arrows at the Mughal soldiers unabated. And then another arrow hit her neck. She fell back but immediately sat up and continued to fight. Her mahout begged to retreat, ready to take the mighty elephant out of the battlefield. Durgavati replied that she would either drive away the enemy or attain *Veergati* fighting on the battlefield. She knew her son might not be alive. With the wounds and the pain, with blood drenching her, Rani Durgavati was persistent in attacking the Mughals, until almost all of her soldiers attained *Veergati* in front of her eyes. Now the enemies approached her. Durgavati would not let them take her prisoner or touch her alive. She preferred death to dishonor. The enemies were about to capture her when she bent forward from the howdah of her elephant, snatched the dagger from the girdle of the mahout at a lightning pace, and plunged it into her stomach. And she attained *Veergati*.

The Mughals plundered the Gondwana kingdom and looted all the wealth from the royal treasury. They killed most of the youth. The women committed *jauhar* (self-immolation) to save their honor.

According to local historical folklore, the sound of war drums and war cries still echoes through the mountain air. Not a battle did the Gonds lose earlier. And the echoes seem to tell loud that they are ready to fight and decimate the enemies!

Naman and tributes to Rani Durgavati, one of the bravest daughters of Bharat Mata. Vande Mataram!

3

Gangu Mehtar

Killed Nearly 150 Britishers in 1857

Not many have heard about freedom fighter Gangu Mehtar, also known as Ganga Baba, Gangu Baba, and Ganga Din. The War of Independence of 1857 that shook the colonial dominion in India was a series of uprisings against the British in several parts across the country, spanning several months. One of the major hotspots of the fight for freedom was Kanpur, then known as Cawnpore. Gangu Mehtar alone killed nearly 150 Britishers in 1857 in Kanpur. He was employed as a soldier in Peshwa Nana Saheb's army. Later he was hanged by the British. The valor and sacrifice of Gangu Mehtar and thousands of freedom fighters have not been acknowledged in our history textbooks.

Gangu Mehtar hailed from Bithoor village in the district of today's Kanpur in Uttar Pradesh. He was born in a Valmiki family, a community or Sampradaya that traces their tradition to Maharishi Valmiki, who composed the *Ramayana* in *Treta Yuga*. Valmikis also have a legacy of warriorhood. Sadly, years of foreign rule and colonialism led to the creation of caste conflicts that are plaguing the country at present–one of the reasons how groups of this community have been labeled as Dalits. Lakhs of *Bharatiyas* (Indians) from each and every corner of *Bharat* from all walks of life, right from householders to farmers, cleaners to barbers, wrestlers to musicians, writers to cooks, took the role of Kshatriyas and defended Dharma and the motherland.

Going by the definition of varna described in the *Bhagavad Gita* and *Manusmriti* (ancient legal text and Constitution), all who defended Dharma and the motherland are Kshatriyas. Hence, Gangu Mehtar, by dint of his *karma* (work or profession), was a Kshatriya. Even Valmiki, born a Brahmin, became a Shudra by *karma*, as he was a robber for several years. Later, from a Shudra, he again turned into a Brahmin by dint of his *karma*. This episode of Valmiki finds description in the *Skanda Purana* as interpreted by J.L. Shastri in *The Skanda Purana, Part 17, (Ancient Indian Tradition and Mythology Series, Vol. LXV).*

Gangu Mehtar was very brave, strong, and kind from his childhood. A well-built physique further added to his passion for practicing wrestling as he grew up. Though he was poor, he helped the needy when they sought his help. If he saw someone hungry, he would give his own food to him/ her and remained hungry. If he saw a poorer person devoid of warm clothes on a wintry day, he would give him/ her his own blanket or winter wear. He was so strong that he had the ability to do any difficult manual task effortlessly.

The brave wrestler was also an expert in hunting without the use of advanced hunting equipment. He had the ability to fight against two tigers together. Gangu Mehtar's house was located near a forest. If in the night, he heard a deer crying for help to be freed from the clutches of its predator, he would immediately leave for the forest to save the animal. He had a track record of saving deer from tigers' clutches in the forest. Gangu Mehtar became popular in his region

Gangu Mehtar carrying a dead tiger on his back; Peshwa Nana Saheb with his army watching in awe.

owing to those traits. Everyone including the young and the old, irrespective of caste, creed, and riches, admired and respected him.

In 1857, the War of Independence had already begun. Nana Saheb, the adopted son of Peshwa Baji Rao II, strategized on leading the rebellion in Kanpur and his operations against the British had by then begun. Peshwa Baji Rao II enjoyed the rights of a Peshwa with certain limitations. After the death of Baji Rao II, the British refused to continue the pension that Nana Saheb was entitled to as a successor. Besides, the British laid more restrictions on his other entitlements.

During this time, Nana Saheb happened to pass by the jungle route where he chanced to meet the young and well-built Gangu Mehtar. What he saw surprised and startled him, and forced him to stop. Gangu was carrying a dead tiger on his back and walking at ease! He was returning from the forest. Seeing the Peshwa and his army stopping in front of him, Gangu Mehtar stopped too. The Peshwa asked him how he managed to carry such a heavy tiger, heavier than the latter's body weight. When the Peshwa learned that Gangu Mehtar had killed the tiger single-handedly without using any hunting weapon, he was full of praise for him. He immediately asked him to join his army. Gangu Mehtar readily agreed. He was only looking for such an opportunity to fight for the freedom of the country. He hated the British and had said to people around him: "This soil, our motherland, smells of the sacrifice made by our ancestors to make Her free. This land will be free one day." His words indeed came true!

The Indian War of Independence of 1857 by Vinayak Damodar Savarkar describes the lead role played by Peshwa Nana Saheb in leading the 1857 rebellion in Kanpur. Ganga Deen finds mention in the book as a *Subahdar* (official) in his army, but there is no detailed description about him except the fact that all the troops under their respected Subahdars wreaked havoc on the British.

Nana Saheb had a troop of around 4,000 soldiers. The troops helped the Peshwa not only capture Kanpur from the British, killing many Britishers during the act but also execute the survivors. Gangu Mehtar alone killed nearly 150 British soldiers with his sword. Uncountable Britishers including their family of women and children were killed by Nana Saheb's army. That was one reason why Gangu Mehtar was accused by the British as a criminal–a murderer of women and children. But the British themselves committed brutal atrocities on Indian men, women, and children, mercilessly killing them at many places before the 1857 rebellion. The Peshwa became the ruler of Kanpur for a few days until the British captured it back.

British labeled many freedom fighters, Dharmic warriors, and clans/ communities, who fought against them, as robbers, dacoits, thieves, rogues, and looters. The key reason was that these groups of people never recognized British supremacy and never took a favor from them. Colonial historians then created literature against them. The British also created a fake story on Gangu Mehtar, labeling him a criminal. Over 300 clans and tribes today in independent India are still tagged the way the British tagged them, though many legally got rid of the labels soon after independence. The British created this fake labeling and it is a pity and disgrace that we Indians have been aggressively carrying forward this colonial legacy.

The British, enraged at Gangu Mehtar's act, tried to catch him dead or alive. After several days of effort, they caught him a few miles away from Kanpur. The fact that he killed one of the highest numbers of Britishers made them mad in anger. They left no stone unturned in torturing him to death. They tied him to the back of a horse and dragged him to Kanpur. The brave freedom fighter survived the brutal torture till he covered the distance of several miles to the city, bleeding with wounds all over his body. Yet he was the least affected in spirits.

The merciless British then hanged him to death from a neem tree in Chunniganj in Kanpur.

A few years ago, the Valmiki community collected funds and commissioned a statue of Gangu Mehtar. The statue was installed in Chunniganj at the place where he attained martyrdom.

The nation, till eternity, will always remain indebted to Gangu Mehtar for his brave role in the 1857 War of Independence. Vande Mataram! Jai Hind!!!

4

Rani Bhavashankari

Defeated Pathans, Retained Hindu Supremacy in Bhurishrestha

Rani Bhavashankari Roy, also known as Tigress, is a complete stranger to crores of Indians. She was the ruler of the Bhurishrestha Kingdom of Bengal. Despite an attack by the Pathans and treachery by her own minister, she retained Hindu supremacy in her region. She herself led armies to battle and defeated the Pathans. Her feats of bravery, her way of handling enemies, and the affairs of her kingdom were the subjects of discussion beyond her geographical boundaries. Akbar, who was then the Mughal ruler, dared not to interfere in her sovereignty. Folklores and ballads of Bengal plenteously glorify her tale of valor, yet not everyone, even at the regional level, knows about her exploits today.

Bhavashankari was born as Bhavashankari Chaudhuri in Pendo Basantapur to a Brahmin family in Bhurishrestha, also called Bhurshut. She was the daughter of Dinanath Chaudhuri, a Nayak who served under the commander of Pendo Fort. The Bhurishrestha kingdom then had three main forts in Garh Bhabanipur, Pendo Basantapur, and Rajbalhat. Raja Rudranarayan was the king. Dinanath Chaudhuri, who was well trained in the art of warfare, commanded a troop of more than one thousand soldiers, and led armies into battle. Going by the varna system prevalent in ancient, medieval, and pre-colonial times, one's varna was judged not by birth but by profession and karma. Dinanath Chaudhuri, born a Brahmin, became a Kshatriya. So was Bhavashankari. There are many such examples from Puranic history wherein Asamanj (Lord Rama's ancestor), born a Kshatriya became a Shudra. Kavash Ailush, born a Shudra, became a Brahmin. Vishwamitra, who was born a Kshatriya, became a Brahmin. The list goes on.

During her childhood, Bhavashankari lost her mother when her brother was born. The little girl grew up under the care and guidance of her father. Dinanath Chaudhuri not only trained people under him but also his daughter in warfare. In the premises of the Pendo Fort, where she was born, Bhavashankari soon became an expert in horse-riding, swordsmanship, and archery. Dressed as a soldier in battle, she often accompanied her father during his military campaigns. The young warrior daughter took lessons in different subjects, ranging from politics, sociology, philosophy to war, diplomacy, and theology. Dinanath Chaudhuri encouraged the youth around him to be militarily trained so that the motherland could be defended in case an emergency arose–a trait that Bhavashankari nurtured and implemented during her reign.

Bhavashankari had pledged to marry the man who would defeat her in a sword fight. But this pledge was never fulfilled. Instead of getting married to a commoner, she was married to Rudranarayan, the king of Bhurishrestha. There is an interesting incident of bravery that led to the consummation of Bhavashankari's marriage with the king. She often went hunting in the forests. One day while hunting a deer with a spear, she was attacked by a herd of wild bisons. Raja Rudranarayan happened to be passing by that route, but the brave warrior girl was unaware about his presence. The king was awestruck seeing Bhavashankari single-handedly killing a bison and driving away the rest of the herd with the spear in no time. The sight enthralled him. The king at once decided to marry her. And the royal marriage took place soon after.

The Bhurishrestha kingdom, also called Bhurshut, comprised present Howrah and Hooghly districts. It was earlier ruled by Sur kings followed by different feudatory kings, including the Dhibar dynasty. In the late 15th century, the region fell under the rule of Roys, a Brahmin family. Krishna Roy established the Brahmin dynasty, also called Bharadwaj Dynasty in Bhurishrestha. From his maternal side, he was the grandson of Raja Chaturanan Neogi of Garh Bhawanipur kingdom, who dethroned the last Dhibar king. From his paternal side, he belonged to the Mukhti royal family of Phulia. He ruled only for a year and was succeeded by his son Shivanarayan. Raja Rudranarayan was the grandson of Krishna Roy. According to the book *Paschim Banger Sanskriti* by Binoy Ghosh, this dynasty ruled Bhurishrestha for around 200 years.

Bhavashankari's dwelling after her marriage was the royal palace at Damodar, outside the fort of Garh Bhawanipur. The king started seeking her advice on all matters related to administration and the military, given her expertise on the said subjects.

Bhavashankari was a staunch devotee of Devi Rajvallabhi (a form of Goddess Chandi) and Mahadev. The Goddess was her *Kuldevi* (patron deity). It is believed that the queen received a sword as a boon from the Goddess. Bhavashankari offered prayers to the Goddess with a wish that no man would ever be able to defeat her in a battle. She remained on fast seeking blessings from the Goddess. On the third day, a divine hearing from the Goddess led the queen to end her fast. Following the instructions of the divine hearing, she took a bath in the lake near the fort where a sword lay at the bottom. The queen picked it up and accepted it as a gift from Devi Rajvallabhi. Today, Devi Rajvallabhi is worshipped in the Hooghly and Howrah region as Betai Chandi or Melai Chandi.

Bhavashankari built several temples dedicated to the Goddess in her kingdom. One temple built outside the bordering moat of the Chhaunapur fortress in Bashari village was connected to the fortress by an underground tunnel that also served as an escape route during emergencies. A residence in the temple premise served as her abode during her regular visits to the fort.

A trained and skilled soldier, Bhavashankari regularly visited and looked after the army and their training. She had a dedicated female battalion, all well-trained. Under her tutelage, the upgradation and modernization of military infrastructure took place. She also renovated existing forts and built new garrison fortresses along the boundaries of Bhurishrestha. Garrisoned troops were stationed at Khanakul, Chhaunapur, Tamluk, Amta, Uluberia, and Naskardanga to readily counter any possible enemy attacks.

During Rudranarayan's rule, the Mughal rulership emerged powerful in Delhi, so also Islamic rulers in the neighboring provinces. There was always a lurking threat from the Islamic invaders. Rani Bhavashankari encouraged the subjects of Bhurishrestha to undergo military training so that they could easily defend themselves in the event of any such attacks. She made recruitment to the military compulsory from every family of her kingdom.

Rudranarayan, during his reign, expanded his empire and consolidated his control over south-western Bengal. Bhurishrestha thus not only included Howrah and Hooghly, but also the southern part of Burdwan, East Midnapore, and major parts of West Midnapore. He organized and reinforced the navy, stationing a strong naval force along the Damodar and the Ron river banks of his territory.

In alliance with the Hindu kingdoms of Bihar, Orissa–now known as Odisha–(Gajapati Mukundadeva was then the king) and other kingdoms of Bengal, Rudranarayan decided to counter the rising Pathan Sultanate of Gaur. Sulaiman Karrani was then the Sultan of the Gaur kingdom. The combined army under the brave and well-built Odiyan general Rajib Lochan Ray (also called Kalapahad because of his huge build) defeated Sulaiman Karrani in 1565 at the Battle of Tribeni. Gajapati Mukundadeva ascended the throne of Orissa in 1559.

Till Rajib Lochan Ray was there with the allied forces, no one could defeat them. Karrani devised a plan. He won Rajib Lochan Ray to his side by treacherously trapping him into a love affair with his daughter Gulnaaz. Rajib Lochan Ray, a Brahmin, converted to Islam under a new name–Muhammad Farmuli, and married Gulnaaz. Farmuli tried to reconvert back to Hinduism but was refused. He took revenge by attacking Orissa and defeating king Mukundadeva besides destroying many temples, including the Jagannath temple of Puri and Konark Sun temple. Rajib Lochan Ray died soon after by drowning.

After the death of Sulaiman Karrani, his son Daud Khan Karrani became the Sultan of Bengal. He sought the help of Raja Rudranarayan to fight against the Mughals. Rudranarayan refused to help. Seeking revenge, the Sultan's forces under Kotlu Khan attacked the Bhurishrestha kingdom from the West, as all other sides were heavily guarded. Rudranarayan's forces killed Kotlu Khan and badly defeated the Pathan forces.

Bhavashankari soon became a mother; she gave birth to prince Pratapnarayan. She became a widow when her son was only five years old. A grief-stricken Bhavashankari attempted to commit Sati, but was stopped by the royal priest. The priest advised her to look after the affairs of the kingdom as the heir to the throne was a child. He advised

Rani Bhavashankari Roy confronting the Pathan forces in front of the Shiva temple in the forest.

her to nurse and train the prince to be an able king in the future. The queen agreed but remained aloof from the affairs of the kingdom for around three months.

The Pathans under the leadership of Osman Khan were once again geared up to attack Bhurishrestha. Meanwhile, entrusting the affairs of the kingdom to two of her most trusted nobles–Chaturbhuj Chakravarti, the commander-in-chief of the armed forces, and Durlabh Dutta, the revenue minister, Bhavashankari with her young son left for the Mahadev temple at Kastasangrah. She was accompanied by a group of the strongest and ablest female bodyguards. The celebration at the temple included worshipping of Mahadev every day, *kirtan*, giving alms to beggars, and a feast to the needy every day. This was to continue for several days. At night, the widowed queen engaged in *sadhana* (meditation) dedicated to Mahadev in front of the Shivalinga.

Bhavashankari knew of a possible attack by Pathan forces, hence she used to be clad in war attire most of the time and armed with weapons. During worship, she wore the war armor beneath her worshipping attire. While she was in deep meditation at night, female bodyguards kept guard outside.

India has a track record of her own people becoming traitors by supporting enemies. It was because of such traitors that the motherland was under enemy rule for several centuries and most of her treasuries were looted, women raped, temples destroyed, and lakhs were converted. Chaturbhuj Chakravarti joined hands with Osman Khan, the leader of the Pathan forces, to fight against the Mughals and, in return, with the Sultanate's help, became the king of Bhurishrestha. They together also planned to capture Bhavashankari and her son Pratapnarayan. Following Chaturbhuj Chakravarti's plan, Osman Khan along with many well-trained Pathans disguised themselves as

Hindu saints. With 200 more Pathans, they entered the Bhurishrestha territory.

The queen's spies could identify a few of the Pathans at Amta. They immediately sent the news to the queen. The queen in turn summoned a detachment of 200 soldiers from the nearest garrison. The soldiers spread themselves in the forests of Kastasangrah where the Mahadev temple was located. Bhavashankari could not stop her celebration or her Shiv *sadhana* at night. As usual, dressed in war attire, she sat for meditation in front of the Shivalinga with armed female bodyguards keeping guard outside. She knew she might be attacked, hence she was all ready for it without interrupting her devotion for Mahadev.

Bhavashankari surmised right. The Pathan troops attacked her. A fierce sword fight followed. Soon hundreds of Pathans were butchered by Bhavashankari's troops. There was a Shaiva *akhara* in the nearby forest. A fresh contingent of Pathans attacked the *akhara* in the wee hours. The brave warrior sadhus, all devotees of Mahadev, at the *akhara*, bravely retaliated. They killed all the Pathans.

Had Bhavashankari not taken action at the right time, Bhurishrestha would have lost its sovereignty to the Pathans. She returned to the capital early in the morning the next day and took control of the administration and military affairs. Due to lack of evidence, she could not punish Chaturbhuj Chakravarti. Instead, she demoted him to a lower post, as under his commandership, Pathan forces breached security and entered the Bhurishrestha territory. She appointed Bhupati Krishna Ray as the new commander-in-chief.

Bhavashankari's coronation as the ruler of Bhurishrestha was to take place at the Bhavani temple in Bashuri near Chhaunapur Fort as per tantric rites. Meanwhile, Chaturbhuj Chakravarti again joined hands with Osman Khan in a conspiracy against the queen. Once a traitor, always a traitor! Bhavashankari should have executed him so that elements of traitorhood were nipped in the bud. (Rajput prince Chain Singh killed the traitors of his kingdom; these traitors sided with the British against their own *Matribhumi* [motherland]! Chain Singh did the right thing, but not all traitors were caught and not all were punished earlier or later. And traitors exist at present too.) They planned to capture the queen on the night of her coronation when there would be fewer bodyguards.

Going by the plan, Osman Khan entered Bhurishrestha territory with a troop of hundreds of Pathan soldiers. They reached a little distance away from Chhaunapur Fort and camped in the forests. A hunter saw them and reported it to the Bhurishresth army. Bhupati Krishna Ray was then away from the capital fort and Chaturbhuj Chakravarti was the acting commander-in-chief. He dismissed the incident as a false alarm. The news reached Krishna Ray. Following Ray's orders, Chaturbhuj Chakravarti marched towards Bashuri. Meanwhile, at the same time, the traitor sent word to Osman Khan to attack the Bhavani temple towards the end of the night after the coronation.

Bhupati Krishna Ray was quick to send a messenger to Bhavashankari, notifying her about everything. The coronated queen was quick to react. She could not trust Chaturbhuj Chakravarti though he was advancing towards Bashuri with troops. She immediately deployed troops from three nearby garrisons, including the female battalion at Bashuri. This included an infantry of 500, cavalry of 500, and an elephant brigade of 100, all ready for battle. Bhupati Krishna Ray marched with a troop to check Chaturbhuj Chakravarti and his troops. Meanwhile, the local Chandal and Bagdi people joined Bhavashankari to fight against the Pathan forces.

A fierce battle between the pathans, led by Osman Khan, and the

Bhurishrestha forces, led by Bhavashankari, took place at Bashuri. Bhavashankari marched forward fearlessly against the enemy forces seated atop an elephant and armed with her hand cannon *Rudragnishakti*. With the blessings of Bhavani, she fought like Goddess Durga, butchering the enemy soldiers fiercely, one by one. The superior warfare skills of the Bhurishrestha army, who were all trained by the queen herself, were no match to the Pathan soldiers. In no time, the Pathans were decimated. Osman Khan fled the battlefield. He could flee the Bhurishrestha territory in the guise of a fakir.

Akbar was then the Mughal emperor. Did you know Akbar accepted the sovereignty of Bhurishrestha? All because of the valor and courage displayed by Bhavashankari in decimating the Pathan forces! The Mughals never interfered in the affairs of her kingdom. According to an *Anandabazar Patrika* report by Suphal Sarkar published in 2008, Akbar sent Man Singh to the court of Bhavashankari for a treaty wherein the Mughals accepted her sovereignty.

After Pratapnarayan came of age to be able to rule the kingdom of Bhurishrestha, Bhavashankari facilitated his marriage and later coronated him king. She then retired to a spiritual life and spent her remaining years in Kashi.

It is unfortunate that the glorious legacy of the past is ignored at present in Bengal. Not much literary evidence on the chronology of the Bharadwaj dynasty is available except the fact that it was founded in the last part of the 15th century. Literary records mention this dynasty to have flourished for about 200 years and describe all rulers in chronological order. The same records deem Bhavashankari's son Pratapnarayan as the greatest ruler of this dynasty. The temple in Kastasangrah, where Bhavashankari was meditating when the Pathans attacked, was in complete ruins. It was reconstructed and renovated. Worshipping continues in this temple even today.

In the honor of Bhavashankari, the West Bengal Government launched the annual Raybaghini Rani Bhavashankari Smriti Mela in 2012. Salute to the brave warrior Bhavashankari! Vande Mataram!

Note: Drawing lessons from this chapter on Bhavashankari, converts who wish for a *Ghar Waapsi*, reconverting back to Hinduism, should never be refused. They should be readily welcomed back following the required rituals and ceremonies. Had Kalapahad been readily welcomed, the history of Orissa (now Odisha) would have been different.

In the current context, India has border issues with Pakistan and China leading to wars with both countries. There is every possibility of war in the future if China and Pakistan do not stop fighting on the border issue. Besides, almost every day our soldiers are martyred at the border. Then there are Naxalite forces, destroying the country from within. A huge number of selected civilians should undergo military training; they should stay prepared to help the military when the need arises.

Besides, with rising crimes against women, it is necessary that women get trained in defense. This training will instill confidence in them and help resist any sort of attacks.

5

10 Very Young Freedom Fighters of India

The Indian Independence struggle was not limited only to adult and elderly freedom fighters. Thousands and lakhs of children and teenage freedom fighters from each and every corner of Bharat resisted the British and sacrificed their lives for the freedom that we enjoy today. The concept that *bina kharag bina dhaal* (without swords or shields) or M.K. Gandhi's *ahimsa* gave us freedom is only a myth, not a fact.

These young freedom fighters knew about the consequences of resistance against the British. They knew they would be rewarded with even death. Yet they were never deterred. Here are 10 tales of valor of very young freedom fighters.

Dattu Rangari

Dattu Rangari was born on 16th August 1929 in a village of Belgaon or Belgaum (now Belagavi) in Karnataka. His father was Laxman Rangari. Dattu had grown up seeing the atrocities of the British and he wanted to be part of the freedom struggle from a very young age. And he got an opportunity in 1942.

The Quit India movement was already in momentum then. Dattu Rangari mobilized the children of his village and motivated them to fight against the British. Taking the leadership role, he led them to the streets and started raising the slogan 'British Quit India', and marched ahead. Dattu Rangari held high the National Flag in the front.

The loud echoing slogans alerted the British police. They at once reached the spot and threatened the children to stop marching ahead and to stop raising the slogan.

Despite the warnings of the British police that they would open fire, Dattu Rangari and the children did not stop. They continued their march. The British then opened fire. Bullets hit Dattu Rangari and he fell to the ground. But he did not let the National Flag fall. He held it high and ordered another child freedom fighter to hold it high. And he attained *Veergati*, he was then aged only 13 years on 23rd August 1942.

Anathbandhu Panja and Pradyot Kumar Bhattacharjee

On 29th October 1911, freedom fighter Anathbandhu Panja was born at Jalabindu village in Sabang of Paschim Medinipur (now called Midnapore) in West Bengal. Anathbandhu Panja lost his father at age three as a result of which the family–his mother Kumudini and elder brother Surendranath faced financial difficulties. He studied in different schools–Bhuban Pal Pathshala and Sujaganj Primary School and could not continue his high school education.

Pradyot Kumar Bhattacharjee was born at Gokulnagar in the Rajnagar region of Medinipur on 13th November 1913. He was the son of Bhavtaran Bhattacharjee. Not much information is available about his childhood.

In 1928, Netaji Subhas Chandra Bose organized a group of volunteers under the banner of the Bengal Volunteers Corps. Soon, the group started activities against the British in different parts of Bengal. It started 'Operation Freedom' in a big way in 1930. This group trained its members for armed attacks against British officers. The British during that time were very brutal wherein they severely punished freedom fighters for even a trivial cause in police stations and jails. Bengal Volunteers started their mission secretly targeting British officers and assassinating them.

In Medinipur, even before the Bengal Volunteers gained momentum, the youth there were already involved in freedom struggle activities. Besides, Yugantar, another secret revolutionary group of freedom fighters was already active in Bengal. The youth of Medinipur connected with three leading secret organizations committed to the freedom of India–Yugantar, Bengal Volunteers, and Anushilan Samiti.

Anathbandhu Panja joined Bengal Volunteers. The organization helped him continue his education and got him enrolled in Collegiate School. Bengal Volunteers by then had already succeeded in the assassination of several British officers. Anathbandhu Panja was greatly inspired by the members of the organization. He decided to take an active part in the assassination of cruel British officers.

At that time, on 7th April 1931, two freedom fighters shot dead James Peddie, the District Magistrate of Medinipur, while he was attending an exhibition of handicrafts at the Collegiate School. It was the school where Anathbandhu Panja was then studying. Peddie died the next day. The masterminds behind the assassination of Peddie were Bimal Krishna Dasgupta, Jyoti Jiban Ghosh, and another student from the Collegiate School. The British arrested 14 freedom fighters on suspicion and tortured 10 of them brutally. Bimal Krishna Dasgupta escaped and in October the same year, i.e., 1931, he attempted to assassinate Edward Villiers, President of the European Association of Kolkata. He was caught and sentenced to 10 years of rigorous imprisonment but as there was no evidence against him for both the incidents, he was released.

Freedom fighters at Medinipur had already decided to assassinate any British officer who took charge as the District Magistrate of Medinipur. Meanwhile, after the assassination of James Peddie, Robert Douglas held the post. Douglas feared the freedom fighters and often stayed guarded in his bungalow. Thus, several attempts by the freedom fighters to assassinate Douglas failed. And the right opportunity arrived on 30th April 1932. Two freedom fighters shot at Douglas while he was attending a meeting in the District Board Office.

Out of suspicion, Pradyot Kumar Bhattacharjee was arrested. Despite lack of evidence, Pradyot was sentenced to death. He was brutally tortured every day for several days by the British Police. They wanted him to utter the names of his fellow freedom fighters involved in the assassination of Douglas. But Pradyot did not utter any name.

The teen freedom fighter Pradyot Kumar Bhattacharjee was not at all perturbed with the award of death sentence by the British. He wrote letters to his elder brother, sister, and mother from his prison cell at Medinipur Central Jail. A Part of the letter to his elder brother read thus: "Nobody is born to live forever and none is immortal. The purpose of life is not somehow to maintain existence. If existence cannot be utilized to serve the purpose of life, there is no justification for it."

Here is part of a letter that Pradyot wrote to his mother: "Tell my brothers that I leave my heart in my unfinished work. If they try to finish my unfinished work, that will be a better offering to my memory than to shed tears for me for a few days… I am sacrificing my life in pursuit of an ideal and for this, my heart is full of happiness to the brim."

And Pradyot Kumar Bhattacharjee was hanged by the British on 12th January 1933 aged 20 years.

The assassination of Douglas led to the implementation of strict measures by the British in Medinipur. Hindus were subjected to heavy taxes, collective fines, restrictions on gatherings, and tortures. But, such measures did not dampen the spirits of the freedom fighters. They continued with their secret activities.

Bernard E.J. Burge, a ruthless British officer, was appointed as District Magistrate of Medinipur. Taking note of the two previous assassinations, Burge started work in his own heavily guarded house instead of the office. Bengal Volunteers youth started looking for opportunities to assassinate him. Few months passed by. Meanwhile, Burge, surrounded by armed bodyguards, started going out occasionally after a year.

On 2nd September 1933, Burge was supposed to take part in a football match organized between two local teams, at the Police Football Ground, in Medinipur. Freedom fighters Anathbandhu Panja and Mrigendra Dutta came to know about this and before Burge's arrival, they were already practicing with a ball at the venue.

The match began. Burge joined the match. Anathbandhu Panja and Mrigendra Dutta mingled with the players and seeking the right opportunity, shot at Burge. The British District Magistrate died on the spot. Burge's bodyguards fired at the freedom fighters. Anathbandhu Panja attained *Veergati* at the Medinipur Police Football Ground and a heavily wounded Mrigendra Dutta attained martyrdom the next day in the hospital. While Panja was aged 22, Mrigendra was 18.

Mainawati

Mainawati was the adopted daughter of Nana Saheb. Did you know that Nana Saheb himself was the adopted son of exiled Maratha

Peshwa Baji Rao II? Both Nana Saheb and Tatya Tope were childhood friends of Rani Lakshmi Bai of Jhansi. During the 1857 War of Independence, Mainawati was 13 years old.

In 1857, freedom fighters at many places across the country revolted against the British, involving in armed conflict. British brutality saw its zenith at Bithoor in Uttar Pradesh. Nana Saheb, whose base was at Bithoor (some 24 kms away from Kanpur) emerged successful in defeating the British at Kanpur (then called Cawnpore) and captured the British garrison. Many Britishers were killed. Nana Saheb exerted control over Kanpur for a few days. The British arrived with additional forces and regained Kanpur. They couldn't arrest Nana Saheb. The British, led by Gen. Havelock, then ransacked Bithoor Fort and vandalized the palaces and temples in the city.

The British held Mainawati captive. Mainawati knew about the whereabouts of her father Nana Saheb. Despite continuous torture, she did not reveal the information. The British had already set fire to the palaces in the fort. They warned Mainawati that they would throw her into the fire if she did not tell them about Nana Saheb's whereabouts. Mainawati, yet, did not utter a word. She pledged she would rather accept death than tell a word about her father. The British then tied her legs and threw her into the raging fire. Mainawati attained *Veergati*. She was burnt alive.

In Bithoor alone, the brutal and savage British killed thousands of men, women, and children of all age groups. But world history or even Indian History does not highlight the genocide committed by the British.

To spread terror, the British hung hundreds and thousands of freedom fighters in rows of trees in Bithoor. But did this act dampen the spirits of the freedom fighters? No! In the coming years till 1947, they continued fighting until India attained freedom!!!

A portrait of Mahadev Vinayak Ranade.

Mahadev Vinayak Ranade

Mahadev Vinayak Ranade was from Pune, Maharashtra. He was born in 1980. Right from his childhood, he was involved in mobilizing the children of his region against the British. As he grew up, he trained himself in the art of warfare and also trained the teenagers so that the trained group could involve in attacks against the British.

In late 1896, bubonic plague struck Pune. Within a few months, it reached epidemic proportions resulting in the death of 0.6 percent of the city's population. Soon half the population deserted the city. Walter Charles Rand was appointed as the plague commissioner to take control of the situation.

In the name of curbing the deadly pandemic, Rand started a reign of terror in Pune. Soon after his appointment, he deployed forces, who were authorized to deal with the situation their way. The forces would barge into any house and forcibly strip men, women, and children naked for 'check-ups'. They would do this even in public. Without considering their opinion, the forces would then evacuate them to hospitals for quarantine. Whenever they entered a house for a 'check-up' they ransacked the belongings and even destroyed property. The British forces also broke *moortis* (statues) of deities and polluted places of worship.

This terrorizing act of the British angered many freedom fighters. Chapekar brothers (Damodar Hari Chapekar–born in 1870, Balkrishna Hari Chapekar–born in 1873, and Vasudeo Hari Chapekar–born in 1879) along with Mahadev Vinayak Ranade and few others decided to assassinate Walter Charles Rand. The Chapekar brothers, who grew up with their *kirtankar* father Hari Vinayak, received little formal education. They were trained by their father in music, Sanskrit, and philosophy.

On 22nd June 1897, Britishers in Pune assembled at a Government House in Pune to celebrate the Diamond Jubilee of the coronation of Queen Victoria. The Chapekar brothers carried arms and it was decided that Damodar Hari and Balkrishna Hari would attack Rand with a pistol and a sword each. Balkrishna carried a hatchet. Mahadev Ranade assisted them in the process.

While Rand was on his way back from the Government House in his carriage, it was already dark. He was escorted by Lieutenant Ayerst in the carriage. As planned, the Chapekar brothers attacked Rand. Balakrishna Hari fired shots, targeting the heads, from behind the carriage. Lieutenant Ayerst died on the spot. Rand died of wounds on 3rd July 1897 at Sassoon Hospital.

The British could not arrest the Chapekar brothers and Ranade, who masterminded and planned the attack on Rand. But two traitors Ganesh and Ramchandra leaked info to the British about Damodar

Hari after which he was first arrested. He was hanged by the British on 18th April 1898.

Vasudeo Hari, Mahadev Vinayak Ranade, and Khando Vishnu Sathe came to know about the traitors. They eliminated both Ganesh and Ramchandra on 9th February 1899 and the same day, they tried to attack chief constable Rama Pandu, who was completely loyal to the British and took part in the atrocities against fellow Indians. Their attempt failed and the trio was apprehended and tried. They were sentenced to death, they were executed in the gallows of Yerwada Jail.

Vasudev Hari was hanged on 8th May 1899, Mahadev Vinayak Ranade on 10th May 1899, and Balkrishna Hari on 12th May 1899. As Khando Vishnu Sathe was a juvenile, he was sentenced to 10 years' rigorous imprisonment.

Bishan Singh

At a time when the British formed a solid base, missionary activities were already prevalent, and the British permitted Muslims in Punjab for open slaughter of cows, resulting in the Kuka movement gaining momentum. Besides, most people had forgotten the message of the Gurus. Kuka members were mainly Namdhari Sikhs. They were the disciples of Sat Guru Ram Singh. He was the 12th guru in the lineage of Namdhari Sikhs. Several decades before Mohandas Karamchand Gandhi started the Swadeshi Movement, the Namdhari Kuka Sikhs started it under their Guru's leadership. They boycotted British goods and wore clothes made of homespun cotton. They revolted against cow-slaughter. Sat Guru Ram Singh was also the first Indian to start a non-cooperation movement against the British.

According to the book, *Kuka Movement: Freedom Struggle in Punjab* by Jaswinder Singh, 150 Kuka Namdhari Sikhs attacked butchers of Maler Kotla (Sangrur, Punjab) in January 1872. The butchers had the support of the British. The British Police arrested 66 Kukas, brought them to Maler Kotla ground, and without any trial, executed them with guns and cannons. The execution was ordered by Cowan, the Deputy Commissioner of Ludhiana, and Forsyth, the Commissioner of Ambala. Among the martyred freedom fighters were three children. One of the children was Bishan Singh, a 12-year-old boy.

Cowan, at the request of his wife, had agreed to spare the life of Bishan Singh on one condition that he should deny that he was a disciple of Sat Guru Ram Singh. Bishan Singh was a boy, shorter in height compared to Cowan. He said that he would reply in whispers in Cowan's ears. Cowan agreed and he knelt down towards Bishan. What Bishan did took everyone by surprise. As soon as Cowan bent his head, Bishan Singh caught hold of his beard and pulled them hard. The Deputy Commissioner shrieked in pain. He ordered his men to take action against the boy. British police first chopped off Bishan Singh's hands and then beheaded him. As Bishan Singh's hands fell lifeless to the ground, Cowan's beard was seen entangled in his tender fingers.

That's how even a 12-year-old revered a Guru and that's how the child resisted the British, the enemy of the motherland.

The British arrested Sat Guru Ram Singh and exiled him to Rangoon (now Yangon), Burma (now Myanmar) in March 1872.

Phooleshwari

Dhekiajuli is a beautiful, serene town surrounded by tea gardens with the river Brahmaputra flowing through it in today's Sonitpur district of Assam. Freedom fighter Phooleshwari was born at this place in the year 1930.

During the 1942 'Quit India' movement, freedom fighters in large numbers, comprising of both the young and the old, marched towards Government buildings, raising the slogan 'British, Quit India'. They held the National Flag high. They planned to hoist the National Flag on different British-occupied Government buildings located across the region.

One such rally was led by Phooleshwari. She was then aged only 12 years old. She held the National Flag high and marched with her followers towards the Dhekiajuli British Police post. Her target for the day was to hoist the Indian National Flag in the police office post.

The British police arrived. They warned Phooleshwari and all freedom fighters with dire consequences if they marched even a step ahead or if they did not stop raising slogans against the British. But Phooleshwari and her followers marched ahead. The British police then gave the last warning that they would open fire. Yet, the freedom fighters continued marching with their loud voices of 'Quit India' echoing far.

The British police opened fire at the freedom fighters. Bullets hit Phooleshwari and she attained *Veergati*.

Kedar Nath Singh

Kedar Nath Singh was born in 1929 in Jaunpur, Uttar Pradesh. He was a student of Standard VII in Singramau School in Jaunpur when the 'Quit India' movement spread across the country.

On 16th August 1942, near Dhaniya Mau in Jaunpur, many freedom fighters gathered to start a rally against the British. Amongst the freedom fighters were also school and college students. Kedar Nath Singh was one of the participants in this rally. Their slogan was 'British, Quit India'. They started the rally.

British police arrived on the spot. They warned the freedom fighters to leave the rally and go back to their respective homes. But, no one followed their orders. Despite repeat warnings, the freedom fighters continued raising the 'Quit India' slogan addressed against the British.

The police then opened fire. It hit a student freedom fighter, who attained *Veergati* on the spot. Enraged, the freedom fighters attacked the British police, throwing stones at them.

The British police then continuously opened fire at the freedom fighters. Many fell wounded. Seven more student freedom fighters attained martyrdom. A bullet hit Kedar Nath Singh and he attained *Veergati*. He was only 13 years old then.

Sita Devi

Sita Devi was born at Neemuchana village in the Bansur area of Alwar, Rajasthan in 1905. She hailed from a farmer's family.

Farmers not only during the rule of Islamic invaders but also during the tenure of British Christians suffered disastrously. Heavy taxes were levied upon them. Many farmers, across India, lost their farming privileges, became homeless, and lived in utter poverty as a result of the draconian law.

The British never considered weather conditions and yields when it came to the collection of revenues from the farmers. They increased the revenue by 50 percent. Farmers in various regions across the country protested. Rajasthan was no exception.

It was 16th May 1925. Place: Neemuchana village. Farmers gathered at an open ground to protest against the British. A group of women, both old and young, led by Sita Devi joined the rebellion. Radha Devi, Sita's friend, also joined her.

British police arrived at the ground. They asked the farmer freedom fighters to disperse. Despite repeated warnings, the freedom fighters continued their protest. British police then opened fire. They started shooting non-stop at the peaceful protestors. Many attained *Veergati* and many fell wounded. Sita Devi, aged 20 years, and Radha Devi attained martyrdom in the police firing.

The British police did not stop at that. They entered Neemuchana village with cannons and destroyed property and crops. They set fire to the entire village. This atrocity of the British doesn't find mention in mainstream literature.

Lakshman (Lakshmanan)

Quilon, the Anglicized term of 'Kollam', has remained a trading center for pepper since ancient times. In Sanskrit, 'kollam' means pepper. Besides the British, the Portuguese and Dutch also tried to build a firm base in Kollam for the trading of pepper and other spices. Kollam was also the business capital city of Travancore.

Freedom fighter Lakshman, also called Lakshmanan, was born in 1918 at Asraman in Kollam, Kerala.

A massive protest meet was held in the Quilon Cantonment Ground, also known as Cantonment Maidan. Freedom fighters from near and far, especially the Travancore region, gathered there demanding the British's 'Responsible Governance' in Travancore on 2nd September 1938. In the Malayalam calendar, it was the Chingam month, dated 17th. Hence, this protest was also known as Chingam 17 Revolution. Lakshmanan participated in the protest.

A speech was to be delivered by a leader to the freedom fighters, who assembled at the Quilon Cantonment Ground. Police arrived and warned the freedom fighters to leave the ground. The freedom fighters did not obey and continued with the protest. The police then opened fire on those assembled. They arrested the speakers.

Six freedom fighters attained *Veergati* due to police firing at the Quilon Cantonment Ground. Among the martyred was Lakshmanan, aged only 20 years.

Let us remember our young freedom fighters, who equally played an instrumental role in the fight for freedom and whose names have been purposely wiped out from the pages of history textbooks.

Vande Mataram! Jai Hind!!!

6

Dahir's Resistance to Arabs; How His Daughters Ended Life of Mohd Bin Qasim

The north-western region of *Akhand Bharat* (undivided India before foreign conquests, British rule, and independence), known as Sindh, was ruled for a period of 143 years from 489 CE to 632 CE by the Rai dynasty. Rulers of this dynasty were patrons of both Buddhism and Hinduism. The last Rai ruler was Rai Sahasi II, who reigned till 632 CE. The dynasty's empire extended from Kandahar-Sulaiman-Ferdan-Kikanan hills in the north to Kashmir in the east, from modern Karachi in the west to Surat in the south. Chach, a Brahmin, served as the prime minister under Rai Sahasi II, owing to his expertise, he rose to prominence within a short span of time. After the death of Rai Sahasi II, Chach became the ruler of Sindh. And thus started the rule of the Brahmin dynasty! Soon after his accession to the throne, Chach appointed his brother Chandar to look after the administration. He then set out on an expansion spree of his kingdom wherein he conquered a number of neighboring autonomous regions. He brought few of those regions under the dominion of Sindh and left a few to be ruled by vassal rulers. Alor, also called Aror (located in the present Sukkur region of Sindh in Pakistan), was the capital of Sindh. Chach ruled up to 671 CE. After his death, his brother Chandar became the ruler of Sindh. Chandar ruled for eight years till 679 CE. After the death of Chandar, his eldest nephew Dahir, the eldest son of Chach, ascended the throne of Sindh.

Around the same time, the Sassanid empire–the Persian imperial dynasty, came to an end after four centuries of rule in 651 CE. The Sassanids were Iranians and were followers of Zoroastrianism. The Arab invasion of Iran, which was a series of attacks starting from 633 CE until 651 CE, led to the fall of that empire. The initial attacks were conducted by Arab commanders working under Islamic Prophet Muhammad, followed by Caliphs. The Caliphate was an Islamic state under a leader called Caliph, who was considered the politico-religious successor to Prophet Muhammad. There were four major Caliphates–Rashidun, Umayyad, Abbasid, and Ottoman respectively. Most of the later attacks of the Sassanid empire were directed under the leadership of Caliph Umar of the Rashidun Caliphate. The long duration for the subjugation process to continue was because the Iranians resisted and fought against the invading Arabs continuously. The Arab conquest led to subsequent Islamization of the region. Iranian historian Biruni and Arab historian Baladori have described how Zoroastrian scriptures were burnt and priests executed, especially where there was violent resistance. During the rule of the Rai dynasty of Sindh, the Arabs had also annexed Makran after defeating the Sindh army at Rasil in 644 CE. That happened under the Rashidun Caliphate. It was again during the Umayyad Caliphate under Caliph al-Walid I that the Arabs attacked Sindh, the kingdom of Raja Dahir.

Muslim historians have described Alor, the capital of Sindh, as a city 'adorned with various kinds of royal buildings, villas, gardens, fountains, streams, meadows and trees'. Raja Dahir ruled for almost 40 years, from 668 CE to 712 CE. He ruled wisely and maintained law and order. Bandits had no place in his kingdom. Once found guilty, they were banished to the seas. Raja Dahir was married to Ladi. He had one son Jaisiah and three daughters–Surya Devi, Premala Devi, and Jodha Devi. According to a few accounts, Raja Dahir also had another wife named Rani Bai.

The spread of Islam and the looting of wealth were always reasons for conquest by Islamic invaders. The other key objective behind the Arab attack of Sindh was because it was the nucleus of not only seaports and maritime routes but also of overland passages to India and other regions. And pirates had already been active in the port regions, which the Arabs wanted to hold control. Muslim shipping on the coasts of Sindh had already been affected by pirates. An Arab Governor wanted Raja Dahir's help and interference to prevent pirates from disrupting their shipping activities. Dahir's refusal was also another reason that led the Arab army to reach the doorsteps of Alor. According to an account, the Arabs attacked the Sindh kingdom several times, and each time they were defeated by Raja Dahir. *Chach Nama* describes volumes about Raja Dahir's bravery and valor, which corroborates the heroic resistance offered and the victory won by the Brahmin king. Continuous defeats led the Arab army to drop the idea of attacking Sindh until they resumed the campaign under the commandment of Muhammad bin Qasim.

The book *Chach Nama*, also called *Fateh Nama Sindh*, written in Persian by Abi Bakr Kufi (it is believed Bakr only discovered it) describes in detail the history of Sindh during the seventh and eighth centuries. The first name of the book 'Chach' is derived from Raja Chach, one of the greatest rulers of Sindh and the father of Raja Dahir. Thomas Postans was one of the translators of the *Chach Nama*, which he considered as 'a record of centuries of Muslim barbarity'. He included the translations in his book *Personal Observations on Sindh*, first published in 1843. Sindh, according to this book, was 'a rich, flourishing, and extensive monarchy' under the Hindu rulers.

After the Arabs under Qasim conquered parts of the Sindhi territory–Debal, Neirunkot, Sehwan, Raja Dahir started preparations for war. He could foresee the advancing Arab army towards his capital. Raja Dahir immediately sent a huge army to prevent the advancement of the Arabs towards his capital. Despite offering a strong resistance, the Hindu army was defeated. Dahir's son Jaisiah resisted Qasim's forces at Jitor but in vain. The Muslim forces then started advancing towards the capital of Sindh. Raja Dahir was all ready for the war. It was 712 CE.

A courtier at Dahir's court advised the king to seek refuge from one of his friendly kings from India. Raja Dahir refused. The courtier then requested him to send his family members to India so that they were safe. Again the king refused. He said it would be utterly selfish on his part to send only his family members without considering the families of the nobles, governors, and other men of Sindh.

Raja Dahir had 30,000 infantry ahead of his cavalry and elephants. On the day of the war that took place on the outskirts of Alor, the king positioned himself in a richly ornamented howdah. Raja Dahir then moved around and arranged his soldiers in battle array. He delivered a fiery speech, motivating his soldiers to fight ferociously to save the kingdom and the people.

The Umayyad Caliphate Arab army was led by their commander Muhammad bin Qasim al-Thaqafi. Al-Hajjaj ibn Yusuf, governor of Iraq and the east under the Umayyad Caliphate, superintended Qasim's campaign. Stationed at Kufa in Iraq, he deployed messengers, between Iraqi port Basra and Sindh and supervised it. Muhammad bin Qasim's army comprised of 6,000 Syrian cavalry, detachments of

Raja Dahir's daughters Suriya Devi and Premala Devi buried alive into a wall at the orders of the Caliph.

Mawla (non-Arab, but Muslim) soldiers from Iraq, 6,000 camel cavalry, an advance guard, and reinforcements from the governor of Makran with five catapults (ballistic devices used to launch projectiles).

According to an account by author and researcher Khurram Ali Shafique, further based on various accounts by Muslim historians, Raja Dahir said thus before the war: "I am going to meet the Arabs in the open battle, and fight them as best as I can. If I crush them, my kingdom will then be put on a firm footing. But if I am killed honourably, the event will be recorded in the books of Arabia and India and will be talked about by great men. It will be heard by other kings in the world, and it will be said that Raja Dahir of Sindh sacrificed his precious life for the sake of his country, in fighting with the enemy."

And the battle began. Heavy bloodshed followed from both sides. Suddenly, the Arab forces started constant discharging of Naphtali ball fireworks, which ignited the howdahs and injured the elephants. The gigantic animals 'turned on their own troops and trampled all before them'. This not only created confusion in the Hindu army but also with the elephants running away from the battlefield, their position weakened. This gave room to the Arab army for an easy attack.

By this time Raja Dahir's elephant too started fleeing from the battlefield despite the king trying to pacify it to continue the battle. A stray arrow suddenly hit Dahir's neck. His elephant rushed to the nearest river for relief from the fire wound. A few Hindu soldiers, having witnessed the fate of their king, had followed him. By the time the elephant reached the river, Dahir died of the wounds. Ensuring that the king's body doesn't fall into the enemy's hands, the Hindu soldiers quickly hid him, burying him on the riverside. Meanwhile, the Arab soldiers arrived at the spot. Raja Dahir's howdah had two female bodyguards. The enemy soldiers held them captive; upon torture, the bodyguards narrated the whereabouts of their king. Dahir's body was 'procured, and the head stuck on a spear as a trophy'. According to another account, Raja Dahir, seeing his elephant fleeing away from the battlefield, jumped onto a horse and resumed a heroic fight, and later attained *Veergati* on the battlefield.

During the time when the battle between Raja Dahir and Qasim continued, Rani Bai challenged Qasim's troops for a battle in the Fort of Rawar in the capital city. There were around 15,000 men in the fort. After the defeat of Dahir, Qasim reached Rawar Fort. Unable to break the robust defense of the fort, Muhammad bin Qasim ordered his soldiers to dig and mine the boundaries of the fortification. Mining continued for days until the fort started falling. Qasim's army started demolishing the fort walls. Finding herself encircled and with hundreds of her men being subdued, Rani Bai, along with other ladies, arranged a huge fire and committed *Jauhar* to save their honor.

Destroying temples was one of the key objectives of the Islamic invaders. They often erected mosques at the vandalized temple sites. The same fate happened in Raja Dahir's kingdom of Sindh. To quote from the book *A Book of Conquest* by Manan Ahmed Asif on Muhammad bin Qasim wherein he further quotes Thomas Postans' book: "The portrait of Qasim that emerges in Postans's work focuses on his habit of 'converting the Pagan temples into mosques and places of Mohammedan prayer.' His destruction of the temple at Daybul 'occasioned a general despondency throughout the country'. After the killing of Dahir, 'as usual, mosques were erected on the ruins of the temples, or those places were transformed for purposes of Mohammedan worship'."

The wealth of Sindh was looted, the surviving soldiers executed, sparing those who accepted Islamic supremacy, and women taken away as slaves.

Two of Raja Dahir's daughters Suriya Devi and Premala Devi were taken captives. They were renowned for their beauty. Muhammad bin Qasim sent both the princesses as gifts for the Caliph's harem along with other looted wealth. Suriya Devi and Premala Devi devised a plan to avenge the death of their father Dahir and the loss of their kingdom. And they were confident that their plan would lead to the death of Muhammad bin Qasim. It was after several days that Raja Dahir's daughters reached the capital of the Umayyad Caliphate and were accommodated at the Caliph's harem. It was only again after several days that the Caliph 'remembered them and called the elder princess Suriya Devi to enjoy her company'. To quote from the book *Indo-Persian Historiography up to the Thirteenth Century* by Iqtidar Husain Siddiqi: "Captivated by her youthful charm, he stretched his hand towards her but she stood up and said, 'Long live his Majesty!' We are not worthy of your Majesty's love because Muhammad bin Qasim shared his bed with us for three days before we were sent here. Is it your custom?' The Caliph believed this."

Suriya Devi's words enraged the Caliph. The princesses' trick worked. Feeling insulted, the Caliph immediately wrote an order that Muhammad bin Qasim be sewn up in rawhide and transmitted to his capital. He did not inquire into the depth of the matter. The order was followed. Qasim was wrapped and stitched in raw oxen hides. En route to the capital of the Umayyad Caliphate, he died due to suffocation. It was the year 715 CE. He was aged 20 years then.

Suriya Devi and Premala Devi were overjoyed hearing about the tragic death of Qasim. But they did not want their honor to be at stake. They knew that if they told the truth to the Caliph, they would be punished with death. And for them only then would death save their honor. They sent word to the Caliph about their ploy of taking revenge against Muhammad bin Qasim. Listening to this, the Caliph was so filled with repentance that he immediately ordered that the two princesses be buried alive in a wall. The Caliph's orders were immediately followed. Suriya Devi and Premala Devi attained *Veergati*.

That's how the king of Sindh offered resistance for years against Arab invaders and attained martyrdom on the battlefield. That's how the queen of Sindh challenged the enemy and committed *Jauhar* with many women of Sindh to save their honor. And that's how, even when subjugating the enemy in battle was impossible, the princesses of Sindh used their wit to put an end to the life of the invader. That's the story of Raja Dahir and his family.

7

How Satnamis Drove away Aurangzeb's Forces from Narnaul in 1672

How many of us know about the Satnami rebellion against Aurangzeb? Over a period of a thousand plus years, Indic warriors fought time and again against the Islamic plunderers and rulers. While many kings and queens regained their respective kingdoms after victorious battles, groups of warriors revolted against brutal policies. Satnamis revolted against Aurangzeb, driving away his forces from Narnaul, and held the position for some time before encountering in a final battle and attaining martyrdom in thousands.

The Encyclopedia of Religion and Ethics edited by James Hastings describes thus: "The Sadhs, under the name of Satnamis, appear to have been the heroes of the revolt of Hindu devotees against Aurangzib in 1672. The leaders were mendicant Satnamis, who were nicknamed by the people 'Mundiyas' or 'Shavelingas' from their habit of shaving the body clean of all hair."

The concept of Satnam, meaning 'True Name' or 'In the Name of Truth' inspired a section of people from certain parts of north India, especially Narnaul, Mewat, Agra, Jaipur, Farukkabad, Mirzapur, and

Rohtak. 'Satnam' is what they refer to God. Followers of 'Satnam' called themselves Satnamis. This sect was founded by a Sadhu named Birbhan in the year 1543. Birbhan was inspired by Uddhava Das, a disciple of Rai Das, whose Guru was Ratnananda, a Vaishnavite. Satnamis, thus, were also called Sadhs (from the term Sadhus).

In the words of R.C. Mazumder, H.C. Raychaudhuri, and Kalikinkar Datta from *An Advanced History of India*, Satnamis "were originally an inoffensive sect of Hindu devotees with their centres at Narnoi (in the Patiala State) and Mewat (Alwar region)... If anyone attempts to wrong or oppress them by force, or by exercise of authority, they will not endure it. Many of them have weapons or arms." Waldemar Hansen in *The Peacock Throne: The Drama of Mogul India* called Satnami devotees as 'an agricultural Hindu sect'.

According to the book *Maasir-I-Alamgiri: A History of Emperor Aurangzib-Alamgir* by Saqi Mustad Khan, and translated by Sri Jadu Nath Sarkar, members of the Satnami sect were mainly 'goldsmiths, carpenters, scavengers, tanners, and members of other menial professions'. Saqi Mustad Khan describes the Satnamis as 'infidels', 'low people', 'weak', 'wicked mischief-makers', and 'wicked people'. It is but apparent for many such authors pertaining to Islamic invaders and plunderers to label the native warriors of the soil this way.

What was the way of life of the Satnamis? Satnamis were peasants and carried weapons. They always dressed like devotees. To quote from *The Encyclopedia of Religion and Ethics:* "Adults are required to wear a white dress and ornament and the use of rich apparel of every kind are prohibited. They never wear a cap, but use instead a turban of a peculiar shape. They are enjoined by their religion never to tell a lie and never to take an oath. They are in the same way prohibited from using any kind of intoxicant or any article which borders upon luxury. Wine, opium, ganja, bhang, betel, and tobacco are abominations to them. They have an intense respect for animal life, which extends to even the smallest insect, and the use of any kind of animal food is strictly denounced. They will salute no one but the Divine principle, which they term Sat or 'The Truth'..."

When it comes to South Asian history and society, many researchers and authors have come up with narratives on Satnamis. The interpretation of these narratives is rather one-sided with emphasis laid more on the unification of 'lower caste groups' and casteism, creating caste-based divisions rather than highlighting how a small group of warrior devotees revolted against the barbaric policies of Aurangzeb. Not much information is available in mainstream media and narratives on how the Satnamis drove away the Mughal forces of Aurangzeb from Narnaul, how they wreaked havoc on the imperial throne, and how thousands of Satnamis attained martyrdom in the final battle against Mughals.

Aurangzeb was among the few monarchs, who established Sharia law and Islamic commercial jurisprudence throughout his dominion, which finds description in the book *Structure of Politics Under Aurangzeb 1658-1707* by S.M. Hussein. The Mughal ruler reintroduced the *jizya* wherein non-Muslims were subjected to paying burdensome tax and other policies that were anti-Hindu in nature. Besides this, Aurangzeb also ordered the demolition of temples and stopped the reconstruction of destroyed shrines or the construction of new temples. Hindus in small groups started revolting against his policies and defied Mughal imperialism. The Satnami Rebellion is one of the earliest revolts by a group of devotees, who were also small peasants, against Aurangzeb.

In 1672, the battle between the Satnamis and Mughals started with the murder of a Satnami devotee by a Mughal foot-soldier. The devotees assembled in huge numbers and retaliated. They first killed the Mughal soldier and 'pressed toward Delhi, plundering Mughal-

Satnamis fighting against Aurangzeb's Mughal forces at Narnaul.

occupied villages and defeating small Mogul forces'. They drove away Mughal forces from Narnaul (located in now Mahendragarh District of Haryana) and occupied it. The sudden uprising of Satnami devotees shook the imperial throne, i.e., Aurangzeb such that the Mughal Emperor 'ordered his tents to be brought out'.

Such was the valor and strength of the Satnamis that Saqi Mustad Khan described them in his book *Maasir-I-Alamgiri: A History of Emperor Aurangzib-Alamgir* that they 'suddenly sprang out of the ground like termites (winged ants) and descended from the sky like locusts'. To quote Khan further: "It was said that these wicked people considered themselves immortal, and believed that if one of them was slain, seventy others would spring up in his place. They defied the imperial authority and caused disturbances near Narnol in a body of about 5,000 men, and plundered the villages and parganahs."

Five thousand Satnamis started fighting against Mughal forces and plundered Mughal territories after their capture of Narnaul. The Mughal fauzdar of the region, namely Tahir Khan, was defeated. Khan reached the Mughal court and described the details of the rebellion to Aurangzeb. The Mughal ruler resolved to crush the 'despicable infidels' on a Friday. Radandaz Khan, Hamid Khan, Yahia Khan Rumi, Najib Khan, Rumi Khan, Kamaluddin, Purdil, Mughal prince Asfandiyar were commanders on the Mughal side with artillery and troops, who marched forward against the Satnamis.

The peasant devotees lacked artillery and advanced war materials like the Mughals. Yet with the very few weapons, which they had, they decided to fight the Mughal forces. To quote from *Maasir-I-Alamgiri: A History of Emperor Aurangzib-Alamgi*r, the Satnamis "acted the battle described in old Hindu books called in the Hindu tongue the Mahbhharat, which means the slaying of elephants in the field... A terrible battle was fought".

Aurangzeb's forces were double the Satnamis. The Mughal ruler wrote prayers for victory. To quote from Waldemar Hansen's *The Peacock Throne: The Drama of Mogul India* about retaliation by Aurangzeb: "Aurangzeb countered with ten thousand men, artillery, and even a detachment of his own imperial drew to neutralize Satnami power, he wrote prayers and drew esoteric designs on paper talismans which were then sewn into Mogul army banners. In a distinctly unsupernatural finale which soon became high massacre, Satnami martyrs fell in cascades of blood."

In the terrible battle that ensued, thousands of Satnamis fought till their last breath with their 'pitiless swords'. They neither ran nor surrendered. Thousands of the devotees attained martyrdom.

This is an untold tale of resistance against invaders, against Adharma. Satnamis did not fear Aurangzeb and his Mughal forces. They did not fear death. They fought for Dharma and the motherland. Our thousands-of-years-old civilizational existence and survival are all because of the resistance and sacrifice of thousands of Dharmic warriors. Vande Mataram!

8

Bhima Bai Holkar

Defeated British Col Malcolm in Guerrilla Warfare

Mahidpur! This place in Ujjain in Madhya Pradesh, which was once part of the ancient trade route connecting the Silk Road and Dakshinapatha, is synonymous with the freedom struggle. This was the place where Bhima Bai Holkar defeated British Col Malcolm in guerrilla warfare in 1817. She was then aged only 22 years. This was the place where the brave freedom fighter led a brigade of 2,500 cavalry against the British forces. And this was one of the first battles against the British by a woman warrior long before the 1857 War of Independence. Rani Lakshmi Bai drew inspiration from Bhima Bai Holkar to rise in revolt against the British. Today, the Mahidpur Fort with six entrance gateways, a fortification wall, and temples stands as a witness to the heroic past.

Bhima Bai Holkar was born on 17th September 1795. She was the daughter of the Maharaja of the Holkar State–Yashwant Rao Holkar, who was one of the ablest military leaders of the Maratha Empire. By the time the British started establishing their colonial power, there were five powerful Maratha dynasties. They were the Peshwas of Pune, who held centralized powers, the Scindias of Gwalior, Holkars of

Indore, Bhonsles of Nagpur, and Gaekwads of Baroda. Yashwant Rao Holkar not only expanded his kingdom through conquests but also worked towards uniting the Hindu rulers.

Bhima Bai Holkar was also a relative of Ahilyabai Holkar, who not only built hundreds of temples across India but also renovated and undertook maintenance of the Char Dhams, Shaktipithas, Saptapuris, Jyotirlingas, and more religious sites. Ahilyabai Holkar became the ruler of the Holkar State after the death of Malhar Rao I in 1766. She administered her kingdom from Maheshwar. Another capital of the Holkars was Indore. Maheshwar, the city of ancient glory, erstwhile known as Mahismati or Mahissati and which also finds mention in the Mahabharata and the Ramayana, was the capital of the Holkar dominion until 1811.

From a very young age, Bhima Bai Holkar took interest in the political and administrative affairs of her father's kingdom. Yashwant Rao Holkar considered his daughter as a son and trained her in warfare. She was so resilient that she was believed to be like Pandava prince Bhim, who was known to be very strong and brave. Hence, she was nicknamed Bhima and came to be known by this name.

Bhima Bai Holkar always wore men's clothing. She soon became an expert in swordsmanship, shooting, and horse-riding. She excelled in Guerilla warfare. During this time, Yashwant Rao Holkar came under the influence of one of his beautiful queens Tulsibai. This queen did not like the growing bond of the father and daughter. She did not like Bhima Bai's participation in the political and military affairs of the Holkar State. She was successful in persuading the Holkar Maharaja to look for a groom for his daughter.

Bhima Bai Holkar was married to Govindrao Boliya II, the grandson of Govindrao Boliya, who was the Saranjami Jagirdar, also called Sardar, under the Holkars on 12th February 1809. Bhima Bai

Bhima Bai Holkar leading her army against the British forces.

was then aged only 14 years. The marriage was consummated with great pomp and show with the participation of royal households from far and near including Nepal. Yashwant Rao Holkar gifted his daughter 200 *tolas* (one tola is equivalent to 10 grams of gold at present) of gold ornaments amid other gifts including the *jagir* of Kut Pargana of Jalon. Unfortunately, Bhima Bai Holkar soon lost her husband. The young widow undertook the administrative and military responsibility of her *jagir*.

Meanwhile, Yashwant Rao Holkar died of a stroke on 27th October 1811 at the age of 35. His only son Malhar Rao Holkar II, was then aged five. He was a minor and hence Tulsibai took the role as Queen Regent, assuming power on behalf of her stepson. She took the help of her favorite ministers Ganapatrao and his associate Tatya Jog and also the support of two Muslims–Amir Khan and Gafur Khan to run Holkar State. Besides, Tulsibai also gained support from Zalim Singh of Kotah.

But Tulsibai faced financial difficulties in a few years while running her kingdom. Maintaining an army was a challenge due to a lack of funds. During this time Daulat Rao Scindia 'pounced upon the undefended possessions of Holkar' and even attempted to put an end to the lives of Tulsibai and Malhar Rao Holkar II. Furthermore, the Maratha Peshwa from Pune ordered Tulsibai to be ready with a force for an anti-British drive. Fearing attacks and defeats, a distressed Tulsibai sought shelter with Zalim Singh of Kotah. The British were only looking for such an opportunity. Malcolm offered her certain terms and conditions so that she could be safe under British protection, Tatya Jog advised her to accept it. But accepting it would only mean the annihilation of the Maratha power in Indore. Hence, Tulsibai refrained from accepting the terms of the British.

John Malcolm was then the British general. He looked for opportunities to attack Bhima Bai Holkar. News that the young queen would personally travel to attend the marriage ceremony of her guard's daughter and perform *kanyadaan* (a concept of giving away a daughter in marriage to the groom) reached a Pindari Sardar's ears. The Sardar was an ally of the British. Both Malcolm and the Pindari Sardar became alert but before they could give shape to their plan, Bhima Bai Holkar had reached her destination. The *kanyadaan* was solemnized.

Bhima Bai Holkar always dispensed justice in her kingdom. According to an account, one Gangadhar from her *jagir* married a British girl Jasmine. But soon after Gangadhar ditched his wife. Jasmine approached Bhima Bai for justice. The young queen forced Gangadhar to give enough money for her maintenance. A frustrated Gangadhar then sided with the British.

The Marathas under Chhatrapati Shivaji Maharaj were united. During the first half of the 19th century, conflict for the post of Peshwa and rivalry between Maratha chiefs gave scope for the British to involve in war and gain territories. And thus the third Anglo-Maratha War took place in 1817 for a year till 1818. The first Anglo-Maratha War took place from 1775 to 1782 and the second from 1803 to 1805.

The Peshwa from Pune sent a considerable amount of money for the maintenance of the Indore Maratha army so that they were ready for war against the British. Tulsibai had given enough freedom to Pathan leaders led by Roshan Beg, making them heads of the disciplined regiments and also Ramdin, who commanded the Maratha horse. Hence, real power rested in the hands of Roshan Beg and Ramdin, when it came to fighting the enemy, i.e., the British. Tulsibai sanctioned the Holkar Maratha army to move towards the south. Besides, Amir Khan, who had supported Tulsibai, had already allied with the British, accepting their terms and conditions and earning a reward–a grant of the Nawabship of Tonk. Roshan Beg and Ramdin, instead of supporting Tulsibai, seized her and her stepson Malhar Rao Holkar II, then 11 years old, and put them under confinement on 19th December 1817. On 20th, i.e., the next day, the two military leaders carried Tulsibai to the banks of the Shipra River at Mahidpur, beheaded her, and threw her into the river.

The British forces under Governor-General Hastings and General Thomas Hislop defeated the Peshwa and placed him on a small estate in Bithoor. The Peshwa's forces had resisted at different places including Mudhoji II Bhonsle of Nagpur and 11-year-old Maharaja Malhar Rao Holkar II of the Holkar State of Indore. The battle by the Holkars was led by three commanders–Malhar Rao Holkar II, Bhima Bai Holkar, and Hari Rao Holkar, who also belonged to the Holkar dynasty. This battle was known as the Battle of Mahidpur. A series of battles was fought, and the final battle took place on 21st December 1817.

This is what John Malcolm wrote about Bhima Bai Holkar in his book *Memoir of Central India:* "In a long conference I had with Bheema Bhye, the daughter of Jeswunt Row Holkar, (detailed in my letter to Mr. Metcalfe, of the first of September, 1819) she expatiated with much eloquence on the duties inculcated as those of a Mahratta princess when the interests of her family and nation were at stake. It was, she said, an obligation for such in extreme cases (where she had neither husband nor son) to lead her troops in person to battle. The young lady appealed to Letchma Bhye, a respectable matron, for the truth of her assertion; and it was confirmed, with a qualifying remark that the case must be extreme, which called for such a departure from female habits. Bheema Bhye was, from eccentricity of character, an exception to common rules. She rode with grace and few excelled her in the management of the spear."

About Maratha ladies in the royal household, Malcolm wrote thus in the same book: "They have always had great influence in their secret council, and usage has latterly given them a considerable and increased share in the Government, and in some cases, they have been the acknowledged heads. They are usually instructed in reading, working, and arithmetic. The management of the horse always constitutes part of their education, which is directed to qualify them for the duties to which their condition makes them liable to be called… They have the reputation of being faithful wives and good mothers."

Bhima Bai Holkar defeated Malcolm using Guerilla warfare techniques at a place now called Bhimakhedi, named after her victory. According to few accounts, she defeated the British several times. To quote Govind Sakharam Sardesai from his book *New History of the Marathas, Vol III:* "Bhimabai then a widow of twenty, showed the same valour during the battle, riding at the head of her corps of cavalry on a fine charger to win the day." It was in the final battle that Bhima Bai Holkar lost. She led a brigade of 2,500 cavalry, sword and lance in hand, and fought till she could resist.

The Treaty of Mandsaur, a peace pact, was signed between the British and the Holkars on 6th January 1818 at Mandsaur. Holkars lost major parts of their territory to the British.

9

Bibi Dalair Kaur

Led 100 Women Warriors in Battle against Mughals

She was a trained Khalsa warrior and a disciple of Guru Gobind Singh. The Guru gave her the responsibility to guard Anandpur Sahib against the Mughals in his absence. He left 10 armed men to assist her. There were around 100 women warriors when the Mughals attacked the fort at Anandpur Sahib. She bravely defended the fort and offered resistance. Before attaining *Veergati*, she, along with her army, killed hundreds of Mughal soldiers. She was Bibi Dalair Kaur.

On the Vaisakhi of 1699, Guru Gobind Singh, the 10th Sikh Guru created the Khalsa, a warrior community, involving a group of six warriors including himself, at Anandpur Sahib, located on the edge of Shivalik Hills. The other five warriors initiated into the Khalsa were known as the Panj Pyare. Amidst recitation from the *Adi Granth* (epic), the initiation ceremony took place with all six taking the surname 'Singh', connoting lion. Thereafter, thousands of devotees consumed nectar from the Guru over time and became part of the Khalsa. Many of the Khalsa warriors at Anandpur Sahib, under the aegis of the Guru, were trained on horse-riding and the use of weapons including swordsmanship, archery, and other martial skills. Bibi Dalair

Kaur and other women warriors, who were initiated into the Khalsa, underwent training in horse-riding and warfare.

Guru Tegh Bahadur, the ninth Sikh Guru, was executed on the orders of Mughal ruler Aurangzeb on 24th November 1675. Following this, hostilities between Sikhs and Mughals further escalated. Guru Govind Singh, before creating the Khalsa, defeated the Mughals in the Battle of Nadaun in 1691 and the Battle of Guler in 1696. After the creation of the Khalsa, Guru Gobind Singh severely defeated the Mughals in the first Battle of Anandpur in 1700 and the Battle of Nirmohgarh in 1702. The Khalsa army defeated the Mughals in the battle of Chamkaur in 1702. The Mughals again attacked Anandpur Sahib in 1704. Initially, the Sikhs emerged victorious. Aurangzeb then sent a larger force under two generals, Wazir Khan, who was also the governor of Sirhind, and Zaberdast Khan, in 1705. At that time, the Mughals followed a different strategy. They laid a prolonged siege of Anandpur Sahib at the borders, cutting off all food and other supplies. The siege continued for several months and several battles took place in between with neither party winning. Thousands of Mughal soldiers were killed in those battles though they massively outnumbered the Sikh soldiers.

The siege by the Mughals lasted for several months, from May 1705 until December. Towards the end of the siege, when Anandpur Fort, located on the top of the hills, looked deserted, the Mughals advanced on horsebacks with swords swinging on their hands to strike. For many months, they were not able to capture the fort but at that time they were confident of their victory. As they mounted up the hill, hundreds of Mughal soldiers fell off from their horses and died. The Khalsa warriors incessantly rained arrows on them from the fort. Wazir Khan and his forces retreated to their base camps.

At their camps, the Mughal generals renewed their strategy. Their siege of nearly eight months did not bear fruits. Instead, changing

Bibi Dalair Kaur with other women Khalsa warriors defending Anandpur Fort from Mughal forces.

weather conditions, floods and diseases took the lives of many Mughals in the camps. Besides, whenever they tried to attack, they only ended up with more casualties on their side and no success. The generals then decided that continuing to lay siege and waiting would further bear no fruit. Hence, they decided to strike again.

Meanwhile, due to the cut-off of the supply of food and other basic necessities to the fort, the stored food was almost out of stock in the fort. The Khalsa warriors resorted to eating the barks and leaves of trees. Guru Gobind Singh had received a letter from Aurangzeb for initiation of peace talks between the two and that no harm would be meted out to them if they were ready for the talks. Many of the Khalsa soldiers approached *Mata* (mother) Gujri, mother of Guru Gobind Singh, for accepting the proposal. Guru Gobind Singh refused citing it was a trick by Aurangzeb, as he was the same person who imprisoned his father and killed his own brothers for the throne. It was then that around 40 Khalsa warriors offered their resignation and left Anandpur Sahib for their respective homes. They crossed the enemy camps safely after creating confusion and deceiving the Mughal soldiers. But the women stayed back to defend the city and the Guru. Among the Khalsa women, numbering around 100, always ready for defending the city, was Bibi Dalair Kaur.

A messenger arrived the next day and in the name of the *Koran* promised that the Mughals would cease their attacks if the Guru agreed to go for peace talks. As there was no food stock left and as the Guru must survive for Dharma and the protection of his people, a few Khalsa warriors appealed to their leader to accept the proposal. And the Guru agreed.

Guru Govind Singh, still skeptical about Aurangzeb's promise of the letter, decided not to leave Anandpur Sahib with all the Khalsa warriors. He divided them into two groups suggesting while he and his group of 1,500 Khalsa warriors would proceed, the other group of 10 men and several women warriors led by Dalair Kaur would follow once they safely pass. Bibi Dalair Kaur sought the Guru's blessings so that she could protect the fort and the city in his absence. The Guru blessed her, tapping her shoulder with the golden tip of his arrow.

The Guru left Anandpur Sahib with 1,500 Khalsa warriors on the midnight of 5th December 1705. The Mughals broke their promise and attacked the Guru and his men. The Guru surmised it right that Aurangzeb was not a man to be relied upon, that he would never keep his promise even in the name of the *Koran*. The Sikhs bravely resisted. When Bibi Dalair Kaur heard about the attack and the betrayal, she anticipated the advancing of the Mughals towards the fort. She immediately ordered an assemblage of the women warriors in the fort and motivated them to be ready with their weapons for battle.

The Mughal forces advanced towards the fort, looting and burning everything on their way. They were confident that the fort was vacant as the Guru had left with his followers. Bibi Dalair Kaur and her group rained arrows and bullets on the Mughals as they neared the fort. Hundreds of Mughal soldiers lay dead outside the fort. The surviving soldiers retreated fast to save their lives.

Wazir Khan could not believe his eyes at the defeat. He immediately ordered his men to advance towards the fort with fire cannons. Using cannons, they broke the walls of the fort. Bibi Dalair Kaur and her army continued attacking the Mughals with arrows and bullets. There were hundreds of more casualties on the side of the Mughals. Wazir Khan sent one additional force after another and the battle continued until the Khalsa warriors ran out of ammunition.

Bibi Dalair Kaur immediately addressed a gathering of the Khalsa women warriors, numbering around 100, and motivated them to fight bravely and die for the motherland and Dharma. She inspired them, saying they had together bravely resisted the outnumbered Mughals for several hours. She ordered them to take up their swords, bows and arrows, and strike at the enemy, and fight until death.

To enter the fort, the Mughal soldiers started crossing the heaps of rubble that piled up near the broken wall. Bibi Dalair Kaur and the women warriors waited, all charged up, at the entrance of the opening. When the Mughals saw the women warriors, they were taken aback. They expected to fight with men and not women. They stopped when Wazir Khan ordered them to attack.

A fierce battle ensued. The Khalsa women warriors fought like lionesses, like Shakti. Hundreds of Mughal soldiers lay dead. The surviving soldiers retreated. Wazir Khan ordered to fire cannons at the Khalsas.

The Mughals fired heavy cannons in the direction of the Khalsas. Many walls and interiors of the fort lay damaged and a heap of rubble accumulated in no time. Wazir Khan and thousands of the Mughal soldiers entered the fort. Not a single Khalsa warrior was seen. There was silence everywhere. While the soldiers surmised the Khalsas were all dead, Wazir Khan believed many of them were alive. He ordered his men to search for them at every nook and corner of the fort. They did not find anyone. When they removed the rubble, they found the bodies of the martyred warriors.

Bibi Dalair Kaur, the 100 women warriors, and the 10 Khalsa men fought till their last breath and attained *Veergati* in the battle.

10

Haipou Jadonang

Built an Army of 500 Men/ Women against British; Hanged at 26

The freedom we enjoy today is not because of a few freedom fighters depicted in history textbooks but because of the sacrifice of lakhs of warriors from every walk of life from every nook and corner of India. The name Haipou Jadonang may be familiar to a few in Manipur and Nagaland but unknown to the rest of the country. At a very young age, Haipou Jadonang led a movement, building an army of 500 men and women as well as gaining allegiance from tribal chiefs to fight against the British. He was a spiritual leader, a political head, and a social reformist. Like countless freedom fighters, he was also hanged by the British at the age of 26. Had he lived further, the history of the region would have been different!

Haipou Jadonang was born on 10th June 1905 to Thiudai and Taboliu at Kambiron village, also called Puiluan, now in the Tamenglong district of Manipur. He lost his father when he was one year old. His mother Taboliu worked on the family farm to bring up Haipou and two other sons. Haipou belonged to the Malangmei clan of the Rongmei Naga tribe. Rongmei, meaning 'rong' for south and 'mei' for people, is an indigenous Naga community from north-east India. Earlier known as Kabui, they lived in the southern portion of the vast tri-junction of Assam, Manipur, and Nagaland, also called Zeliangrong. They follow the lunar calendar and worship Haipou Tingkao Ragwang, who they believe, is the Supreme God. According to the Constitution of India (Scheduled Tribes): Order, 1950 under the Ministry of Law and Justice (India), Rongmei Nagas, categorized under 'any Naga tribes' fall under Scheduled Tribe.

Haipou was deeply religious right from his childhood. He visited places of pilgrimage of the Nagas. He would spend hours, invoking the deity and worshipping in solitude. He also saw visions that included prophecies and healing powers. Haipou had knowledge of local herbs for curing certain ailments. By teenage, he became popular in the region. People from far and near came to listen to him, to get healed, to seek his advice.

The Treaty of Yandaboo in 1826, a peace pact signed between Gen Campbell representing British and Maha Min Hla Kyaw Htin from Burma, led to an end of the First Anglo-Burmese War. But while signing the peace treaty, the consent of local chiefs of the north-east was not taken into account. In the name of the terms and conditions of the treaty, the British cleverly extended their jurisdiction to parts of Manipur, Assam, and Tripura. By the 1830s, they set up tea plantations in these regions. The British gradually started interfering in the affairs of the other regions of the north-east. In 1891, they imposed taxes in Tamenglong of the Zeliangrong region where the Rongmei Nagas were in majority. The Rongmeis revolted and refused to pay any tax to the British. This defiance continued for three years until in 1894, the British, under C.L. Crawford, Assistant Political Agent of Manipur, used force to collect tax from the people of the region.

Haipou Jadonang was a witness to the British oppression right from his childhood. He nurtured a passion to drive away the British one day. The porter system was prevalent during those days wherein the tribal population was exploited and forced into rigorous work as porters and coolies to carry the belongings of the British in the hilly terrains with little or no payment. They were also forced to carry the British on their backs at times in the hills. Besides, they were used as labor for the construction of roads. The majority of the tribal population, including the Rongmei Nagas, were involved in cultivation. When forced into coolie work, they had no other option but to surrender to the oppression. During monsoons, the British could hardly provide them food and shelter in the hills. That often resulted in disease and death of the porters and coolies. Most of these details find mention in accounts by Burns, the Superintendent of Cachar under the British, the records of which are now available in 'Superintendent's Letter Book, 1837–38, No 130' in the Cachar District Record Room. The forced porter system of the British offended the Rongmei Nagas and also affected their prestige. Besides, the British levied heavy hill house tax and imposed more barbaric laws. Haipou Jadonang raised his voice against those oppressions and he started motivating as well as influencing the youth to fight for their freedom. He also tried to unite the local chiefs and villagers to jointly fight against the colonial rule. The British oppression led to a patriotic consciousness amongst the Rongmei Nagas. This consciousness of freeing the motherland from the clutches of the British saw the rise of Haipou Jadonang as a leader.

The people of the north-east, like in other regions of India where the British established their dominion, faced two challenges–fighting for freedom and checking Christian missionaries that became active in the region. Zeliangrong region was no different! Haipou Jadonang saw the growing control of Christian missionaries in the Naga territories as a sign of foreign imperialism and considered it a threat to the traditional Naga religion. To keep the Naga people grounded and

Haipou Jadonang motivating tribal freedom fighters to revolt against the British and to check missionary activities.

rooted in their ancestral indigenous religious practices, he established the Heraka socio-religious movement. Heraka means 'pure' and the term is derived from 'Paupaise', an ancestral Naga practice. Through this movement, Haipou sought to standardize the ancestral Naga belief systems. Rongmei Nagas worshipped several Gods but Haipou emphasized the worship of 'Tingkao Ragwang' as the Supreme Being, describing Him as omnipotent and omniscient. Followers of the Heraka movement, led by Haipou, thus started giving more importance to Tingkao Ragwang though other gods were also respected. They offered regular prayers to the Supreme Being and sang hymns in His praise. The Heraka religious movement started gaining many followers. Haipou further brought socio-religious reforms, abolishing superstitious taboos, reducing ritual sacrifices, doing away with certain rituals pertaining to weapon injuries, and felling of trees. He retained rituals related to harvests and the safety of crops from pests. He encouraged nurturing of qualities pertaining to truth, love, and respect for the whole creation, which he believed were pleasing to the Supreme Being Tingkao Ragwang. Haipou also encouraged the building of Heraka temples called 'Kao Kai' for worshipping Tingkao Ragwang. He himself constructed a 'Kao Kai' cave temple in the Bhuvan cave premises in the Zeliangrong region in Assam.

Tamenglong located in the west of Manipur bounded by Peren of Nagaland in the north, north Cachar Assam in the west, Senapati region of Manipur in the east, and Churachanpur of the same state in the south was a principal city of the Zeliangrong region. During Haipou's time, Tamenglong was the headquarters of Manipur's north-west sub-division under the British. Though Meidingngu Churachand, the Raja of Manipur enjoyed privileges as a titular king, the British held complete administrative powers. British political agent J.C. Higgins looked after the administration while S.J. Duncan undertook responsibility as the sub-divisional officer (SDO) of Tamenglong. More regions of the north-east including Naga Hills, Cachar where Rongmei Nagas were in majority, were also under British control.

During this time, Christian missionaries had already converted many tribals. The Christian converts started opposing Haipou's Heraka socio-religious movement. But Haipou already had thousands of followers, who considered him as their leader. He traveled extensively across the Zeliagrong region and mobilized people to fight for freedom and their religious identity. Haipou, to differentiate himself from the rest, rode a pony and dressed similar to British officials. This came to the notice of British SDO Duncan. The British officer did not allow Haipou to dress like them or ride a pony. But Haipou did not obey Duncan's orders. This resulted in Haipou's imprisonment for a week. Haipou was only 23 years then. His arrest only accelerated his popularity amongst the Nagas.

Soon after his release, Haipou Jadonang decided to gather an army for war against the British. In no time, he built an army called the Riphen, comprising of 500 soldiers that included both men and women. He trained them in military strategies and tactics as well as handling of weapons including guns. The army was also well trained in civilian tasks, right from the collection of firewood to farming. They were further trained in intelligence operations. This army also equally participated in Heraka gatherings, rituals, and ceremonies. The 500 Riphens were then entrusted to move from one village to another to gather support and gain allegiance from the Zeliagrong tribes to unitedly fight against the British. Haipou Jadonang succeeded in this endeavor. It took several months.

In 1930, Haipou Jadonang decided to declare war against the British. The chosen time was the end of 1931. By the beginning of 1931, he had already gained support from thousands of the Rongmei

Nagas and other tribals. The challenge that lay ahead was the accumulation of weapons, especially guns, which he felt would take over a year's time. Haipou started collecting guns. He, along with the Riphen, started holding secret meetings to strategize on the war against the British. Meanwhile, he also asked the tribals to stop paying taxes to the colonial masters.

At the beginning of 1931, the British somehow came to know about the activities of Haipou Jadonang and his army and their plan of declaring war against them. On 19th February 1931, the British arrested Haipou while he was on his way from Bhuvan Cave with 600 of his followers including Rani Gaidinliu. Haipou Jadonang was a mentor to Rani Gaidinliu, also his cousin. She joined the freedom struggle under him at the age of 13. Under his mentorship, Gaidinliu became an expert in modern warfare, especially Guerilla techniques and by the age of 16, she became a leader in Guerilla warfare against the British.

Haipou was imprisoned in Silchar Jail. The arrest of Haipou led to unrest amongst the Nagas, who decided to revolt. Immediately, the British set to action. They imposed a ban on the gathering of the tribals in groups. They also banned them to carry spears and related weapons and equipment. J.C. Higgins marched with an army towards the Zeliagrong, confiscated guns from the villagers after a search operation, arrested many, imposed further fines, and destroyed the Heraka temples. The British handed over Haipou to Higgins. It was decided that the Naga leader would be taken to Imphal Jail. Higgins took a long route, placing Haipou in chains, across the Naga territory, and after several days, nearing a month reached Imphal. Higgins tried to demonstrate that whoever would dare to raise their heads against the British would face a similar fate.

At Imphal Jail, Higgins could not extract any information pertaining to the proposed war from Haipou. Not a single Naga including Rani Gaidinliu uttered anything about the same though they were repeatedly interrogated and also tortured. Meanwhile, during this time, Christian converts led by Jinlakpou, who were looking for opportunities to put an end to the Heraka movement and get Haipou punished, falsely blamed Haipou saying that it was under his orders that four traders from Manipur were killed in early 1930. They testified in front of Higgins and thus Haipou was falsely implicated in the murders. Haipou Jadonang was hanged to death behind the Imphal Jail on the bank of the Nambul River on 29th August 1931 at 6 a.m. at the age of 26. His body was allowed to be taken to his native village Puiluan, where the last rites were performed.

Rani Gaidinliu continued the Heraka movement and the fight for freedom. In later years, Gaidinliu was arrested too and imprisoned for life; she was released post-independence. Both Jadonang and Gaidinliu being Rongmei Nagas, are revered by the Naga communities, but hardly known in the rest of India. In 2006, the Manipur Government constructed a small park behind the Imphal Jail (the place where the young Jadonang was hanged by the British) in Jadonang's honor.

11

How Pazhassi Raja Resisted Troops of Hyder Ali, Tipu Sultan, British

Pazhassi Raja! He was a brave warrior known to many from Kerala but almost unknown to the rest of India. At the young age of 21, he became the Prince Regent of the Princely State of Kottayam of Malabar. He ruled as king from 1774 to 1805. He bravely resisted Hyder Ali's troops using guerrilla warfare techniques. In later years, he also resisted Tipu Sultan's troops. He was one of the earliest freedom fighters of India. Even Arthur Wellesley, who later defeated Napoleon Bonaparte and became first Duke of Wellington and twice the British Prime Minister, could not defeat Pazhassi Raja! He was called the Lion of Kerala–the lion who never bowed in front of foreigners, the lion who defended Kerala from foreign clutches.

Kerala Varma, Cotiote Rajah, Pychy Rajah–these were the names by which Pazhassi Raja was also known as. Pazhassi is the place where he was born and hence his first name! He was born on 3rd January 1753 as the youngest Prince at Kannur, Malabar to the ancient royal clan of Puranattu Swarupam that had three branches of rulership. He was the nephew of Vira Varma, who was the ruler of Kottayam at the time of his birth. The Kottayam dominion encompassed the hilly regions of Wayanad and Northern Malabar. When Hyder Ali marched towards the Malabar kingdoms, Vira Varma fled to Travancore. He instructed Pazhassi Raja to protect the region. The young Pazhassi Raja then took over the throne of Kottayam and offered stiff resistance to Hyder Ali's troops in 1774. He was then only 21 years old. Pazhassi was married to Kunjani.

From the time he became king (as Regent) of Kottayam, Pazhassi Raja was involved in conflicts with the Sultans of Mysore–first against Hyder Ali and then Tipu Sultan. Both Hyder Ali and Tipu Sultan had been barbaric rulers, who destroyed the very roots of Indic culture during their military expeditions in their dominion by converting many forcibly to Islam, destroying and razing hundreds of temples to the ground, confiscating temple wealth, and collecting heavy taxes from the Hindus. Later Pazhassi was involved in prolonged conflicts with the British until his death. He successfully resisted Hyder Ali's, Tipu Sultan's, and British troops. His conflicts can be divided into three phases as follows:

1. 1773 to 1782 against Hyder Ali
2. 1784 to 1793 against Tipu Sultan
3. 1792 to 1805 against British until death

Vira Varma remained in Travancore as the conflict between Kottayam and the Mysore Sultans continued. Later, to regain his kingdom from his nephew, he sided with the British. The colonials agreed to reinstate him to the throne of Kottayam on one condition–their levying and collection of taxes from his people to which Vira Varma agreed. The British demanded receipt of one-fifth of the revenues of the districts of Thamarassery and Kurumbranad besides the introduction of their administration for this purpose. Pazhassi Raja considered it an offense and resisted it. This was how Pazhassi's conflict with the British started.

1773 to 1782 against Hyder Ali

In a 1766 war, Hyder Ali had subjugated most of the kingdoms in Malabar including Kottayam. The Rajas regained their respective kingdoms against payment of regular annual tributes. By 1773, the Rajas stopped paying tributes to the Mysore Sultan. That led Hyder Ali to march with a huge army towards Malabar. Most Rajas including Raja Vira Varma of Kottayam fled to Travancore seeking political asylum. Pazhassi Raja became the king Regent in Vira Varma's absence.

Pazhassi Raja, rather than fleeing from the enemy, vowed to protect the people from the invader. But he had neither guns and other modern weaponry nor troops to face Hyder Ali and his troops in an open battle. He devised a plan. Accordingly, he motivated the youth of Kottayam and arranged a force. They trained themselves in the art of guerrilla warfare. He set up a number of guerrilla bases in the forested mountains of Puralimala and Wayanad, which he and his men were well familiar with. And they started attacking Hyder Ali's troops in small groups at short intervals. This resulted in casualties in the Mysore (now known as Mysuru) Muslim army with every attack until the Mysore troops were reduced to a considerable extent. Hyder Ali entered into an alliance with two neighboring chiefs to collectively crush Pazhassi Raja but in vain. This continued till 1780 with no success for the Mysore army.

Pazhassi Raja further followed another tactic to be a terror for the enemies. He successfully raided and looted wealth in the neighboring kingdoms that sided with Hyder Ali. He also looted sandalwood and treasuries from enemies in southern Karnataka. The enemies could offer no resistance to his raids. Ravi Varma and Krishna Varma, princes from southern Malabar kingdoms, entered into alliances with Pazhassi Raja. With their help and with the help of locals, Pazhassi continued with his successful raids.

With his seven years of successful and stiff resistance, Pazhassi came to be noticed both by the British as well as Hyder Ali. During that time, Hyder Ali and the British were not on good terms with each wanting to gain supremacy over the other. Both the enemies, in their own ways, tried to gain the support of Pazhassi to use as a shield against the other. Pazhassi grabbed the opportunity to possess enough arms and ammunition through the help of any one of his enemies. That required him to either side with the British or Mysore Sultan, though temporarily. But to drive away Hyder Ali's troops completely from the Kottayam kingdom, he thought it wise to support the British in decimating Hyder Ali's troops in British-dominated territory where the Sultan's army laid siege. Pazhassi Raja helped the British recapture the Thalasseri Harbor Fort from Hyder Ali's clutches in 1781. Towards giving shape to this task, Pazhassi received enough guns and ammunition from the British. By 1782, the Muslims of Mysore, i.e., Hyder Ali's troops, were completely driven away. Kottayam kingdom became free from the clutches of Hyder Ali.

1784 to 1793 against Tipu Sultan

Meanwhile, Hyder Ali died in 1782 and he was succeeded by Tipu Sultan. Misfortune befell Kottayam and the entire Malabar region in 1784 after the British recognized Tipu Sultan's authority of the Malabar. That was as per the Treaty of Mangalore (now known as Mangaluru) signed in 1784 between Tipu Sultan and the British after the Second Anglo-Mysore War. That war started in 1780 and ended on 11th March 1784 following instructions from the British headquarters in London. Kottayam thus became a vassal state of

Pazhassi Raja using guerrilla warfare techniques against Hyder Ali's forces in the forested area of Wayanad.

Mysore as per the treaty. Tipu Sultan demanded an annual tribute of 81,000 rupees from the Kottayam king. That meant great hardships for the peasant community as the majority of the population were then agriculturists. Pazhassi Raja took up that issue and launched a mass resistance against Tipu Sultan with the help of his people.

Ravi Varma, Pazhassi's brother from the same royal clan, met Tipu Sultan in 1786 for peace talks. Without seeking guidance from the royal family, he signed a peace treaty with Tipu Sultan. According to the treaty, Wayanad was ceded to Tipu Sultan. Soon after, Mysorean troops filled up the region of Wayanad.

This action of Ravi Varma and Tipu's Muslim troops occupying Wayanad angered Pazhassi Raja. He devised a plan to drive away the Mysorean Muslims from Wayanad. His advantage was that he was well acquainted with the twists and turns, and the many paths of the Wayanad hills and forests, which Tipu Sultan's army lacked. As per his plan, Pazhassi Raja did not let the Mysore troops stay in peace. He started attacking and harassing them adopting guerrilla warfare techniques. That became a regular affair. What started in 1786, ended in 1793 after seven long years! Using guerrilla warfare techniques, Pazhassi succeeded in driving out all the Mysore garrisons from the soil of Wayanad!

Meanwhile, after Tipu Sultan assumed power, he followed a forcible conversion of Hindus to Islam. Those who converted were spared and the rest were executed. Many fled from his kingdom to save themselves from the Sultan's atrocities. That was a grave issue for Hindus in the entire Malabar region. Pazhassi Raja allied with the other Malabar chiefs and princes to save Hindus. He helped many inhabitants of Malabar retire to the jungles and assisted them in the development of a new homeland, away from the clutches of Tipu Sultan. As the Nairs revolted against Tipu Sultan, the latter entrusted a French army, who were their allies, to hunt down the former from Malabar and exterminate them. Many Nairs joined Pazhassi's forces.

Though a peace treaty was signed between the British and Tipu Sultan, both parties often went against the terms of the treaty. Pazhassi Raja was only looking for opportunities to help the British recapture forts or territories from the Mysore Sultan. Indirectly, that would only worsen relations between the two enemies and he would gain modern weapons from the British. Following that tactic Pazhassi supported the British in regaining Katirur Fort (with further support of 1,500 Nairs) and Kuttiyadi Fort from Tipu's men. But before helping, the Raja got the British to sign a pact saying that they would never interfere with the sovereignty of Kottayam. He did the same when he helped the British in defeating Hyder's troops earlier.

1792 to 1805 against British until Death

The Third Anglo-Mysore War resulted in the signing of the Treaty of Seringapatam (now known as Srirangapatna) in 1792 between the British and Tipu Sultan. As Tipu lost in this war, he ceded Malabar to the British. Then the British wanted to establish their supremacy in Malabar, which Pazhassi Raja objected to. The Raja had always wanted his kingdom to be free from foreign clutches. The British rejected the pact they signed earlier with Pazhassi. They enforced certain terms and conditions on the Rajas of Malabar–that the Rajas would continue their kingship but under British control; that British residents would be appointed in Malabar kingdoms; that British would be entrusted with determining land valuation; that the British would ascertain the tax to be paid by each citizen; that British would determine the price of pepper that would be sold to them; that the remaining pepper would be bought by merchants appointed only by the British; that the Rajas should pay annual tributes to the British, and more.

Vira Varma met the British in 1792 and accepted all the terms and conditions put forward by them much against the wishes of his nephew Pazhassi Raja. The uncle was jealous of his nephew rising in popularity. He did not want him to continue ruling Kottayam as Regent and wished to take complete power in his hands. The two hated each other.

Pazhassi Raja neither agreed to the terms and conditions set by the British nor followed the acceptance of the treaty by his uncle Vira Varma. In resistance to British sovereignty over Kottayam, he fought a series of wars against the British, one from 1793–1797 and the other from 1800–1805 until his death. Those two wars were termed the Cotiote War. Pazhassi Raja never recognized the supremacy of the British and fought until death upholding the sovereignty of his kingdom.

The British recognized Vira Varma as the ruler of Kottayam and not his nephew. Vira Varma sought the permission of the British to collect taxes from the peasants directly on their behalf.

Collection of heavy taxes would only mean extortion of the peasants. Pazhassi Raja stood up for their cause, vowing never to let the British collect taxes from Kottayam. He did not allow his uncle to collect taxes from his kingdom either. Besides, he threatened the British authorities that he would destroy all the pepper vines of Kottayam if they enforced their terms on pepper on the subjects of his kingdom. Meanwhile, during the same time, he took back certain territories of Wayanad that were under Tipu Sultan. He also gave shelter to Narangoli Nambiar, a Nair nobleman, who was hiding from the desperately searching British. Narangoli Nambiar had revolted against the British. Pazhassi Raja giving shelter to the Nair nobleman further irked the British. They planned to arrest Pazhassi Raja but gave up the idea as the Raja then had 500 strong Wayanad Nairs around him, all ready with arms to resist any type of attack.

From 1792 to 1795, neither Vira Varma nor the British were able to collect taxes from Kottayam following the stiff resistance put up by Pazhassi Raja. In 1796, the British forces under Lieutenant James Gordon marched towards Pazhassi and looted and plundered the Raja's palace. The Raja was away from his palace then. Few of his men had sided with Vira Varma and the British. Pazhassi Raja shifted his base to Purali Range and then to Wayanad. The Kurichia bowmen of the jungles supported the Raja's cause. Most of Vira Varma's men and more people, who earlier sided with the British, later joined the Raja's force. The Nair military as well as the Kurichia bowmen under the leadership of Pazhassi Raja raided British outposts in 1797, driving away the Britishers posted there.

Following guerilla warfare techniques, Pazhassi Raja defeated Major Cameroon in Periya Pass. Cameroon had come with a force of 1,100 soldiers. The Raja's army was able to slaughter many of the British soldiers. Lieutenant Nugent, Lieutenant Madge, Lieutenant Rudderman, and Cameroon were killed in action. Following the defeat of the British, a peace pact was signed in 1797 between Pazhassi and the British. The treaty was in favor of the Raja.

In the first war between 1793 and 1797, 1,000 British soldiers and 3,000 British-employed native sepoys were killed by Pazhassi's army.

Though the peace treaty was signed, the British continued with their efforts to collect taxes from Kottayam but in vain. After the death of Tipu Sultan in 1799, the British started annexing territories of the Mysore Sultanate. They decided to annex Wayanad into the British Empire. Pazhassi Raja put up a stiff resistance with a large Nair force further reinforced by Mappilas and Pathans.

Major General Arthur Wellesley was then the British army commandant of Mysore, Canara (later known as Kanara and now covering the Mangaluru region of Karnataka), and Malabar. Wellesley was the officer who later defeated Napoleon Bonaparte in the Battle of Waterloo and was promoted as the Duke of Wellington besides twice holding office as the British Prime Minister. Between 1800 and 1803, Wellesley was involved in a series of inconclusive wars against Pazhassi Raja. He could never defeat the Raja. In fact, it was the Raja who foiled all of his attacks and defeated him! The British experienced many casualties during this period. Pazhassi Raja got the support from many princes, nobles, and tribal folks from the Malabar region and collectively they created havoc on the British forces. The Raja's army captured the British-occupied Panamaram Fort.

In 1803, Wellesley was called back to Britain. Thomas Hervey Baber was appointed as the British Sub-Collector in 1804. Pazhassi Raja had been leading the revolt from the jungles of Wayanad. The British were able to crush one of his rebel groups in eastern Chirakkal in 1804. It was led by Kalyat Nambiar, a powerful Chirakkal noble. The defeat was a result of a Kolkar party of Malabar siding with the British by providing them information. Indian History has a legacy of traitors with many natives betraying their own people, and helping foreigners establish their supremacy on Indian soil. Another traitor, a Chetti, informed Baber about Pazhassi Raja's whereabouts. The Raja was then camping on the shore of a stream named Mavila close to Karnataka. The British launched a surprise attack. Pazhassi Raja attained martyrdom in the attack on 30th November 1805.

Pazhassi's wife Kunjani was taken prisoner and imprisoned at Kappanaveedu. She committed suicide in captivity. The British confiscated Pazhassi's property and demolished his palace. They constructed a road in its place, thus leaving no trace of his dwelling.

And the 32 years of brave resistance by a brave son of Bharat Mata from Kerala came to an end. He never surrendered. He fought like a lion until his death. Pazhassi Raja will inspire generations to come. Vande Mataram! Jai Hind!!!

12

How Samgramaraja of Kashmir Repulsed Attacks of Mahmud of Ghazni

Not everyone is familiar with this king from Kashmir, who ruled from 1003 to 1028 CE. He was the founder of the Lohara dynasty. Mahmud of Ghazni plundered and looted many kingdoms in India besides razing hundreds of temples to the ground, beheading thousands of Hindus, taking women as sex slaves, and converting many to Islam. Raja Samgramaraja repulsed several attacks of Mahmud of Ghazni in Kashmir. Plunderer Mahmud could never defeat the Kashmiri king! Besides, Raja Samgramaraja also helped Trilochanpala, the Hindu Shahi ruler of Lahore, with an army against Mahmud of Ghazni. The combined army defeated Sultan Mahmud.

Samgramaraja ascended the throne of Kashmir in 1003 CE after the death of Didda, the queen of Kashmir. Didda belonged to Lohara, a region located in the Pir Panjal range of mountains between western Punjab and Kashmir. She was married to Ksemgupta, the king of Kashmir. After the death of Ksemgupta, Didda became the Queen Regent, as the heir to the throne Abhimanyu II was a minor in 958 CE. Abhimanyu II died 13 years later. Didda assumed sole power of

Kashmir. As she had no sons left, she adopted Samgramaraja, her nephew in her old age, and declared him her heir though she had already vested administrative affairs of the kingdom to Vidraharaja, one of her brothers. After Didda's death, Samgramaraja became king of Kashmir, thus laying the foundation for the Lohara dynasty, though there were internal conflicts with several claimants to the throne.

The Arabs made several attempts to conquer Kashmir after they established themselves in Sindh at the beginning of the eighth century but in vain. Junaid, the Arab governor of Sindh, attacked Kashmir a few years later following the orders of Caliph Hisham. Lalitaditya Muktapida was then the king of Kashmir. The Kashmiri king defeated Junaid and thus the Arab attempt of plundering Kashmir failed. Junaid also attacked North India but failed in this expedition. Another attempt to attack Kashmir was made by Hisham ibn 'Amr al-Taghlibi, the Arab governor of Sindh after Junaid, appointed by Caliph Mansur. But Taghlibi failed to subjugate Kashmir too. After the Arabs, the Ghaznavids attempted to conquer Kashmir. During Samgramaraja's reign, Mahmud was the Sultan of Ghazni. Sultan Mahmud heard a lot about the wealth of India. He started a plundering expedition on Indian soil. He himself attacked Kashmir several times but failed. Samgramaraja bravely repulsed all his attacks.

Tunga was the prime minister of Kashmir during Didda's reign. He continued holding office under Samgramaraja. He was a herdsman before his stint in the Kashmir court and was in love with the queen. During Didda's reign, he misused powers to satisfy his own greed. He inducted corrupt officials, who were more interested in meeting their respective selfish motives and usurping money from the subjects. Samgramaraja could not curtail Tunga's power. The practice continued for several years until Tunga was murdered. But even after his death, corruption in Kashmir continued. Despite internal conflicts,

Samgramaraja was always alert against any possible military attacks by Arabs. He fortified his kingdom, kept a strong standing military force, and upgraded the military infrastructure.

During Samgramaraja's time, Trilochanpala was the Hindu Shahi ruler of Lahore (also parts of Kabul) with capital at Waihand. Earlier, this kingdom expanded to cover eastern Afghanistan, Gandhara of Punjab, and more areas. During the beginning of the 10th century, the Hindu Shahi kingdom comprised little parts of Afghanistan, Punjab, and Pakistan with capital at Waihand near Peshawar. In 1001, Mahmud of Ghazni started his military expeditions, attacking regions in Afghanistan, Pakistan, and then India. He attacked Waihand in 1002 and 1009 respectively. Jaipal was then the Hindu Shahi ruler in 1002 CE and his son Anandpal in 1009. Both faced defeat. Sultan Mahmud had vowed to raid, plunder, and loot the wealthy Hindu kingdoms regularly. This was the reason why he attacked India several times.

After the two attacks by Sultan Mahmud, the influence of the Hindu Shahi kingdom was confined only to the Salt Range. Trilochanpala feared another possible attack by Sultan Mahmud and sought military aid from Samgramaraja. The Kashmir king agreed to help. Samgramaraja sent a large army contingent to Trilochanpala's aid. The combined army of the two Hindu kings defeated Sultan Mahmud's forces. But later, months after Samgramaraja's army left for Kashmir, Sultan Mahmud personally advanced with a huge army and attacked Trilochanpala once again and defeated him.

Sultan Mahmud was annoyed by Samgramaraja's conduct of helping Trilochanpala. In 1014 CE, he marched towards Kashmir with a huge force to attack the city, take revenge, and teach Samgramaraja a lesson. He tried entering Kashmir via the Toshamaidan Pass. Samgramaraja's kingdom comprised not only Kashmir but also the Pir

Raja Samgramaraja's soldiers in action against the army of Mahmud of Ghazni.

Panjal range of mountains that housed the strong Loharkot Fort. A strong army was stationed there to check the advancement of enemy forces. Sultan Mahmud could not move beyond that fort. He laid siege to Loharkot Fort at the base but failed to capture it. Loharkot Fort finds mention in Persian historian Firishta's book as Lokote. Samgramaraja's army offered stiff resistance. It continued for a month until heavy snowfall began. It cut off Sultan Mahmud's communication with his base. He was thus compelled to retreat.

According to Firishta whose book was translated to English under the title *History of the Rise of the Mohammedan Power in India* by John Briggs: "The first of those forts was Lokote, remarkable on account of its height and strength, and which entirely defeated the King's utmost efforts; for not being able to reduce it during the summer season, he was obliged, on the approach of winter, to abandon his enterprize and return to Ghizny. On his route he was misled by his guides and falling into extensive morasses, from which he for several days could not extricate his army, many of his troops perished, and he failed in all the enterprises of this campaign." Firishta does not mention the name of the Kashmir king but describes Sultan Mahmud's failed expedition.

Seven years later, i.e., in 1021 CE, Sultan Mahmud again set out to invade Kashmir with a huge army. He had by then already plundered several kingdoms in the Indian sub-continent including Bhatinda, Thaneshwar, and Mathura. Sultan Mahmud failed in his Kashmir expedition again. It was not only a strong defense by the Kashmiri forces but also the bad weather conditions that foiled his attack. He was compelled to retreat. And Sultan Mahmud never attempted to attack Kashmir again!

Till 1320 CE, Kashmir remained unaffected by Islamic invasions. Islamic settlements started in the region after the kingdom was conquered by Zulju, a Mongol chieftain. He entered Kashmir via the

Jehlum Valley route. This marked the end of the Lohara dynasty after the then Lohara king of Kashmir Suhadeva fled to Kistwar after failing to offer stiff resistance. Amid the chaos after Zulju left, Rinchana, a Buddhist and son of a Ladakhi chief, got Ramchandra, the prime minister turned Raja murdered and ascended the throne. He married Ramchandra's daughter Kota Rani to gain the sympathy of the Kashmiris. Later Rinchana converted to Islam under the influence of Bulbul Shah (also called Sayyid Sharfudin), a Sufi preacher, and attained a new name–Sultan Sardarudin Shah. He, in turn, converted Ramchandra's son, the commander of the Kashmiri army, and many other ministers of the court and subjects to Islam. And thus started a Muslim rule in Kashmir under the first Muslim ruler Sultan Sardarudin Shah, a convert! Today Islam is the major religion practiced in Kashmir with the maximum of the region's population being Muslims as per the latest Census. Who isn't familiar with the Kashmiri Pundits Exodus in 1990, wherein the Hindu Kashmiris were forced to leave the Valley turning them to the status of refugees in their own motherland!

Kashmir was saved from being looted, raided, and plundered by the barbaric Sultan Mahmud of Ghazni. It was Samgramaraja who repulsed his attacks.

13

Sanyasi Rebellion

How Jagannath Pilgrims Attacked British in 1770-75

Sanyasi (religious mendicant) Rebellion! Many of us have hardly heard about this rebellion against the British by a group of wandering sanyasis, especially from 1770 to 1775 in British Bengal, especially today's Bengal and Odisha. While colonial historians including few Indian historians labeled the sanyasis who revolted against the British as 'banditti', 'robbers', or 'looters', Bankim Chandra Chatterjee in his book *Anandamath* describes a true account of the rebellion citing a series of British records and letters. Few of these records include details of what Hastings wrote to George Colebrooke on 2nd February 1773, to Josias Du Pre on 9th March 1973, to Purling on 31st March 1775, to Lawrence on 30th March 1771 besides also quoting from Hunter's *Annals of Rural Bengal*.

Warren Hastings was the first de facto Governor-General of India from 1774 to 1785. George Colebrooke was the chairman of the East India Company, Josias Du Pre the Governor of Madras (now Chennai) from 1770 to 1773, John Purling the commander of East India Company, and Stringer Lawrence the first Commander-in-Chief of British India. These records and descriptions by Bankim Chandra Chatterjee give us a glimpse of how ascetics revolted against the

British, how they impacted the early phase of the colonial rule, and how they were the subject of discussion among top British officials for several years. It was the song and slogan of 'Vande Mataram' depicted in *Anandamath* that inspired many freedom fighters to rise in rebellion and free the motherland from British rule.

In ancient and medieval India, kings donated villages to temple authorities in respective kingdoms wherein priests collected revenues from those villages for not only maintenance of the temples but also to run Gurukuls for primary education, to host pilgrims, and for related socio-cultural activities in the temple premises. Ascetics also earned the patronage of the kings and ministers, and later zamindars as well as traders for pilgrimage to shrines across the country. During the 1770s, the British established their stronghold in the Bengal region and later Madras. They started collecting heavy taxes from peasants, zamindars, landlords, and traders. Besides, the great famine that affected the lower Gangetic plain from Bihar to Bengal from 1769 to 1776 turned the region from riches to rags. The British proved harsher than Nature. They took away as tax whatever little the peasants cultivated, thus leaving them to die in starvation. This fury of Mother Nature combined with the barbaric policies of the British resulted in over 10 million deaths.

According to a report by Warren Hastings, then Governor-General of British India, one-third of the population in the affected region starved to death. For every peasant family, it started with one meal a day, then half a meal, and then starving the whole day, followed by several days of starving and ultimately death. In such a situation, tax collectors employed by the British levied more taxes on the poor starving peasants.

Here is a grim description by Bankim Chandra Chatterjee of the situation of the famine-affected people: "First, people began to beg.

But soon there was none to give alms–they then began to starve. Then they began to suffer from diseases. They sold their cattle, sold their ploughs, ate up the seed grains, sold their houses and their holdings, and at last their daughters and sons, and wives. Then there could not be found buyers of men, everybody wanted to sell. They then fed on leaves, grass and weeds for want of other food; the lower classes and wild tribes fed on dogs, mice, and cats. Many fled and died of starvation away from their homes. Those who did not fly away died from starvation or from diseases brought on by eating unwholesome food."

After the British took control of Bengal, the landlords, zamindars, and traders weren't able to give alms in cash and kind freely to the sanyasis for their pilgrimage. Whatever they gave came under the notice of the British. This act of donation irked the colonial masters. When they interfered, the sanyasis took action. They started slaughtering the British. This action came to be known as the Sanyasi Rebellion. Moreover, they hated the British looting the people and the country. The exploitation of the people of the region by the British even during famine further angered them. Most of the sanyasis came from the northern and western parts of the country to visit the Jagannath temple of Puri–one of the *char dhams* and other pilgrimage sites.

The sanyasis, as described by Warren Hastings to Josias Du Pre, the then Governor of Madras dated 9th March 1773 were 'mostly naked'. The phrase here can be interpreted both as 'partly covering the bodies' and 'most of them being naked'. The naked sanyasis were undoubtedly Naga Sadhus. Among the Hindu ascetics, a section of Naga Sadhus stays naked.

The sanyasis have been described as wanderers with no homes or families, that they came to Bengal from as far as Tibet, Afghanistan, and China. In short, the description of their whereabouts meant they came from the Himalayan region given the fact that the British then weren't very much aware of the complete geography of upper northern India. British records describe them as 'the stoutest and the most active men in India' and as 'hardy, bold and enthusiastic'. Warren Hastings wrote thus to Josias Du Pre about the sanyasis: "The history of the people is curious. They inhabit or rather possess the country lying south of the hills of Tibbet from Caubul to China. They go mostly naked, they have neither towns, houses, nor families; but rove continually from place to place..."

In a letter to George Colebrooke, chairman of the East India Company, dated 2nd February 1773, Warren Hastings wrote how a group of 3,000 sanyasis (Hastings also terms them as *fakeers*) attacked the Pergona Sepoys who were steered by Captain Thomas near Rungpore (now Rangpur in Bangladesh). He described how Captain Thomas was killed in action during the fight. Hastings also described the sanyasis, numbering in groups from 1,000 to 10,000, to be annual pilgrims who came to visit the Jagannath (Puri Jagannath) shrine. He admitted and fretted the fact that the sanyasis were hailed more than they deserved by the people for their rebellion–'which has made them more talked of then they deserve'.

To Josias Du Pre, Warren Hastings wrote that the sanyasis defeated two bands of Pergona Sepoys and 'cut off' the bands' two commanders.

Warren Hastings described the sanyasis as 'the Gipsies of Hindustan'. Such was the people's reverence for these pilgrims that the British could not gather information about their movement. The British became alert after two of their bands were defeated by the sanyasis. Despite deploying people to gather intelligence about their whereabouts and despite passing rigid orders, the villagers stood united in not providing any info about them. Thus, the sanyasis appeared from nowhere; to quote Hastings, 'they often appear in the heart of the province as if they dropt from heaven'.

Warren Hastings also wrote to John Purling, the Commander of East India Company, dated 31st March 1775 quoted in *Anandamath*. The letter is evidence of how the sanyasis wreaked havoc on the British. Hastings wrote: "We have lately been much troubled here by hordes of desperate adventurers called Sannyasis, who have overrun the province in great numbers and committed great depredations."

After the successful defeat of two bands of Pergona Sepoys and 'cutting off' their two commanders, the sanyasis further troubled the British at different places. They then attacked British posts in different parts of the Dinajpur and Rungpore provinces of Bengal. They came in several groups of 2,000 to 3,000 members each. The people, despite being subjected by the British to the strictest orders of passing information about the sanyasis' whereabouts, remained mute. The sanyasis attacked and defeated another detachment of British soldiers commanded by Captain Edwardes. They killed Edwardes and all the sepoys. Edwardes tried to escape crossing a nullah (a water body or ravine) but in vain. Hastings labels the reverence of the people for the sanyasis as 'superstition'.

The Sanyasi Rebellion took a toll on the British in Bengal. Hastings then deployed three troops–the 19th battalion of Sepoys commanded by Captain Stewart, another battalion from Burrampoor (now Berhampore), and another from Dinapoor (now Patna) to pursue the sanyasis. An additional battalion from Cooch Behar commanded by Captain Jones was to join the pursuit.

The Sanyasi Rebellion took a different turn. Groups of sanyasis then entered Purneah province (now in Bihar) and started plundering British-held villages and properties. Captain Brook was in-charge of that province. He had a newly raised battalion of light infantry. Before the British army reached the spot the sanyasis had already left. The losses incurred as a result of the plunder 'inconsiderably' affected the revenue of the British East India Company. According to Hastings, the sanyasis looted the British treasury besides destroying more of their properties in other districts of Bengal, which also affected the overall revenue. The British then stationed troops in small detachments at various posts to prevent any future incursions by the sanyasis.

Attacks by the sanyasis continued throughout the year. The local people supported them, giving them refuge. According to Warren Hastings, zamindars also supported them. The British were subsequently able to expel sanyasis from the north-eastern part of Bengal. Indians including zamindars who gave refuge to the sanyasis were 'severely' punished. He wrote about it to Stringer Lawrence, the first Commander-in-Chief of British India dated 30th March 1771.

The sanyasis who revolted in Bengal attacking the British army and posts were annual pilgrims. They did not stay in one place. Merchants also accompanied the sanyasis to visit the shrines. The Sanyasi Rebellion thus lost momentum in a few years with the sanyasis returning to where they came from after visiting the shrines. But they were successful in defeating several bands of British soldiers besides killing their commanders. They were successful in destroying British-held properties in villages and plundering their posts thus severely affecting the revenue of East India Company. The locals supported them and gave them refuge despite knowing how harsh the British were. But these series of victories by the sanyasis and how the Sanyasi Rebellion impacted the initial phase of the colonial rule don't find a place in our history textbooks.

Sadhus and sanyasis played an instrumental role in defending Dharma and the motherland. Vande Mataram!

14

Dantidurga II

Rashtrakuta King who Defeated Arabs in the Eighth Century

Islamic invasions in India started with the Arabs attacking the northern part of India and the Himalayan regions for a period of several years. Every Hindu ruler resisted. Raja Lalitaditya Muktapida of Kashmir successfully resisted their attacks and Guhilot Raja Bappa Rawal defeated them and captured Chittor. While few rulers lost their kingdoms initially, later, they regained their territories. To further put an end to the Arab attacks, the Indian rulers united. Two inscriptions tell us about two united battles of the Hindu rulers that put an end to Arab attacks. The Arabs were so badly defeated that they did not dare to invade the Indian territories for the next 250 to 300 years.

The two inscriptions are the Navsari record of Navsari and Gwalior engraving of Mihir Bhoj. While the Gwalior inscription describes a confederation of Hindu rulers under Gurjar Pratihar ruler Nagbhat I defeating the Arabs, the Navsari inscription tells us about Avanijanashraya Pulakeshin, a Chalukyan vassal ruler, and Dantidurga II, a Rashtrakuta together decimating the Arabs. Besides, the latter victory of the Hindu rulers stopped the advances of the Arabs towards the south of India.

In addition, according to the book *The Rashtrakutas and Their Times* by Dr. A.S. Atlekar: "Arabs of Sindh were now and then attacking their western neighbours and Dantidurga seems to have defeated some of these raids." During this time, Dantidurga II was consolidating and expanding his kingdom. When Dantidurga II along with Avanijanashraya Pulakeshin defeated the Arabs, he was a feudatory Rashtrakuta prince of the Chalukyas and had not yet established the Rashtrakuta empire.

Who was Dantidurga II, also called Dantivarman II, who defeated the Arabs? Who were the ancestors of Dantidurga II? He re-established the Rashtrakuta dynasty in the Deccan, hence he is also deemed the founder. According to Kalhana's *Rajtarangini* and Pandit Bisheshwar Nath Reu's *History of the Rashtrakutas (Rathodas),* Dantidurga II's ancestors ruled a major area of the Deccan. Reu mentions that out of 75 inscriptions and copper grants available on Rashtrakutas, eight describe them to be of Yadava lineage with one copper grant describing Rashtrakuta Dantidurga being born 'in the line of Yadava Satyaki'. Reu also describes Rashtrakutas as 'Ratta', which also finds mention by Kalhana of a Rashtrakuta queen named 'Ratta'. Besides, Reu delves on a fact rarely pointed by historians that the Rashtrakutas originally resided in the north-western part of India and later migrated towards the south, tracing them as Arattas of Punjab during the *Mahabharata* period, Rashtrikas during Mauryan times, and the Rathodas of later era.

The Yevur (a historical site in the present-day Yadgiri District of Karnataka State) inscription mentions about Rashtrakuta ruler of the Deccan Indra (the son of Krishna), who owned 800 elephants, being overthrown by Solanki Chalukya Jayasimha. Solanki Chalukyas then assumed the title of 'Vallabharaja' and started ruling the Deccan. The Rashtrakuta rulers (who then became feudatory) after Indra were Dantidurga I, Indraraja I, Govindaraja I, Karkaraja, and Indraraja II

Dantidurga II seeking blessings from his mother Ratta in a temple before going to war.

respectively. The Ellora inscription of Dantidurga II describes him as the son of Indra II. Indra here is Indraraja. Dantidurga II was thus the son of Indraraja II. He defeated Kirtivarman II, the 11th Solanki Chalukya King in descent from Jayasimha, and thus regained major parts of the Rashtrakuta kingdom in between 747 and 753 CE. This was after defeating the Arabs. Rashtrakutas retained the title of 'Vallabharaja' for themselves; they find mention in Arab chronicles as 'Balharas', a corrupt form of 'Vallabharajas'. Dantidurga II's mother was a Solanki Chalunkyan Queen, hence the Rashtrakutas and Chalukyas were on friendly terms.

According to Kalhana's *Rajtarangini*, Raja Lalitaditya Muktapida of Kashmir helped Rashtrakuta queen Ratta also known as Bhavagana, the mother of Dantidurga, with an army to maintain her supremacy from rivals. It was Ratta who sought Lalitaditya's help. Hermann Goetz in *Studies in the History and Art of Kashmir and the Indian Himalaya* describes Bhavagana as Ratta and also as Queen Regent of Dantidurga for some time, as he was a minor when Indra II died.

Dharashraya Jayasimhavarman, brother of Vatapi Chalukyan king Vikramaditya I, was appointed governor of parts of the southern Gujarat region including other regions subjugated by the Chalukyas. He was succeeded by Jayashraya Mangalarasa followed by Avanijanashraya Pulakeshin. There is inscriptional evidence of all the three vassal rulers. Avanijanashraya Pulakeshin ascended the throne in 731 CE.

The Navsari inscription was found by a resident of Satem village in Navsari, he gave it to the Epigraphical Society of India. The inscription is dated year 490 of the Kalachuri era corresponding to 1st November 738 of the Gregorian calendar. Another estimated date is 21st October 739 CE. Going by the inscription of Navsari, the fierce battle against the Arabs took place in 738 CE or 739 CE.

The Umayyad Caliphate emerged powerful in the Arabian region. After the death of Muhammad, four major caliphates were established. Umayyad was the second of the caliphates; they hailed from Mecca. Also termed Tajikas, another connotation for Arabs, they plundered few kingdoms of Akhand Bharat, especially Sindh, and advanced inwards. Their empire, after the conquest, stretched from Spain in the west to Afghanistan and Pakistan in the east.

Dantidurga II and Avanijanashraya Pulakeshin confronted the Arab forces in Navsari in a battle described as fierce. The might of the Arab forces can be well conjectured by the fact that the same troops plundered Sindh, Kutch, Saurashtra, Chavolakas, Maurya, and Gurjara kingdoms by then (later, most of the rulers united and the combined army defeated the Arabs in the north). The strength of Dantidurga was perceptible by his later victories and the establishment of the Rashtrakuta empire. Pulakeshin's role in the battle was exemplified by the titles he received after the battle victory. The combined forces of the Indian rulers severely defeated the Arab forces. The terrible defeat dampened the spirits of the Arabs to such an extent that they dropped their idea of intruding into the southern kingdoms of India.

After the victory of the Battle of Navsari against the Arab forces, both Dantidurga and Avanijanashraya Pulakeshin were felicitated by Vikramaditya II, the Chalukyan ruler of Vatapi.

Eight years after this victory against Arabs, Dantidurga laid the foundation of the lost Rashtrakuta empire by defeating Solanki Chalukya king Kirtivarman, i.e., in 747. He captured more parts of the Chalukyan territory by 753 CE. And then followed the expansion of his empire.

Several inscriptions and epigraphs in copper plates describe Dantidurga II's might. The copper grant of Dantivarman II, dated 753

CE features a couplet that describes Dantidurga II proving his reverence for his mother by granting lands in charity in almost all the 400,000 villages of his kingdom. The number of villages mentioned in the copper grant gives us an idea about the vastness of the Rashtrakuta kingdom during Dantidurga's reign. The magnificent Ellora Kailasha cave temple was built by the Rashtrakutas. Rulers of this dynasty, including Dantidurga II, built several temples in Ellora caves. The Dashavatara temple in Cave 15 has a stone inscription of Raja Dantidurga II that has a line describing 'who is not aware of the world-famous Rashtrakuta race'. The copper grant of Samangadh describes Dantidurga II's elephants going up to the Mahi, Mahanadi, and Narmada, which refer to expansions through conquests. During the peak of his rule, his kingdom extended from Rameswaram in the south to the northern borders of Gujarat and Malwa. The Ellora inscription of Dantidurga II describes him taking the titles of *Rajadhiraja* and *Parameshvara*.

Dantidurga died in 758 CE without a heir and the Rashtrakuta kingdom fell into the hands of his uncle Krishna. That Dantidurga died in his late thirties proved he was 18 or 19 years old, or even younger when he defeated the Arabs.

15

Hambirrao Mohite

Defeated Mughals and Adilshahi Army Several Times

He was a blunt, energetic, fearless, and gallant soldier, whose nature matched with Chhatrapati Shivaji Maharaj! In the history of India, he was one of the few commanders who won numerous battles against Islamic invaders, especially Aurangzeb's Mughal forces and the Adilshahi forces of Bijapur. This Maratha general was a brilliant war strategist. He was Hansaji Mohite, more popular as Sarnobat Hambirrao, a title conferred by Chhatrapati Shivaji Maharaj for his brave battle exploits. Sarnobat means 'Chief of Army' and Hambirrao means 'the brave one', an honor well deserved! His legacy of valor was continued by his daughter Tarabai Bhosale, Shivaji's daughter-in-law, who resisted Mughal attacks many times, leading armies to battle and because of whom the Maratha Empire survived the awful crisis from 1700 to 1707!

Hambirrao Mohite was born on 1st May 1632 (few sources mention 1630) at Talbid, located in today's Satara region of Maharashtra. His father Sambhajirao Mohite was a valorous Maratha Sardar and the ruler of Talbid. He had four siblings–two brothers Harifrao and Shankarji as well as two sisters Soyarabai and Annubai. While

Soyarabai was married to Shivaji Maharaj, Annubai was married to Venkoji, the step-brother of the Maratha king. Hambirrao Mohite spent his childhood at Supe, located 70 kms from Pune. He inherited the military talent and energy of his father besides further training in the art of warfare to perfection. He joined Shivaji's Maratha Army as a commander in 1670, soon to be promoted as the 'Chief of Army' or commander-in-chief, the second-highest post among Shivaji's principal ministers after the Peshwa.

In 1674, the Adilshahi forces under general Bahalol Khan attacked the Maratha territory. The Marathas under Prataprao Gurjar surrounded Bahalol Khan's camp at Nesari. In a fierce battle that ensued, the Maratha *ffect* (commander) took Bahalol Khan captive. They captured the Adilshahi forces along with their war material. Shivaji had warned all of his senapatis and the sardars to never trust enemies, and never let them go free. When Bahalol Khan repeatedly begged for pardon and promised never to attack Maratha territory again, Prataprao Gurjar gave a second thought. The enemy general's repeated requests to let him and his captured army free made him forget Shivaji's warning. His impulsive emotional nature came into play. And he released Bahalol Khan along with his troops including the seized war material. Prataprao Gurjar's action irked Shivaji Maharaj. "Never come into my presence until you have extinguished the army of Bijapur!" Shivaji ordered Prataprao. Meanwhile, few days after his release, Bahalol Khan started preparing for a fresh invasion of the Maratha territory. He did not keep his promise made to the Maratha ffect. He advanced towards Nesari with a troop of 15,000 soldiers. He camped at Nesari. Prataprao Gurjar had a strength of 1,200 soldiers, who were no match to the Bijapuri army, numbering 15,000. Prataprao left alone towards Bahalol Khan's camp. Six Maratha Sardars joined him when they saw him galloping in his horse towards the enemy all alone. Seven Marathas against 15,000 Muslim soldiers! Prataprao Gurjar and the six Maratha

Sardars fought until death. At the fall of the Maratha ffect, Shivaji's army was paralyzed. The Adilshahi army, then led by Abdul Kareem, took the opportunity and committed 'great slaughter' of the Hindu army until the latter found shelter behind the ramparts of Panhala Fort.

Hansaji Mohite, a commander of 5,000 Maratha soldiers, marched towards the battle site and Panhala Fort. The Maratha armies under Prataprao had faced a crushing defeat and were chased by the enemy forces. Hansaji Mohite encountered the enemy at Jessary. A fresh breath of life prevailed amongst the decimated forces with the arrival of the commander. Hansaji fell upon the enemy recklessly and 'changed the whole aspect of the battle'. He employed his war tactics to the advantage of the Maratha army. Soon in no time, defeat turned into victory! Two brave warriors under Hansaji's command were Santaji Ghorpade and Dhanaji Jadhav. To quote from *The Life of Shivaji Maharaj: Founder of the Maratha Empire* by N.S. Takakhav and K.A. Keluskar: "Thousands of Mahomedans were overtaken and slain. Such was the Battle of Jessary (1674)." The surviving Adilshahi army including their commander Abdul Kareem, heavily wounded, fled from the battlefield to save their lives. They were so gravely defeated with thousands of casualties that their army as a whole remained crippled for some time. Such was the havoc created by Hansaji Mohite on the battlefield! For the next few years, the enemy forces did not dare to attack the Maratha territory!

The outcome of the Battle of Jessary greatly impressed Shivaji Maharaj. He promoted Hansaji Mohite as the chief of the Maratha army and conferred him the title of Hambirrao. Henceforth, Hansaji Mohite came to be known as Sarnobat Hambirrao Mohite. To further quote from *The Life of Shivaji Maharaj: Founder of the Maratha Empire: "Shivaji* was highly gratified with the marvelous bravery of the

Chhatrapati Shivaji Maharaj commending Hambirrao Mohite for his victories in war against the Adilshahi Sultanate of Bijapur and Aurangzeb's Mughal forces.

man who in the hour of darkest disaster had so triumphantly turned the scales against the enemy. He extolled the conduct of Hansaji Mohite, appointed him to the chief command or sir-nobut, and gave him the title of Hambirrao, by which he is generally known… The victory of Hambirrao over Abdul Kareem had cost many lives to the Bijapur army which remained appreciably crippled for some time. Neither was it possible to muster a new army against Shivaji nor did a capable general offer himself for a renewal of the contest."

Hambirrao never stayed idle. He was always involved in exploits against the enemies–Adilshahi Sultanate of Bijapur and Aurangzeb's Mughal forces. Once Hambirrao with his forces climbed the ghats near Surat and thereafter divided his forces into several groups and dispersed them in different directions. The commander-in-chief entrusted each of these groups of soldiers to ravage the Mughal territories. A group entered the district of Broach (now known as Bharuch), a Mughal domain in Gujarat, and collected heavy war booty. Diler Khan, a Mughal commander, had to rush back with his forces stopping his military expeditions in the territories of Shivaji. Meanwhile, Hambirrao Mohite himself 'carried on a vigorous offensive' in Mughal dominions in Gujarat and gathered an immense booty. The Maratha commander-in-chief anticipated Diler Khan's intervention while on his way back with the booty towards the Maratha kingdom. He strategized and accordingly marched forward. Diler Khan did try to attack Hambirrao but in vain. Hambirrao thus brought to Raigad all the booty. In a few days, Hambirrao again intruded into Mughal territories and repeated his onslaughts. No Mughal commander 'came forth to challenge him'.

The Koppal province, located in the basin of the Krishna and the Tungabhadra rivers in karnataka during Shivaji's reign, was under two generals of Adilshahi Sultanate, brothers–Abdul Rahimkhan Miyana and Hussain Miyana. The Adilshahi Sultan Sikandar Adil Shah was a minor, the officers under him thus considered themselves as leaders. Both the generals collected heavy taxes from the inhabitants besides forcibly taking away crop yields from farmers. According to one account, the oppressed people of Koppal sought Chhatrapati Shivaji's help in 1677. Shivaji sent a huge force under the command of Hambirrao Mohite to attack Koppal. A fierce battle ensued between the Maratha and Adilshahi forces. So aggressive was the battle and unparalleled valor shown by Hambirrao that half of Adilshahi soldiers were slain. Hambirrao killed Abdul Rahimkhan Miyana and imprisoned Hussain Miyana. 'The whole of the country was overrun and subdued. The feudal lords of the region accepted the suzerainty of Shivaji'. Adil Shahi Sultanate 'never attempted thereafter to recover these districts from Shivaji'.

Hambirrao Mohite also attacked more territories of the Adilshahi Sultanate. He attacked the fort of Devur where he encountered an army of 10,000 commanded by Hussain Khan. Hambirrao defeated the enemy forces and captured the fort. Another force of Adil Shah under the commandment of Lodi Khan reached Devur but he too was defeated and taken prisoner. Hambirrao also captured the forts of Gondal and Bahadurbanda including more forts. Hambirrao's military warriors Dhanaji Jadhav and Bayaji Ghorpade led every battle to victory. Chhatrapati Shivaji honored and acknowledged all three–Hambirrao Mohite, Dhanaji Jadhav, and Bayaji Ghorpade–as well as other Maratha officers and soldiers for their successful campaigns.

After the death of Shivaji Maharaj, Hambirrao Mohite supported Sambhaji Maharaj as a claimant to the Maratha throne. He served Sambhaji just as he served Shivaji.

In 1681, Hambirrao Mohite and Sambhaji Maharaj attacked Burhanpur, then a major trade center under the dominance of the Mughals with an army of 20,000. Khan Jahan was the Mughal Subedar of Burhanpur. The Maratha army easily defeated the Mughals. In this expedition against the Mughals, the Marathas collected a large booty and assets. Hambirrao also defeated Ranamast Khan, a Mughal chieftain in Kalyan Bhiwandi in 1683.

In 1687, another battle between the Marathas–led by Hambirrao Mohite and Mughals led by Sarja Khan–was fought near Wai in now Satara district of Maharashtra. Hambirrao, a brilliant war strategist, as always pushed the Mughals into the dense jungles near Wai and Mahableshwar. This was a terrain the enemy forces were not very familiar with. The Marathas emerged victorious in this battle near Wai. But a cannonball accidentally hit Hambirrao Mohite. The gallant Maratha commander-in-chief attained *Veergati* on 16th December 1687 at the age of 57. Had Hambirrao Mohite lived further, Sambhaji would have repelled the Mughals and the history of the region would have been different!

Naman to Hambirrao Mohite for his valor! Vande Mataram!!!

16

Jayi Rajaguru

Royal Priest who Waged War against British in 1803-05

India has a legacy, since ancient times, of Brahmins who not only were *pujaris* and Gurus (teachers) but also warriors and commanders of armies, rulers, besides holding administrative posts. Since time immemorial, they have been known for their martial abilities. Dronacharya was not only a priest and Guru, who taught various subjects including military exploits to the Kauravas and Pandavas but was also a commander of the Kaurava army. He was the 2nd commander-in-chief of the Kauravas during the Mahabharata War. Bhai Singha, a Brahmin, was *Kul-purohit*, the royal priest and lieutenant of Guru Hargobind, 6th Sikh Guru. He rescued the Guru's young daughter from the Mughals' clutches and killed Mughal commander Mohd Ali before attaining martyrdom in the battle against the Mughals in Amritsar. Not many of us, except from Odisha, have heard about Jayi Rajaguru, the royal priest of Gajapati Mukunda Deva II of the Khurda kingdom. He was also the commander-in-chief of the Khurda army and administrative representative of the king. He was one of the first freedom fighters who waged war against the British around 1803-05 and was one of the first martyrs of India's freedom struggle.

Jayi Rajaguru was born on 29th October 1739 at Biraharekrushnapur village near Puri in Odisha. His mother was Haramani Devi and father was Chandra Rajaguru. His grandfather Gadadhara Rajaguru was a Sanskrit scholar and was well versed in the ancient Hindu scriptures. Jayi Rajaguru inherited the scholarly qualities of his grandfather. He was an exceptional scholar in Sanskrit and a *Tantra Sadhaka*. He was trained in warfare from a very young age. Jayi Rajaguru remained a *Brahmachari*, i.e., he never married. He was the royal priest of the Bhoi dynasty under Gajapati Dibyasingha Deva II and later under Raja Mukunda Deva II. He was also the chief minister Of Dibyasingha Deva II. Later under Raja Mukunda Deva II, he was entrusted with another additional responsibility as the chief of the army and as the king's representative.

Khurda was a kingdom in Odisha during the reign of the early Bhoi dynasty founded by Govinda Vidyadhara in 1541. The Bhois trace their origin to Krishna's Yaduvamsa. Cuttack was their power center. Mukunda Deva, the founder of the Chalukya dynasty in this region, deposed Bhoi ruler Raghuram Chhotaraya in 1560. As a result of attacks by the Bengal Sultanate and then the Mughals, the kingdom shrank. The power and territories of the Bhois diminished. Ramachandra Deva, later Bhoi ruler, shifted base to Khurda. Jayi Rajaguru served under Bhoi rulers Gajapati Dibyasingha Dev, who ruled from 1793 to 1798, and Mukundeva Deva II, who ascended the throne of the Khurda kingdom in 1798 and ruled till 1804.

Initially, the British only had commercial and no political interests in India. They set up a factory in Harishpur near Cuttack in 1633 CE and at Balasore in 1642 CE where they dealt in fabrics. The Mughals allowed them as these regions existed as vassal kingdoms under them. After the Marathas captured most of the Mughal territories including major parts of Odisha, the trade of the British declined and they shifted base to Hooghly. Kingdoms lying south of the Subamarekha river came under the control of the Marathas–the Bhonsle Raja of Nagpur. After the British won the Battle of Plassey in 1757, their political interests gained ground and they started occupying one province after another. In 1765, Mughal ruler Shah Alam issued a *firman*, a permit, granting *diwani* (the right to collect taxes directly from the people on behalf of the Mughals) of Bengal, Bihar, and parts of Odisha. British under Robert Clive obtained the *diwani* of these regions including Cicacole, Raj Mahendri, Ellore, and Guntur as free gift. They were granted *diwani* rights of the present Ganjam district in Odisha, especially Midnapur. After the British established their power in Bengal, Bihar, and Madras, the strategic importance of Odisha amplified. With major parts of Odisha under several regional kings, who were vassal rulers under Marathas, the movement of British troops between the southern and northern dominions became difficult. Hence, the British started interfering in the affairs of those regions for the complete acquisition of Odisha. They tried to take the Marathas into confidence but in vain. Clive, Warren Hastings, and Cornwallis tried to win over the Marathas for possession of Odisha but did not succeed. But under Wellesley, the Maratha Peshwa entered into a subsidiary alliance with the British, which enraged the other Maratha chiefs; the latter did not agree. As a result, Wellesley declared war against the Marathas in 1802. To quote from Prafulla Kumar Pattanaik's book, *The First Indian War of Independence: Freedom Movement in Orissa, 1804-1825:* "Lord Wellesley planned a three-pronged invasion of Orissa. From Ganjam in the south, a military campaign was to be launched under the command of Lt. Col. Campbell. In the north, an attack was to be made from Jaleswar. Balasore was to be occupied by an invasion from the sea." Many rulers, except that of khurda and counted few kingdoms, gave permission to British troops to pass through their respective kingdoms. British forces from Ganjam started marching from 8th September 1803 under the command of Campbell. But the commander fell ill, hence, Lt. Col. Harcourt took over the command. They were to march through Meetacoah, Manikpatna, Puri, Narsinghpatna, and more cities. At Narsinghpatna, the British realized that four-fifth of the road further from there covered Khurda.

During that time, as Raja Mukunda Deva II was a minor, Jayi Rajaguru undertook complete responsibilities of the administration, army, and major decisions pertaining to the kingdom. To pass through Khurda, the British needed to take permission from the king. But they were apprehensive that the Raja might be in a secret alliance with the Marathas. The British, after a discussion between Colonel Harcourt and J. Melville (civil commissioner for the settlement of the revenue of Cuttack), wrote a letter to Raja Mukunda Deva II for safe passage, including assistance from the king to speed up the advance of the store, baggage, and artillery of the British besides some military support.

Jayi Rajaguru was suspicious of the British motive. He thus did not allow them to pass through his kingdom. He was the first in Odisha to oppose the British movement. The British continued with their negotiations. Part of the Khurda territory–the parganas of Limbai, Rahang, Serai, and Chabiskud were already taken by the Marathas in 1760. During the time of Chhatrapati Shivaji Maharaj, the Marathas attacked only those kingdoms that were under the Mughals, Bijapur Sultanate, Portuguese, and other foreign invaders. He did not interfere in the affairs of the kingdoms run by native rulers. This legacy was followed by his successors Sambhaji, Rajaram and Tarabai, and Shahu Maharaj. Later, Peshwas gained control of the Maratha Empire followed by Maratha confederacies. The Marathas, under Raghuji Bhonsle, attacked Odisha, a major part of which was under the Mughals. But deviating away from the policies followed by Shivaji and later Maratha rulers, Raghuji Bhonsle also attacked and annexed few territories ruled by native Hindu kings. Had Raghuji acted like Shivaji,

Jayi Rajaguru training the youth the art of warfare.

things would have turned different. Raja Mukunda Deva II asked Rajaguru to let the British pass through his kingdom despite the latter's disagreement. Jayi Rajaguru then thought of a strategy. He wanted to get back the four parganas taken by the Marathas of Nagpur, hence he decided to put his own terms and conditions. He thus sent a *vakil* (lawyer) to Ganjam to meet Colonel Harcourt to negotiate with the conditions. During the meeting, Harcourt, who wanted safe passage of his soldiers through Khurda by any means, agreed to Jayi Rajaguru's terms and conditions besides also agreeing to pay some cash; they paid Rs. 10,000 and promised to pay the rest of Rs. 90,000, as agreed, later.

The British emerged victorious in several battles against the Marathas at several places in Odisha. The treaty of Bassein was signed on 17th December 1803. As per the treaty, the Bhonsle chief ceded the coastal belt of Odisha, i.e., Cuttack to the British. With the addition of Cuttack to British dominion, the strength, and power of the British increased. They decided to sign treaties with the other native kings including the *zamindars* of Odisha. The British also decided to demand a fixed annual tribute from these kingdoms. Even before the treaty was signed, kings of 11 kingdoms submitted to the British, acknowledged British suzerainty and agreed to pay the fixed tribute. Jayi Rajaguru, as the representative head of the kingdom of Khurda, did not agree to the terms and conditions of the treaty. Besides, the British retracted from their promise of giving the four *parganas* to Jayi Rajaguru.

Jayi Rajaguru marched with an army of 2,000 soldiers to Cuttack. He utilized the amount paid by the British to strengthen and maintain his soldiers. He met Colonel Harcourt and J. Melville and reminded them of their promise. But Harcourt refused to keep up the promise, saying the *parganas* now belonged to the British. To avoid war, the British paid Rs. 40,000 and also promised to pay the remaining Rs. 50,000 after the signing of the treaty. An angry Rajaguru returned to

Khurda with his soldiers. He decided never to sign a treaty with the British and never accept British suzerainty. Thereafter, the British sent one letter after another to Raja Mukunda Deva II for signing the treaty and requested acknowledgment of a receipt of Rs. 50,000 in total. Jayi Rajaguru ignored the letters. As the king was young, the British surmised he was under the ill-advice of Jayi Rajaguru. Hence, they decided to curb Jayi's authority and win over the king to their side. Repeated letters and pressure from the British forced the Raja of Khurda to sign the treaty with the British to the utter disagreement and disappointment of Jayi Rajaguru. But he did not pay the tribute as the British did not return the four *parganas* as promised. The British again felt the king was under the influence of Jayi Rajaguru. Hence, they ordered Jayi Rajaguru to visit them but in vain. The British then sent Gola Amin, their representative, to the court of Raja Mukunda Deva II. The king was asked to follow the advice of only Gola Amin.

Meanwhile, Jayi Rajaguru decided to wage war against the British with the help of neighboring kings and *zamindars*. He took the king into his confidence. Himself the royal *pujari*, Rajaguru engaged a sadhu for the purpose of mediation. In no time, he gained the support of the neighboring kings of Kanika and Kujang. A triple alliance was thus formed among the rajas of Khurda, Kanika, and Kujang. Jayi Rajaguru moved from place to place to garner support. *Zamindars* of several regions including Bishenpur, Harishpur, and Merichpur joined him for the cause of the freedom of the motherland. Rajaguru also gained the confidence of Antaji Naik, a Maratha officer under Raghuji Bhonsle. He sought Maratha help of '1,000 horses and foot soldiers including guns' for which he was ready to pay. Antaji Naik wrote a letter to Raghuji Bhonsle requesting the same. Besides, Rajaguru gained the support of the Raja of Berar. Unfortunately, Antaji Naik was caught by the British and was imprisoned for his role as a messenger of Rajaguru, their enemy.

Balabhadra Sendh Narendra Bahadur was the Raja of Kujang. He had already accepted the British suzerainty but his people did not. Hence, when British officers came to survey Kujang, the people opposed and did not allow them. The king was soon murdered by his *diwan*, a minister, in September 1804. Chandradhyaja, the younger brother of Balabhadra was heir to the throne but the British interfered. They later agreed and Chandradhyaja was recognized as the king around November 1804. Chandradhyaja fully supported Jayi Rajaguru and secretly started preparing for war. Besides, he also indulged in hostile activities against the British. The Raja of Kanika, Balabhadra Bhanja, unwillingly accepted the British suzerainty too and as per the treaty paid a tribute, and agreed to sell the salt of his kingdom only to the British. But he did not want British interference in his kingdom. Besides, his people misbehaved with British revenue collectors at Utkan Bisi, a part of his kingdom, due to which the British sent an officer to enquire into the matter. This act of the British irked Raja Balabhadra Bhanja and he obstructed the passage of British vessels at Dhamra. British officers in Kanika were further ill-treated by the natives. When Jayi Rajaguru approached Raja Balabhadra Bhanja for a joint war against the British, the latter readily supported. As three kingdoms–Khurda, Kujang, and Kanika continued with their aggressive activities, the British further surmised and were confident that there was a secret pact between the rulers of these three kingdoms.

The most aggressive of all the freedom fighters was Jayi Rajaguru. It alerted the British authorities and they feared that his actions would motivate other rulers to rise in rebellion and breach the terms of the treaty that they had signed with the British. Meanwhile, more rulers and *zamindars* extended their support to Jayi Rajaguru.

During that time, Jayi Rajaguru not only trained ordinary men soldiers but also advised Raja Mukunda Deva II to assert his right against the British by force. He started recruiting Paikas into the

Khurda army and strengthened the military infrastructure besides building roads for smooth movement of the soldiers in times of need. The Paikas, all armed, were stationed in strategic locations.

Who were the Paikas? They were traditional soldiers of Odisha, who served as warriors under different kings. Paharis, Banuas, and Dhenkiyas were the three ranks of Paikas. While the Paharis were experts in the use of the sword and the shield, Banuas excelled in matchlocks and the Dhenkiyas in archery. Banuas were additionally involved in distant military expeditions under Odia kings. Few Paikas also held *jagirs* (lands) besides holding important positions in the Odia army. By 1802-03, the British cut down the privileges of the Paikas. The power and prestige of the Paikas thus started declining. Besides, the British did not consider the Paikas as warriors but mere cultivators. Many of them were deprived of their *jagirs*. The Paikas readily supported Jayi Rajaguru for his cause. Jayi Rajaguru also placed a troop of Paikas under a Maratha Sardar, who was further entrusted to train them to perfection in warfare and the use of modern arms and ammunition such as guns and cannons. Rajaguru needed funds for the maintenance and strengthening of his army. He used the amount given by the British for the same.

Jayi Rajaguru started taking bold decisions against the British. He stopped following the conditions of the treaty that the king signed with the British. To challenge the British, who were stationed in the Jagannath temple in Puri, he entrusted 2,000 carpenters for the construction of *rath* (chariot cars) of *Bhagavan* Jagannath. He claimed the right of collection of revenues from Batgoan, Barpada, Kharad, Matiapara, which the British were otherwise entitled to as per the treaty. The British controlled the management of the Jagannath shrine; Mukunda Deva II under the guidance of Jayi Rajaguru attempted to take over the management. He also sent troops to raid British-occupied villages. All of those activities were implemented in the name of the king.

Colonel Harcourt notified Wellesley about the turn of events at Khurda and sought permission for an immediate attack. As the battle between the British and Marathas under Holkar had not yet ended and the attack of Khurda might lead the Marathas to support the native ruler, Harcourt was asked to follow strategic measures to cleverly deal with the matter and not resort to war until Holkar was defeated.

Following Wellesley's advice, Harcourt immediately set to action. He imprisoned Sambhu Bharati, the messenger of Jayi Rajaguru entrusted to visit the court of the neighboring kingdoms to gain support for the war against the British. Harcourt then directed several neighboring rajas and *zamindars* not to help Jayi Rajaguru and threatened them with dire consequences. As the colonel realized that all the aggressive activities at Khurda were conducted under the direction of Jayi Rajaguru, he decided to get him removed from his post. He sent a messenger to the court of Raja Mukunda Deva II with a message that Captain Blunt would visit him. Jayi Rajaguru told the messenger that the king would not meet Blunt. He told the messenger that he would give the message in writing and kept him waiting for 14 days. Without a letter, the messenger thereafter was then asked to leave immediately.

By November 1804, British forces defeated Holkar. Harcourt decided to use force against Khurda. Jayi Rajaguru too was prepared for war. He, in the name of the king, started by raiding the four parganas that were under the control of the British. The Khurda forces could defeat and disarm a band of British soldiers at Kotdesh.

Colonel Harcourt marched towards Khurda from Cuttack. He entrusted two British troops under Captain Storey and Major Fletcher to attack Khurda Fort. Jayi Rajaguru's soldiers offered stiff resistance, which continued for three weeks. At last, the British captured the fort. Raja Mukunda Deva II could flee to the jungles from where Waz Muhammad, a servant under the British, got him treacherously arrested. The British granted the traitor a reward of 3,000 rupees for this act. Jayi Rajaguru was arrested too. The British took action against the other neighboring kings and zamindars, who extended their support to Jayi Rajaguru. Few offered resistance but in vain. Many Paikas attained martyrdom in all of those battles. The Raja of Kujang was subdued and British representatives were appointed for administration. The Raja of Kanika was held captive.

Both Jayi Rajaguru and Raja Mukunda Deva II were kept in confinement in the fort of Barabati at Cuttack. The raja was then removed to Midnapur jail as a state prisoner. Jayi Rajaguru was produced before Colonel Harcourt, who asked him if he was the cause for all the aggression or the raja instigated the same. Rajaguru honestly and fearlessly declared that he caused the disturbance, "that the rajah was a child and what had been done, had been done by himself." He was then taken to Midnapur jail.

The trial of Jayi Rajaguru was held at Baghitota in Midnapur. He was held guilty and sentenced to death. The British acted very brutally. Rajaguru's legs were tied upside down on opposite branches of a banyan tree in broad daylight and were pulled resulting in his body getting split into two parts. The brave son of Bharat Mata remained calm during the savage execution process on 6th December 1806.

Jayi Rajaguru was one of the bravest and earliest freedom fighters who did not recognize British suzerainty and opposed their interference. He motivated the warrior Paikas to give their 100 percent for the freedom of the motherland. He collaborated with neighboring kings and *zamindars* though unfortunately, the tide turned in favor of the British. He offered a brave resistance with his forces at Khurda Fort until defeat befell. Jayi Rajaguru's tale of valor and resistance will be remembered by generations till eternity. Vande Mataram!

17

Chennabhairadevi

Protected Karnataka Coast from Portuguese

Chennabhairadevi! She isn't a familiar name across the country except for Karnataka. This queen of Gersoppa under the Vijayanagara Empire is attributed with building the robust Mirjan Fort in Uttara Kannada. She was perhaps the longest-serving Indian queen, ruling her kingdom for 54 years. Gersoppa, since ancient times, was an international trading center for pepper. The Portuguese named her 'Rainha de Pimenta' meaning 'Rani, the Pepper Queen'. Chennabhairadevi protected her kingdom from Portuguese attacks and intrusion for 54 long years!

Gersoppa (also Gerusoppa) is located on the banks of the Sharavati, a westward flowing river, which originates and flows entirely within Karnataka. This 'once upon a time' flourishing town for cashews and pepper, was also known as Kshemapura, Nagire, and Bhallatakipura. This region was the capital of the Salva dynasty between the 14th to 16th centuries CE. Chennabhairadevi was the last ruler of this dynasty. She ruled from 1552 to 1606 CE. Her kingdom was known as *Haivanadu*. According to the Gorantla inscription, this dynasty traces its origin to the Uttara Kannada region from the 10th century onwards when the Western Chalukyas and then the Kalachuris ruled. Narasimha Deva Raya was a famous Saluva emperor of the Vijayanagara Empire, his grandfather Mangaldeva won battles against the Madurai Sultanate. The Vijayanagara Empire was ruled by four dynasties in succession–Sangam, Saluva, Tuluva, and Aravidu. Chennabhairadevi draws her lineage from both the Saluva and Tuluva warriors of the Vijayanagara Empire. Saluva rulers were Jains and Hindus. The Saluva kings including Chennabhairadevi built beautiful temples.

The rulers of the Vijayanagara Empire decentralized their administration, entrusting various royal families respectively to rule the kingdoms. These rulers were known as Mahamandaleshwaras, which means subordinates. In short, these kingdoms were feudatories of the Vijayanagara Empire. Chennabhairadevi was a Mahamandaleshwara, the ruler of Haivanadu. After the fall of the Vijayanagara Empire in 1565 following their defeat in the Battle of Talikota against an alliance of the Deccan Sultanate, Chennabhairadevi became an independent ruler. She is from the matriarchal tradition that follows the lineage of the sister's son for inheritance. It is known as *Aliyakattu* or *Aliyasantana*. This tradition is still followed majorly in the coastal belt of Konkan and Kerala including some regions in south India. Chennabhairadevi's kingdom covered Uttara and Dakshina Kannada including south Goa. The ports of Mirjan, Honnavar, Malpe, Bidnoor, Ankola, and Karwar were part of her kingdom. All of these ports were important centers of international trading, especially pepper as well as other spices and dry fruits.

Chennabhairadevi built the robust Mirjan Fort, spread over an area of 10 acres. Her main objective behind constructing the fort was monitoring Portuguese activities on the west coast. The Portuguese then were a threat to her kingdom. High double walls and bastions with high turrets in laterite stones mark the uniqueness of Mirjan Fort.

It has one main and three subsidiary entrance gates. A number of interlinked wells dot the fort with access channels leading to a circular moat. This defense measure was followed by many Indian kings to protect the fort. The moat completely surrounds the fort, water to this destination is further supplied through canals outside the fort premise. Mirjan Fort also houses a secret passage with doors, which Rani Chennabhairadevi must have built with a purpose. The queen lived in this fort for several years. Several years after the fall of the Vijayanagara Empire, she shifted base from Mirjan Fort to a safer location on an island in the middle of river Sharavati. From there, she kept an eye on the activities of her kingdom, traveling throughout and defending her kingdom as and when the need arose.

Excavations at the Mirjan site led to the discovery of a number of artifacts dating back beyond the timeline of Chennabhairadevi though the timeline of the fort structure corresponds to her reign period. This suggests the queen built the fort over few existing ruins. Laterite structures dating back to the medieval period were also found. This fort is located on the banks of the Aghanashini River, which originates in Sirsi in Uttara Karnataka and flows into the Arabian Sea.

Chennabhairadevi's kingdom was known as the pepper country and this spice from this region is high in demand in Europe and the Middle East. The mounting trading activities, which made this region rich, led to attacks by neighboring kingdoms, especially the Bijapur Sultanate and from Keladi. Chennabhairadevi bravely defended her region. Then, the Portuguese were engaged in the export of pepper and other spices from her kingdom.

Meanwhile, going a step ahead of commercial activities, the Portuguese started using military power to capture parts of the Indian territory. On 25th March 1505, Francisco de Almeida was appointed the first Viceroy of the Portuguese territory in India with headquarters at Kochi. He came with a troop of 1,500 Portuguese soldiers initially and was entrusted to build forts in four locations on the Indian coast. Then they occupied Bardesh, Matagram, and Tiswadi–three talukas of Goa from the Sultan of Bijapur in 1510 and stationed more forces. By 1526, the Portuguese took possession of Mangalore and Kasargod in Kerala. The Portuguese had their eyes on the ports of Haivanadu.

A strong military force and building of forts at several places marked the presence of Portuguese in regions they occupied. News of events pertaining to the Goa inquisition by Portuguese wherein thousands of Hindus were tortured and temples razed to the ground, spread far and wide. Chennabhairadevi noticed the growing Portuguese power and also their attempt to establish their suzerainty over Haivanadu. Foreseeing the threat from the Portuguese, Chennabhairadevi drove them away from her kingdom including the ports of Bhatkal, Honnavar, and Gokarna.

Besides the small conflicts, Chennabhairadevi was involved in two major wars against the Portuguese, first in 1559 when D. Constantino de Braganza was the Viceroy and again in 1570 when D. Luis de Ataide held that position. Years of governance, expertise in military warfare, and acumen in battle strategies helped Chennabhairadevi defeat the Portuguese in both battles. So badly were the Portuguese defeated that they gave up the idea of attacking her kingdom and resorted to diplomatic ties for continuing trade relations. A Portuguese chronicle states thus about the brave queen, "We must deal with her, most carefully and diplomatically. We must be courteous, polite, and diplomatic to win her to our side."

Rani Chennabhairadevi was a devout follower of Jainism. She built numerous Jain temples. She was tolerant of all other religions and sects in her kingdom. She donated plentifully for the construction of Shaiva, Vaishnava, and Shakti temples in her kingdom. Art and culture flourished under her regime. Besides, many Hindus, Jains, and Buddhists, who faced tyranny from the Portuguese in Goa and other regions, sought refuge in her kingdom. Rani Chennabhairadevi provided shelter to all of them.

In 1607, the rulers of Keladi and Bilagi (near present Bagalakote) formed an alliance and unexpectedly attacked Rani Chennabhairadevi. The brave queen, then old, offered resistance but in vain. She was taken prisoner and kept confined in a prison in Keladi where she breathed her last.

The Portuguese had already established their hold in several coastal cities of India when they encountered Chennabhairadevi in battle. It was because of the stiff resistance offered by the valiant Rani that Haivanadu remained safe from Portuguese occupation.

18

Babu Kunwar Singh

Won Several Battles against British at Age 80

At the age of 80-81 years and failing health, he led several successful battles against the British in Bihar. It was the year 1857 to 1858. He traveled hundreds of kilometers across the northern part of the country to mobilize forces against the British. Once, while crossing the Ganga with few men on a boat, the British incessantly shot at them. A bullet shattered his left wrist. Immediate medical attention was then a far-fetched affair. To avoid infection spreading in his body that would further weaken him, he drew his sword, cut off his left hand with one blow near the elbow, and offered it to the Ganga. On 23rd April 1858, he regained his kingdom from the British. He brought down the British flag from Jagdishpur Fort and hoisted the native flag. He succumbed to battlefield wounds three days later, i.e. on 26th April at his palace. He was Babu Kunwar Singh, the Raja of Jagdishpur, a principality in Bihar.

Babu Kunwar Singh (spelled Kooer Sing in British records) was born on 13th November 1777 at Jagdishpur to Rani Panchratan Kunwari Devi and Raja Shahabzada Singh. He belonged to the Ujjainiya clan of the Parmars, who trace their origin to Ujjain in

Malwa. Ujjainiyas were known for their valor, they won battles against the Jaunpur Sultanate and Bengal Sultanate. In the 14th century, Ujjainiyas saved pilgrims and Brahmins in Buxar from the cruel Jaunpur Sultan. Shahabzada Singh was extremely gallant, a 1794 British record describes how he got involved in a brawl with a British commissioner and how he fearlessly drew out his sword and wounded a few British officials. Shahabzada Singh also killed a tiger when it created havoc in Jagdishpur. Babu Kunwar Singh carried forward the legacy of valor of his father and his ancestors.

A British judicial officer describes Kunwar Singh as 'a tall man about seven feet in height with long arms extending down to his knees. He had a big face with broad jaws and high cheekbones, an aquiline nose and a broad high forehead… He was a first-rate horseman, spearman, and swordsman, also an accurate hand at the gun'. This finds mention in *The Greased Cartridge: The Heroes and Villains of 1857-58* by E. Jaiwant Paul. Kunwar Singh manufactured weapons and gun powder at Jagdishpur. Before he became the Raja, Kunwar Singh often stayed in the jungles a little far away from Jagdishpur where he built a bungalow and followed his passion of hunting. Jagdishpur is presently a town under Bhojpur district, earlier called Shahabad. During the reign of Raja Shahabzada Singh and later Babu Kunwar Singh, the Jagdishpur estate included several neighboring towns and villages. This estate hosted a fort with palaces where the royal family resided.

The British gained suzerainty over major parts of Bihar after the Battle of Plassey of 1757 and Buxar in 1764. In 1845-46, Kunwar Singh secretly entered into an alliance with few neighboring chieftains and also sought help from the Raja of Nepal for eliminating the British from India. But before he could give shape to his plans, the British came to know about it, resulting in restrictions and interference.

When the War of Independence of 1857 happened, Kunwar Singh was aged 80. He led this war in the Bihar region along with his brothers Babu Amar Singh and Hare Krishna Singh. The commander-in-chief of his forces was Hare Krishna Singh. He was greatly supported in his battlefield exploits by his nephew Ritbhanjan Singh and his friend Nishan Singh. He also fought against the British in the now UP region.

Freedom fighters, especially Indian sepoys, revolted against the British at Danapur, located around 72 kms away from Jagdishpur, on 25th July. The Indian sepoys, who were recruited from Shahabad, were from the seventh, eighth, and 40th Regiments of the East India Company's Bengal Native Infantry. Despite being employed under the British, majority of them were loyal to Kunwar Singh. They joined him in the fight for the freedom of the motherland. On 27th July, these forces under Kunwar Singh occupied Arrah where the district headquarter of the British was located. There is Bhojpuri folklore about Kunwar Singh and Arrah, which describes volumes about how the natives of Arrah under the British regime wanted Kunwar Singh to liberate them from oppression, which finds mention in 'Popular Culture and 1857: A Memory against Forgetting' by Badri Narayan in *Social Scientist*:

Mahua ke pedwa, tabai, nik ffect,
Jaba mahuari hoae
Ara sabariya tabai nik lage,
Kunwar Singh ke rajwa hoae

Translation: The mahua tree looks beautiful in its blossoming season, and Arrah town will look beautiful when it is ruled by Kunwar Singh.

To quote another folklore from Badri Narayan:

Bhado mas andheria, badariya gagan ghere ji,
Tahl rate challe, Kunwar Singh lare laraiya ji.

Translation: It was *Bhadon* (July-August) month; night and dark clouds were covering the sky when Babu Kunwar Singh went to war at the end of the night.

Kunwar Singh and his forces laid siege to Arrah for eight days. Major General Vincent Eyre, an officer in command of the East India Company's Number 1 Company, 4th Bengal Foot Artillery marched towards Arrah. When Kunwar Singh heard about it, he went with an army of around 2,500 soldiers and intercepted Eyre and his forces 9.7 kms ahead of the city. A fierce battle ensued between the British and the freedom fighters. The British were superior in arms and ammunition, especially bayonets and artillery, which proved a bane for the freedom fighters. Eyre won the battle; Singh's muskets had 'no chance over howitzers'. Around 600 freedom fighters attained martyrdom in this battle. Vincent Eyre then marched towards Arrah and relieved the town on 3rd August. The cruel British did not leave the wounded. They hung to death the wounded freedom fighters in trees along the road in Arrah, stretching a distance of one and a half miles (approximately 2.4 kms).

Vincent Eyre received news about Kunwar Singh's whereabouts at Dulloor, not far from Jagdishpur. Kunwar Singh had been gathering forces to attack the British. But before Singh could give shape to his strategies, Eyre along with his forces marched towards Dulloor. Another battle started between Kunwar Singh and Eyre on the 11th of August. Three hundred freedom fighters attained martyrdom whereas casualties of the British soldiers were estimated at six. Major Eyre then marched towards Jagdishpur. He destroyed the royal palaces including the residences of Babu Amar Singh and Hare Krishna Singh. Eyre was notorious for burning villages, looting wealth, destroying crops, and pillaging entire cities. He followed the same policy, but on a larger scale, at Jagdishpur. He not only looted wealth but also killed many villagers, all followers of Kunwar Singh, destroyed the entire town besides also destroying a grand temple built by Kunwar Singh.

Meanwhile, Kunwar Singh started following Guerilla warfare techniques, attacking the British now and then. He was so proficient in this art that his strategies left the British puzzled. The British commanders never understood the moves of Kunwar Singh so much so that they always feared a sudden attack by him. Sometimes he and his forces would spit fire on the enemy forces, sometimes he would himself move backward or push them backward, or suddenly attack their posts. Veer Savarkar in his book *1857 Ka Bhartiya Swatantrata Samar* described Kunwar Singh's Guerilla warfare skills thus: "In the 1857 revolution, this brave man had no peers in the strategy and skill of war. After Shivaji, he was the first to prove the efficacy of guerrilla warfare. He was the only one, who had complete knowledge of this skill. Not only this, if we compare the achievements of Tatya Tope and Kunwar Singh in the field of Guerilla warfare during the 1857 revolution, the first place will go to Kunwar Singh." The British could not capture Kunwar Singh. They declared a price upon his head–initially Rs. 10,000 and then raised it to Rs. 25,000, which corroborated the importance of his capture!

Sepoys at Bijaygarh near Mirzapur joined Kunwar Singh on 26th August and together proceeded to Singrowlia (presently Singrauli) and marched towards Rewah. More local chiefs joined Singh. The combined forces defeated the British at both places.

Such was the influence of Kunwar Singh that the very utterance of his name created panic in British posts and created much alarm. There was every possibility, as assumed by the British officers, that he might march towards Calcutta (now Kolkata), seize the railways in Raniganj,

Babu Kunwar Singh cutting off his injured wrist with his sword in one blow and offering it to the Ganga.

or move southwards the reason being that he had feudal suzerainty over a fifth of the sepoy army. A *Times* report carried the question thus, "What if Kooer Sing, who has feudal suzerainty over a fifth of the sepoy army, should make a dash southward, surprise Raneegunge, seize the railway, and march upon Calcutta?" Many freedom fighters across Bengal, Bihar, Odisha, Assam, and more regions drew inspiration from him. A Hindu chieftain in Assam revolted and the British not only captured him, his mother, and his entire family and imprisoned them but also seized his treasures.

The old raja of Gond (presently Jabalpur)–Shunkur Shah, whose 60 generations of ancestors (Gondwana dynasty) ruled the region, waged war against the British in 1857. Shunkur Shah was inspired by the valor of Kunwar Singh. He and his son Raghunath, both staunch devotees of Shakti, motivated their men to fight for the freedom of the motherland. Both were excellent poets and they used the medium of poetry to inspire the freedom fighters. At every step of their freedom struggle activities, they invoked the Devi. The British also found an invocation of the Devi written on a silk bag. They came to know about the Gond Raja's plans of attacking Chawni, which was under their suzerainty. With the help of a traitor, the British treacherously caught them and imprisoned them. Both Raja Shunkur Shah and Raghunath were ordered to be blown away by canons at Jabalpur. When they were tied at the mouth of a canon each and about to be blown off, Shunkur Shah told thus to his followers through the medium of poetry, invoking Goddess Kali:

मलेच्छों का मर्दन करो, कालिका माई |
मूंद मुख डंडिन को, चुगली को चबाई खाई,
खूंद डार दुष्टन को, शत्रु संहारिका ||१||

(The above is a part of the following poem composed by Shunkur Shah):

मलेच्छों का मर्दन करो, कालिका माई।
मूंद मुख डंडिन को, चुगली को चबाई खाई,
खूंद डार दुष्टन को, शत्रु संहारिका ||१||
मार अंग्रेज रेंज, कई देई मात चंडी,
बचै नाहि बैरी, बाल बच्चे संचारिका।
शंकर की रक्षा कर, दास प्रतिपाल कर ||२||
दीन की सुन आय, मात कालिका,
खाई लेई मलेछन को, झैल नहीं करो अब।
मच्छन कर तछन, धौर मात कालिका ||३||)

And Raghunath Shah uttered thus, invoking Devi:

कालिका भवानी माय अरज हमारी सुन
डार मुण्डमाल गरे खड्ग कर धर ले...।

And they were blown off on 18th September 1857. The gory half-burnt remains were gathered by relatives for the last rites on behalf of the Gond Rani. The British officers watched with smiles on their lips.

More chieftains from other kingdoms revolted against the British, drawing inspiration from the aged Kunwar Singh. Sepoys near Jabalpur, under the leadership and guidance of Kunwar Singh, revolted and took Lieutenant Macgregor prisoner. Twenty-five miles away from Jabalpur, they successfully encountered the British where they killed MacGregor on 27th September 1857. More sepoys, under the guidance of Singh, revolted at Nagod; the British officials and soldiers fled. The sepoys got hold of the British treasury. In October 1857, Kunwar Singh reached Banda and then Kalpi. He supported the Gwalior troops in the Battle of Kandhapur. From there, he marched towards Lucknow. Kunwar Singh sought the support of chieftains from far and near. He visited Kanpur, Ayodhya, and more neighboring places.

In March 1858, Kunwar Singh occupied Gorakhpur. Thereafter, he marched towards Azamgarh. When Col. Milman, an officer in command at Azamgarh, heard about the approaching freedom fighters, he advanced ahead. Both the armies met at Atrowlee, 20 miles from Azamgarh. Singh had a large force and was well equipped with guns and ammunition. The British were defeated. British survivors fled from the battlefield, leaving behind their guns and baggage. Kunwar Singh took possession of Azamgarh. The next day, the British tried to re-occupy the place. Another fierce battle took place between Singh and the British under Colonel Dames. Kunwar Singh defeated them once again, killing several British soldiers including Captain Bedford. Edward Lugard, British Adjunct General, marched from Lucknow towards Azamgarh on the 20th of March with a huge force. Kunwar Singh, learning about the approaching army, destroyed a bridge over the Gomti at Sultanpur, thus impeding their advance.

The British also feared Kunwar Singh, anticipating his attack of Arrah or even Benares. The commissioner of Patna wrote to the British office in Calcutta that if Kunwar Singh landed in Arrah, not only would the city fall but also result in revolt in surrounding districts. Troubled by two successive defeats of the British at the hands of Kunwar Singh, Governor-General Canning shifted base from Calcutta to Allahabad. Following Canning's orders, Lord Mark Kerr advanced towards Azamgarh from Allahabad with the 13 Light Cavalry. Kunwar Singh had then left Azamgarh, and the two forces met not very far away from the city. At the first attempt, Singh could ambush the enemy forces, there were heavy casualties on the side of the British. He received news about approaching British reinforcements with enough artillery. He left, leaving behind 2,000 men to continue the fight. Singh's forces employed guerilla strategies and started harassing the British forces. Kunwar Singh marched towards Jagdishpur to regain it from the British.

Kunwar Singh and his troops had to cross the Ganga on boats at Shivrajpur (presently a *nagar* [town] panchayat in Kanpur). But as the British spied on him and were always on the move searching for his whereabouts, he spread a rumor that he and his forces would be crossing the Ganga with weapons on elephants at Ballia, located seven miles away from Shivrajpur. British forces under Commander Douglas reached the bank of the Ganga at Ballia and waited for Kunwar Singh. The 80-year-old warrior's strategy worked! His forces started crossing the Ganga on boats at Shivrajpur. Douglas came to know of the trick and he rushed immediately towards Shivrajpur. By the time the British reached Shivrajpur, all of Kunwar Singh's men except a few had already crossed the river. Douglas and his forces noticed the last boat carrying Kunwar Singh and few soldiers. The British began to shoot incessantly at the freedom fighters. Kunwar Singh and his soldiers retaliated with guns as well as bows and arrows. A bullet shattered Kunwar Singh's left wrist. With no immediate medical facility and risk of infection spreading in his body, Kunwar Singh decided to get rid of the useless body part. He drew his sword and cut off his left hand near the elbow and offered it to the Ganga. Kunwar Singh was also wounded on the thigh. They crossed the river safely. Edward Lugard remarked about Kunwar Singh as a 'born strategist'.

Kunwar Singh reached Jagdishpur in April. The people were overjoyed seeing their king. His brother Amar Singh had kept the flame of 'freedom struggle' alive by continuously fighting against the British with his base at Kaimur hills. Hearing the news about the return of the Raja, Amar Singh rushed towards Jagdishpur with his forces. Kunwar Singh drove away the British, brought down the British flag from Jagdishpur Fort, and hoisted the Hindu flag. Anticipating an attack from the enemy, Kunwar Singh was all ready for battle. Sepoys from surrounding areas reached Jagdishpur and joined the old raja.

Le Grand was the British commander for Arrah and Bibiganj. He set out for Jagdishpur with a huge force and canons. To reach Jagdishpur, the British forces had to cross the thick jungles surrounding the city. Kunwar Singh was all ready with his forces in the jungles. They ambushed the enemy forces. They fired at the British soldiers from all directions. Sensing defeat, the British retreated. Kunwar Singh, with one hand and a wounded thigh, pursued the British with his forces, killing two-thirds of the enemy forces including the commander Le Grand on 23rd April 1858. Kunwar Singh was badly wounded in the battle. He succumbed to his wounds on 26th April 1858 in his kingdom.

Age doesn't matter when it comes to fighting for the freedom of the motherland. This is well proven by Babu Kunwar Singh. Lakhs of freedom fighters offered resistance and sacrificed their lives for the freedom we enjoy today. Yet, we are taught *ahimsa* got us this freedom!

Naman to the brave son of Bharat Mata! Vande Mataram!!!

19

Marthanda Varma

Defeated the Dutch in Battle, Crushed their Indian Expansion

Who was Raja Marthanda Varma? Except few from Kerala and Tamil Nadu, the rest of India hardly knows about this brave son of Bharat Mata from Travancore. He was one of the first Asian kings to defeat a robust Dutch army in a naval battle at Colachel. According to the book *Battle of Colachel* by Frederic P. Miller, Agnes F. Vandome, and John McBrewster, it was the earliest example of the defeat of European power in Asia in 1741. Marthanda Varma captured all the Dutch forts and crushed their expansion in India. Had Marthanda not checked or destroyed their expansion, there would have been an extended Dutch rule in India like the British! Marthanda Varma is also known as the 'maker of modern Travancore'.

It was from 1500 CE that Travancore emerged as an independent kingdom first under the Travancore Royal Family from Padmanabhapuram, and later Thiruvananthapuram. The kingdom's territory covered most of modern-day central and southern Kerala including Kanyakumari of Tamil Nadu. Travancore was earlier known as Venad. It was under the reign of Raja Marthanda Varma, who ruled from 1729 to 1758, that the dominion of Travancore further expanded.

Did the British establish supremacy in India in one go? No! They first came to trade and later established their power in Bengal. What started in 1600 as British East India Company with few aristocratic traders to India via Bengal became a major military and political power by 1803 backed by a private army of about 260,000 soldiers. This count, which comprised of both British soldiers and Indian sepoys they employed, was twice the army count of the British homeland!

Likewise, the Dutch East India Company (also called VOC), founded in 1602, came to India for trading, especially for spices. This Dutch trade group became the world's first formally listed public company in the early 1600s. The Dutch East India Company first established its trade base in the Coromandel Coast followed by Surat, Bengal, and the Malabar. Its presence in India lasted from 1605 to 1825. What started as a trading entity gradually turned into a military and political power like the British East India Company in no time. Had Raja Marthanda Varma not captured the Dutch forts and gave them a crushing defeat in 1741, the History of India would have been different with Dutch supremacy extending across other parts of the country!

Marthanda Varma was born as Anizham Thirunal Marthanda Varma to Raghava Varma and Karthika Thirunal Uma Devi in 1705 at Attingal, Thiruvananthapuram. His regnal name was Sree Padmanabhadasa Vanchipaala Maharajah Sree Anizham Thirunal Veerabaala Marthanda Varma Kulasekhara Perumal. His father Raghava Varma belonged to the Kilimanur royal house. Marthanda's mother Karthika Thirunal Uma Devi was the queen of Attingal, a principality located in the north of Thiruvananthapuram. She and her sister were adopted into the Travancore Royal Family, her sister died soon after.

Marthanda Varma's predecessor was his uncle Rama Varma, who ruled from 1724 to 1729. He was the heir apparent after Rama Varma as per the system of matrilineal inheritance prevalent then in Venad (Travancore). This traditional system that gave women liberty and the right to property was called *Marumakkathayam*. It was through females that descent and the inheritance of property were traced. Besides the Travancore Royal Family, other royal families that followed the Marumakkathayam system were Nairs, Mappilas, Ambalavasis, Thiyyas of Malabar, and few tribal groups. Women empowerment is inherent in the Indic culture systems since ancient times.

Marthanda Varma was far-sighted since his childhood. He was born with the art of statecraft ingrained in him. During his childhood, Venad was a small kingdom and the ruler was in name only. The real powers rested in the hands of the nobles. The *Matampimar* (barons) and *Ettuveetil Pillamar* (Lords of the Eight Houses) exerted the highest influence. So were the managing committee of Padmanabhaswamy Temple of Thiruvananthapuram and the *Yogakkar* (the Council of Eight and a Half). During that time, both the Dutch and the English were on an empire-building spree, sprucing up their political and military powers.

The teenaged Marthanda devised a plan to curb the power of the nobles, rebellious chiefs, and the aristocracy. He advised his uncle and king Rama Varma to enter into a collaborative deal with the powerful Madurai Nayaks. Rama Varma, who was a weak ruler and whose life was in danger from the nobles, agreed. His predecessor and brother Kerala Varma was assassinated by the Ettuveetil Pillamar. As per the pact, a Pandyan force was stationed in Venad to check any rebellion by the nobles and to protect the king. Marthanda Varma was only 14 years old then. After the death of Rama Varma in 1729, Marthanda Varma succeeded the throne at the age of 24.

Soon after ascending the throne, Marthanda crushed the power of the Ettuveetil Pillamar. He inducted soldiers into the existing army. He had a standing army of about 50,000 soldiers. He fortified the northern boundaries of his kingdom. He laid the foundation of the Travancore kingdom, expanding the Venad territory by subjugating and assimilating a number of neighboring kingdoms through war campaigns. Few of those neighboring kingdoms were rich in pepper cultivation. One was Odanad, which was the heartland of the pepper trade. The Dutch East India Company exercised its monopoly in pepper trade in a few of these regions. With Marthanda Varma exercising his sovereignty of those regions besides signing a treaty with the British on the pepper trade, the Dutch monopoly, and commercial interests were at stake. Hence, they started interfering in the supremacy of the Travancore ruler and supported the local rulers who lost their sovereignty to Marthanda.

Kayamkulam, one of the neighboring kingdoms, feared annexation by Marthanda. The Kayamkulam chief built a strong defense in alliance with the chiefs of Kochi, Purakkad, and Vadakkumkur to resist the possible attack. The Dutch offered to extend their support to that alliance. The joint forces recaptured Marta, a kingdom that Marthanda had seized. That led to a war between Marthanda's army and the allied forces. The Travancore army not only seized Nedumangad and Kottarakkara but also killed the Kayamkulam chief in subsequent campaigns. The chief's brother continued with the resistance.

It was then that Gustaaf Willem van Imhoff, the Dutch Governor of Ceylon (now Sri Lanka) wrote to Marthanda Varma demanding that he should end the aggression against Kayamkulam. It irked the Travancore chief, who wrote back to the Dutch Governor, ordering him not to interfere in matters that did not concern him.

Then followed a meeting between Marthanda Varma and Gustaaf Willem van Imhoff. The main base of the pepper trade for the Dutch was Odanad, which was ruled by a princess. Their trade was hampered after it was annexed by Marthanda. Imhoff demanded that Odanad be restored to its former ruling princess. He also threatened the Travancore king that if he refused his demand, he would invade his kingdom. The Hindu king refused to comply with the Dutch demand. He confidently countered Imhoff's threat of a Dutch attack on his kingdom, replying that his army was robust enough to defeat the enemy forces. Marthanda even went to the extent of saying that he had been planning for an invasion of Europe.

The Dutch East India Company set to action in 1741. It installed a princess of the Elayadathu Swarupam as the ruler of Kottarakara much against the wishes of Marthanda Varma. Kottarakkara was already annexed to the Travancore kingdom during the military operation against the joint forces of the Kayamkulam chief in 1734.

The Kottarakkara army in alliance with the Dutch forces was all ready for resistance. A war ensued between the Travancore army and the allied forces. Marthanda Varma easily defeated the combined army and assimilated Kottarakara back into Travancore. The Dutch forces were forced to retreat to Cochin (now Kochi).

The Travancore army captured all of the Dutch forts in that region. The Dutch had a firm base in Ceylon. With the loss faced by the Dutch army in the war, a fresh contingent of the Dutch army, especially marines, arrived to support their Indian wing. It was led by Captain Eustachius De Lannoy. They landed with artillery in Colachel port on the west coast of Kanyakumari in Malabar. In no time they fortified the port and started giving shape to their war strategies. They captured the nearby villages–Thengapattanam and Eraniel–and continued with their expedition until they marched till Padmanabhapuram, the erstwhile capital of the Travancore kingdom under Marthanda's predecessor Rama Varma. Marthanda had shifted the capital to Thiruvananthapuram.

During that time, Marthanda Varma was camping in Thiruvananthapuram in the north of his empire. He marched towards the south to defend his territory from the Dutch. Meanwhile, the Dutch were all ready to advance further and capture the Kalkulam Fort near Nagercoil in the Kanyakumari region. The Raja reached just on time, thus foiling their attempt and preventing their capture of the fort. The Dutch army was forced to retreat to their defensive position in Colachel.

Marthanda's army was reinforced by the troops brought by Ramayyan Dalwa, who was appointed Dewan of Travancore by the king. A robust Travancore army backed by infantry, cavalry, and artillery in addition to native fishermen, was all geared up to attack the Dutch at Colachel. They were further reinforced by a number of native boats manned by robust native fishermen and Travancore soldiers for the naval battle.

The battle of Colachel between Marthanda's Travancore army and the Dutch took place on 10th August 1741. The fierce battle between the two parties went on for four days. Ultimately, it was a decisive victory for the Travancore army. Many Dutch soldiers including 24 military officers were taken as prisoners. Leaving behind 389 muskets and some artillery, the surviving Dutch soldiers fled the battlefield and the port and sailed towards Cochin.

Despite winning the battle of Colachel, Marthanda Varma did not stop. He wished to crush the power of the Dutch completely in India. He knew they flourished in India and exercised their power owing to their prosperous trade in pepper and other spices in South India, especially in Kerala and Tamil Nadu. He thus set out to conquer the major spice-producing regions to put an end to Dutch supremacy and their trade.

During a period of nine years, between 1743 and 1752, Marthanda Varma won in his expeditions and was able to annex major spice-producing areas in Kochi and adjoining kingdoms to the Travancore Empire. Besides, he declared a state monopoly on pepper. Thus, Dutch supremacy and their trade were affected. Further strife between Marthanda Varma and the Dutch ended after a treaty was signed between the two parties on 15the August 1753 at Mavelikkara. As per the treaty and subsequent peace treaties, the remaining Dutch forts were incorporated into the Travancore dominion.

In the words of historian A. Sreedhara Menon from his book *A Survey of Kerala History:* "A disaster of the first magnitude for the Dutch, the battle of Colachel shattered for all time their dream of the conquest of Kerala."

That marked the end of Dutch supremacy and prevented their expansion in India. It was for the first time in Indian history that a European naval force was defeated by an Indian king. Jai Hind!

20

How Naga Sadhus Defeated Aurangzeb's Forces Defending Kashi Vishwanath in 1664

Naga Sadhus! For them 'valor and Dharma' are two sides of the same coin. They were warrior saints and fought many battles against Islamic invaders and plunderers and then the British. They defended Hindus and temples for several centuries. Naga Sadhus defeated Aurangzeb's Mughal forces near the Kashi Vishwanath temple in Varanasi in 1664 and defended the temple. Aurangzeb did not dare to attack Varanasi again until 1669.

The antiquity of the existence of Naga Sadhus dates back thousands of years. Literary records and folklore attribute their founder to Dattatreya, the incarnation of the Trinity–Brahma, Vishnu, and Mahadev. The Dashanami sampradaya of the monastic tradition attributed to Dattatreya was organized into four mutts by Adi Shankaracharya. Besides the mutts, he also organized a section of warrior sadhus to protect Sanatana Dharma. Later they came to be known as Naga Sadhus. They have no fear of death and their weapons have been the *trishul* (trident), sword, stick. They also carry other weapons as well as musical instruments and conch shells. Their ash-covered bodies and matted locks differentiate them from other sadhus.

A section of the Naga Sadhus was further reorganized by Madhusudana Saraswati of Bengal in the 16th century. They stayed naked and their role was to protect Hindus from the tyranny of the Mughals. Madhusudana Saraswati, a philosopher from the Advaita Vedanta tradition, was a contemporary of Akbar. Witnessing attacks of sadhus by Muslims, Madhusudana Saraswati visited Akbar's court in Agra and complained to him. When his complaint was not addressed, he reorganized the Naga Sadhus and initiated them into action to protect Hindus from atrocities meted out by Muslims. Though many historians do not believe in this theory, few historians justify it to be true. Irrespective of the debate on whether this theory is true or not there is evidence that after Madhusudana's return from Agra, Naga Sadhus assembled in Varanasi and took an oath to defend Hindus.

Baba Rampuri in his book *Autobiography of a Sadhu: A Journey into Mystic India* has given a detailed account about Naga Sadhus and their akharas. An American born as William A. Gans, he is probably, as he claims, the first Westerner to become a Naga Sadhu after he got answers to his questions on truth from Indian philosophy and culture. He has been the Shri Mahant at Shri Panch Dashnam Juna Akhara.

Kashi Vishwanath Temple is one of the 12 *Jyotirlingas*. This temple finds mention in the *Puranas* including the *Skanda Purana*, which is one of the 18 *Mahapuranas* attributed to Rishi Veda Vyasa. And Veda Vyasa lived during the Mahabharata period. The antiquity of this temple is thus several thousand years old–at least from the Mahabharata era. Beyond the Puranas, this temple finds mention in various historical written records. Like almost all temples, this temple was also renovated, rebuilt, and expanded over time.

Naga Sadhus in battle against Aurangzeb's Mughal forces in Kashi.

The Kashi Vishwanath Temple was attacked several times by Islamic plunderers. It was first destroyed by Qutb-ud-din Aibak in 1194 CE. He was then a commander under the army of Mohammad Ghori. The destroyed ruins lay neglected for a few years. Like most other temples, this temple was also rebuilt. The rebuilding was done under the patronage of a Gujarati trader before the mid-13th century. Kashi was plundered again by the Sharqi rulers of the Jaunpur Sultanate followed by the Muslim army of Sikandar Lodhi in the 15th century. It was rebuilt by Raja Todar Mal in the last part of the 16th century, i.e., in 1585.

Aurangzeb and his Mughal forces attacked Kashi Vishwanath Temple in 1664. The Naga Sadhus resisted and defended the temple. They defeated the Mughal forces. This crushing defeat of the Mughals finds mention in James G. Lochtefeld's book *The Illustrated Encyclopedia of Hinduism*, Volume 1. According to this book, the Naga Sadhus of Mahanirvani Akhara of Varanasi offered resistance against Aurangzeb. The book also describes the defeat of the Mughals. The author came across this historical event in a handwritten book in the archives of the Mahanirvani Akhara in Varanasi. He described the event as the 'Battle of Gyan Vapi' in his book.

But our academic history books find no mention of this victory of the Naga Sadhus against Aurangzeb's Mughal forces. Instead, the Mughal ruler has been profusely glorified. James G. Lochtefeld mentions that historians have inferred the defeated Sultan as Aurangzeb. To quote James G. Lochtefeld on the Battle of Gyan Vapi from his book: "Battle reportedly fought in Benares by the Naga ascetic warriors of the Mahanirvani Akhara. According to a handwritten book in the akhara's archives, in 1664 the akhara's soldiers won a great victory near the Gyan Vapi well. This document simply states that the Sanyasis were victorious against the forces of 'the Sultan,' although historians have inferred that this figure was the Moghul emperor Aurangzeb. If the story is true, this battle may have been a contributing factor in Aurangzeb's decision to raze the Vishwanath temple in 1669. In light of this claim, it is possible that the temple's destruction was motivated not simply by intolerant iconoclasm but by the desire to inflict punishment for resistance and rebellion."

The 'victory' of the Naga Sadhus against Aurangzeb and his forces has been termed 'great' in this description by Lochtefeld. So, even if the battle hasn't been described well, it can be imagined how the Naga Sadhus created havoc on the Mughal army!

Jadu Nath Sarkar, in his book *A History of Dasnami Naga Sanyasis,* has recorded the same event thus under the title of 'Battle of the Jnan Bapi': "At the Kashi Kshetra in Samvat 1721 (-1664 AD) they own the victory in a fight with the Sultan (Aurangzib) and gained great glory. From sunrise to sunset the battle raged and the Dasnamis proved themselves heroes; they preserved the honour of Vishwanath's seat. They defeated the Muslims Mirza Ali and Turang Khan and Abdul Ali."

Jadu Nath Sarkar describes how from sunrise to sunset the Naga Sadhus fought against the Mughals and gained 'great glory'. The term 'great glory' further corroborates the immense valor of the Naga Sadhus.

Aurangzeb might have or might not have been personally present in that battle but it is true that his Mughal army was severely defeated by the Naga Sadhus in 1664. Aurangzeb attacked Varanasi again after four years, i.e., in 1669, and vandalized the temple. He built a mosque in its place called the Gyanvapi mosque. This mosque still exists in the temple premise.

There are very few recorded events of Hindu warriors or local communities offering resistance to save temples and to save the land.

It is said the British set on fire and destroyed many such written records, thus destroying evidence of victories and resistance. The records have been preserved through oral history and local historical folklore that have been passed down from one generation to another.

When Aurangzeb attacked Varanasi the second time in 1669, the Naga Sadhus retaliated till their last breath. According to local folklore and oral narrations, around 40,000 Naga Sadhus sacrificed their lives defending the Kashi Vishwanath Jyotirlinga.

Maratha King Malhar Rao Holkar strategized to demolish the Gyanvapi mosque and rebuild the Kashi Vishwanath Temple in 1742 but his plan failed to materialize. The Nawabs of Lucknow intervened. After eight years, i.e., in 1750, the Maharaja of Jaipur planned another strategy to rebuild the temple after demolishing the mosque. He decided to buy the land where the entire temple and mosque premises was located. But his plan failed too.

In 1780, Ahilyabai Holkar, daughter-in-law of Maratha King Malhar Rao, constructed the present temple structure adjacent to the Gyanvapi mosque. Ahilyabai Holkar also renovated many more temples across the country, including the Char Dhams besides taking care of their maintenance. Baiza Bai, the widow of the Maratha ruler Daulat Rao Scindhia of Gwalior, further expanded the Kashi Vishwanath temple followed by more expansions in later years under patronage of more Hindu rulers and traders. The Raja of Nepal gifted a seven-foot high stone statue of the Nandi bull to be installed. While the Bhosales of Nagpur donated silver, the one-ton gold used for plating the dome of the shrine was donated by Maharaja Ranjit Singh. Each time our temples were destroyed, they were rebuilt. This was how faith triumphed over fanaticism.

Naman to the valor of the Naga Sadhus! Har Har Mahadev!!!

21

Chaitanya Mahaprabhu

Started Kirtan Movement in Bengal Defying Orders of Bengal Sultanate

Chaitanya Mahaprabhu! The very utterance of the name of the Vaishnavite saint will ship one to the terrain of Hare Krishna Mahamantra, a chanting which he popularized. He was the founder of Brahma Madhva Gaudiya Sampradaya (Gaudiya Vaishnavism) and the chief proponent of Achintya Bheda Abheda Vedantic philosophy. Bhakti yoga saw its peak under him. Chaitanya Mahaprabhu started the *kirtan* (ecstatic song and dance, invoking the deities with the accompaniment of musical instruments) movement, a form of public worship in Bengal at a time when persecution of Hindus under the Bengal Sultanate saw its worst days. Despite restrictions from Muslim *qazis* and authorities, Chaitanya Mahaprabhu motivated thousands of *bhaktas* to come to the streets for *kirtan*.

He was born Vishvambhar Mishra on 18th February 1485 to Jagannath Mishra and Sachi Devi at Nabadwip in Nadia, Bengal. Chaitanya's complexion was like molten gold for which he was also called Gauranga and Gaura. He was born on a full moon night during a lunar eclipse. He was a scholar in Sanskrit and was well versed in the ancient Hindu scriptures. He met his Guru Ishvara Puri at Gaya under whom he was initiated with the Krishna mantra. Upon return to his hometown, he became a leader of the Vaishnava group in Nadia. Chaitanya Mahaprabhu was initiated into the sannyasa order by Swami Kesava Bharati. Chaitanya's friend and disciple was Nityananda, also called Nitai, who was always with the former when performing *kirtan* in the streets of Bengal. Chaitanya is considered the incarnation of Krishna and Nitai that of Balarama. Both are often named together as Gaura-Nitai.

Hindus in Bengal faced continuous religious persecution under the Bengal Sultanate from the early 13th century. What started with suzerainty from Delhi under the Khiljis, followed by Mamluks, and Tughlaqs turned to independent rule by Bengal Sultans with Balbans holding power for some time after the Mamluks. Chaitanya Mahaprabhu was born at a time when the persecution of Hindus was at its zenith. Not only the Sultans but also their Muslim subjects and *qazis* were involved in atrocities against the Hindus. Shortly before the birth of Chaitanya, Brahmins in his birthplace Nabadwip were subjected to brutal torture. To quote R.C. Mazumder from *History and Culture of the Indian People: The Delhi Sultanate*, Vol. 6, sourced from Jayananda's *Chaitanya Mangala:* "The king seizes the Brahmanas, pollutes their caste, and even takes their lives. If a conch shell is heard to blow in any house, its owner is made to forfeit his wealth, caste, and even life. The king plunders the houses of those who wear sacred threads on the shoulder and put sacred marks on the forehead and then binds them. He breaks the temples and uproots tulasi plants, and the residents of Navadvipa are in perpetual fear of their lives. The bathing in the Ganga is prohibited and hundreds of sacred Aavattha and jack trees have been cut down. The numerous Yavanas (Muslims) who reside in the Piralya village ruined the Brahmanas." During that time, Jalaluddin Fateh Shah from the Ilyas dynasty was the Sultan of Bengal from 1481-1487. Shamsuddin Yusuf Shah ruled from 1474–1481. This was followed by the rule of Sultans from the Habshi dynasty from 1487 to 1494. And then began the rule of Alauddin Husain Shah in 1494; he laid the foundation for the Hussain Shahi dynasty in Bengal and ruled until 1519. The persecution of Hindus and destruction of temples turned worse during the rule of Husain Shah though he has been regarded as a liberal-minded Muslim with one poet even considering him as an incarnation of God Krishna! Another poet compared him, notorious for destroying temples, with Pandava prince Arjuna! It was due to the continued interference from Husain Shah and his men that Chaitanya Mahaprabhu had to leave Bengal and settle in Puri in Odisha under the patronage of Raja Prataparudra.

Vijaya Gupta, a 15th-16th century Bengali poet describes how two *qazis* Hasan and Husain under Husain Shah took delight in tormenting the Hindus in all possible ways. Anyone found with the tulasi leaf on his head was profusely beaten with hands and feet bound. Anyone wearing the sacred thread was subjected to spitting of saliva into the mouth and tearing of the thread. Once a *mullah*, upon seeing a family worshipping Goddess Manasa, a form of Shakti, informed it to the two *qazis*. As punishment for daring to perform puja rituals, a mob under the orders of the *qazis*, demolished the house of the family and the offerings to the Goddess thrown away. The family members who fled to the forest were hunted down and punished. 'Forcible marriage of a Hindu girl by a Muslim, and dubious methods adopted to make the Hindus lose their caste' was a regular feature.

Isana Nagara, an author and contemporary of Alauddin Husain Shah described the Sultan's atrocities on Hindus thus as quoted in *History and Culture of the Indian People: The Delhi Sultanate*, Vol. 6:

Chaitanya Mahaprabhu performing kirtan with devotees in the streets of Nabadwip, defying restrictions laid by Muslim qazis.

"The wicked *mlechchhas* pollute the religion of the Hindus every day. They break the images of the gods into pieces and throw away the articles of worship. They throw into fire *Srimad Bhagavat* and other holy scriptures, forcibly take away the conch shell and bell of the Brahmanas (two necessary articles of worship) and lick the sandal paints on their bodies. They urinate like dogs on the sacred tulasi plant, and deliberately pass faeces in Hindu temples. They throw water from their mouths on the Hindus engaged in worship, and harass the Hindu saints as if they were so many lunatics let large."

The aforementioned is only a short account of the atrocities committed on Hindus and temples under the Bengal Sultanate during the time of Chaitanya Mahaprabhu and how Husain Shah was described by many as liberal but unleashed terror on Hindus.

During that time, Chaitanya Mahaprabhu introduced the *kirtan* movement on the streets of Nadia. It involved an assembly of a large number of devotees singing aloud together a *bhajan* invoking the deities or the Krishna *Mahamantra*, moving in a procession with the accompaniment of special musical instruments. Despite warnings and restrictions, the devotees continued with their *kirtan* activities. This enraged the *qazis*. Once a group of devotees was performing *kirtan* on the streets of Nabadwip. One of the *qazis*, in a fit of rage, attacked a few devotees and broke their musical instruments. He warned them of dire consequences if they were ever seen performing *kirtan* on the streets again. Both, the *qazis* and their followers often patrolled the streets of Nadia to keep a check on *kirtan* activities.

What did Chaitanya Mahaprabhu do when he heard about the restrictions laid by the *qazis* on *kirtans*? The young sadhu decided to defy the *qazis*' orders though the Hindus were terrified. He motivated the Hindus to stand up for Dharma and fear none. Chaitanya Mahaprabhu then announced the performance of *kirtan* in Nadia.

Thousands of Hindus joined the *kirtan* as the procession continued in the streets of Nadia. When one of the *qazis* heard about the violation of their orders, he set out with his men to stop them and attack them. But 'terror seized him when his eyes fell upon the vast concourse of people in a menacing attitude'. They fled. Their house soon turned into ruins!

Soon after, Chaitanya Mahaprabhu visited the capital city of Gauda, the base of Alauddin Husain Shah. His followers and disciples dissuaded him but in vain. They feared he might be attacked and punished by the Sultan. But numbers have their might! When Chaitanya Mahaprabhu walked the streets of Gauda, performing *kirtan*, hundreds and thousands of Hindus joined him, paying their obeisance. The ovation Chaitanya received and the support of thousands of followers that he was able to garner surprised the Sultan. He did not interfere in Chaitanya's activities.

Sanatana, a Hindu official at the court of the Sultan, became an ardent devotee of Chaitanya. He feigned illness to avoid attending court and devoted more of his time to religious rituals and following the footsteps of his Guru. Husain Shah paid a surprise visit to Sanatana's home. He found him hale and hearty and saw him interacting on Dharma with a group of around 30 Vaishnavites. Enraged, the Sultan arrested him and put him in prison. Sultan Husain Shah was then all ready for a military expedition to Odisha. He offered to free Sanatana from confinement on the condition that he should accompany him on the expedition. Sanatana refused saying, as quoted in *History and Culture of the Indian People: The Delhi Sultanate*, Vol. 6: "You are going to torment our Gods (i.e., destroy the images and temples); I cannot go with you." It is to be noted that Husain Shah already led several military expeditions to Odisha between 1497 to 1500 but was defeated. Raja Prataparudra of Odisha was then only 17 years old. The young king not only drove away the Muslim army out of Odisha successfully but also reinforced the borders. Husain Shah sent Ismail Ghazi to Odisha with a huge army in 1509 CE at a time when Prataparudra was out on an expedition to the south. Bhoi Bidyadhar, the Odia general, offered a brave resistance in the absence of the king until the latter, upon hearing about the attack, returned. Prataparudra defeated Ismail Ghazi. Pursuing the enemy forces, the Odia army led by Prataparudra reached Bengal. They won the first battle at Mandarana Fort and laid siege to it, Husain Shah was then stationed in that fort. Govinda Vidyadhara, a commander of the Odia army, changed sides at this juncture and became a traitor. He sided with Sultan Husain Shah as a result of which the fort fell back into the hands of the Sultan.

Chaitanya traveled across the country visiting all the holy places, performing kirtan. He stayed in Bengal for a year thereafter and then left for Puri. Raja Prataparudra welcomed him and became his disciple. For the rest of his life, i.e., for 20 years, Chaitanya Mahaprabhu lived in Puri and continued with his devotional activities without any interference under the Hindu king. There are several literary references to how Sultan Husain Shah tortured the Hindus whenever they were seen performing kirtan or even singing *bhajans* in their respective homes. Though there are no direct references as to why Chaitanya Mahaprabhu left Bengal for Odisha, the reason is evident. Chaitanya left his mortal being on 14th June 1534 at the age of 48 in Puri.

Chaitanya Mahaprabhu was instrumental in ushering a Hindu revival in Bengal at a time when Hindus were the most persecuted. He infused a new spirit and confidence into the minds of the Hindus. Despite being subjected to brutal attacks and interferences, the Hindus of Bengal upheld Dharma, diligently following all religious rituals.

Hare Krishna!

22

Baba Deep Singh

Defeated Afghans in the Battle of Amritsar in 1757

At the age of 17, he was initiated into Khalsa at Anandpur Sahib by Guru Gobind Singh, the 10th Sikh Guru. At 23, he helped Sikh scholar Bhai Mani Singh in making copies of the *Guru Granth Sahib*. At 27, he joined Banda Singh Bahadur in the Battle of Sadhaura against Sayyids and the Battle of Chappar Siri against Mughals. At 51, he was appointed the leader of *jatha*, a military squad, under Kapur Singh, a Sikh leader and organizer of the Sikh Confederacy and the Dal Khalsa. At 66, he became the leader of Shaheedan Misl, one of the 12 Misls (sovereign states) of the Sikh Confederacy. He was also the first head of Damdami Taksal, an orthodox Sikh cultural and educational organization. At the age of 75, he freed a large number of young Hindu prisoners taken captive by Ahmad Shah Abdali near Kurukshetra and also raided the Afghan ruler's treasury. After a few months, he defeated the Afghans in the Battle of Amritsar and attained martyrdom of battlefield wounds at the Harmandir Sahib (Golden Temple). He was Baba Deep Singh, one of the bravest warriors of India.

Baba Deep Singh was born on 26th January 1682 in a Sandhu Jat family to Bhagta and Jioni at Pahuwind village in Amritsar, Punjab.

He was the only son of his parents, who remained issueless for 15 years. It is said a Gursikh, who had food at Bhagta's place, had predicted that 'a great valiant warrior and scholar' would be born in the family. The foretelling turned true. From a very young age, Baba Deep Singh assisted his parents in household chores and farmland. Bhagta recited the *Baanis* of the Sikh Gurus to his son.

In 1699, on Vaisakhi at Anandpur Sahib, Guru Gobind Singh created the Khalsa, a warrior community, involving a group of six warriors including himself, with all six taking the surname 'Singh', connoting lion. Thereafter, thousands of devotees, including Baba Deep Singh and his parents, consumed nectar from the Guru. Deep Singh was then 17 years old. The family of three stayed at Anandpur Sahib for a few days during which Deep Singh came across the army of Guru Govind Singh getting trained in horse-riding and the use of weapons including swordsmanship, archery, and other martial skills. The Guru also entrusted teachers to teach the warriors Sanskrit, Persian, Punjabi, and Hindi. Deep Singh joined the Guru's army much against the wishes of his parents. He soon became an expert in warfare. Under the guidance of Sikh scholar Bhai Mani Singh, he learned reading and writing Gurmukhi. He also learned how to interpret the teachings of the Gurus. At the age of 23, he helped Bhai Mani Singh in making copies of the *Guru Granth Sahib*.

In December 1705, Guru Govind Singh had to temporarily leave Anandpur as a condition for peace. Aurangzeb died in 1707 AD following which a fight ensued between his sons for the emperorship. His eldest son Bahadar Shah, a Shia Muslim, sought Guru Gobind Singh's help. With the Guru's help and against a promise, Bahadar Shah became the next Mughal emperor. The promise was that as king he would do justice in Punjab by punishing the Governor of Sirhind under Mughals, Nawab Wazir Khan, and his accomplices for their crimes against the common people and for killing the Guru's mother

Mata Gujri and two younger sons Zorawar Singh and Fateh Singh. His sons, aged five and eight, were buried alive in a wall after they refused to convert to Islam. But after becoming emperor, Bahadur Shah did not keep up his promise.

In 1708, Guru Gobind Singh along with his family and followers reached the Nander ashram of Banda Singh, then known as Madho Daas, in Maharashtra. After Guru Gobind Singh initiated him into the Khalsa, he was named Gur Bakhash Singh and later became popular as Baba Banda Singh Bahadur. Knowing about Banda Singh Bahadur's expertise in the art of warfare, he appointed him his general. The Guru appointed five Sikhs for counseling–Daya Singh, Binod Singh, Kahan Singh, Bijay Singh, and Ram Singh as his counselors. The Guru ordered him to go to Punjab and fight the Mughals. Reaching Punjab, Banda Singh Bahadur managed to garner support from both Hindus and Sikhs for fighting against enemy forces in battle. Guru Govind Singh had prophesized about Sikh sovereignty in Punjab. Banda Singh led several battles to victory. Baba Deep Singh joined Banda Singh in two battles–The battle of Sadhaura in 1709 and the Battle of Chappar Chiri in 1710. The Sikhs emerged victorious in both battles. In the Battle of Sadhaura, only a few Sikh soldiers defeated the Sayyids and Shaikhs and killed the ruler Osman Khan. In the Battle of Chappar Chiri fought near Sirhind in Fatehgarh, the Sikhs gave a crushing blow to the Mughal army. Wazir Khan, the murderer of Guru Govind Singh's mother and two younger children, was killed in this battle. Following victory in this battle, the Sikhs established their first rule in Punjab. Guru Govind Singh's prophecy turned true.

To withstand the atrocities committed by the Mughals, Sikh Gurus established military forces and fought against the enemies. Later, they organized into military bands called *jathas*. There were 65 *jathas*, which in 1748 at the biannual meeting called the Sharbat

Khalsa, were reorganized into 12 Misls. The Misls were sovereign states of the Sikh confederacy. Each Misl, comprising of warriors numbering a few hundreds to a few thousands, was attributed a territory. And each Misl had a leader under whom the chosen warriors remained loyal. Misls primarily employed cavalry in warfare. Baba Deep Singh was appointed the leader of the Shaheedan Misl with 5,000 horsemen, which also included Nihang Sikhs. Talwandi Sabo and northern Ambala, i.e., today's Bathinda and Panchkula districts, were under the Shaheedan Misl with its capital at Shahzadpur.

From 1748 to 1767, Ahmad Shah Abdali, the founder of the Durrani Empire in Afghanistan, attacked parts of India eight times. He had accompanied Nadir Shah during the latter's expedition to Delhi in 1739 and was well aware of the wealth and riches of the Indian kingdoms.

In April 1757, when Ahmad Shah Abdali raided the northern part of India for the fourth time, he not only committed a massacre of the weak and innocent, plundered and burned entire villages but also looted wealth and held women as captives, especially Hindu women from Agra, Mathura, and Vrindavan. With the loot and the captives, Abdali started his journey back to Kabul from Delhi. The Sikhs decided to relieve Abdali of the looted wealth and free the captives. Baba Deep Singh, with his forces, was all ready to strike near Kurukshetra. They were successful in freeing the captives and also relieving much of the wealth looted by the Afghan ruler. Batch after batch, the Sikhs attacked Abdali's men in camps killing them in thousands, releasing captives, and taking away their booty. At one camp, Abdali himself kept guard but he was looted again. A frightened Abdali hurried towards Lahore without any further delay with only one-fourth of the booty he had looted.

Upon arrival in Lahore, Ahmad Shah Abdali decided to take revenge on the Sikhs for his loss. He ordered his men to prevent the

Sikhs from entering the Golden Temple in Amritsar. He also ordered the desecration of the temple. At Lahore, Abdali assigned the Punjab region to Timur Shah, his son, also leaving behind an army of 15,000 men under General Jahan Khan, and left for Kabul. General Jahan Khan marched towards the Golden Temple with his forces to fulfill his master's orders.

During this time, as Jahan Khan reached Amritsar, Gur Bakhsh Singh Sandhu, a leader of the Panjgarhia Misl, was serving the Gurudwaras of Amritsar including the Golden Temple with 30 of his men. The Sikh warriors fought bravely; the 30 killed 300 of Abdali's soldiers. All of the Sikh warriors attained martyrdom defending the Golden Temple. Jahan Khan desecrated the temple and filled the waters of the Amrit Sarovara, the holy tank, with entrails of slaughtered cows.

The news of the desecration of the Golden Temple and impurity of the Amrit Sarovara (temple lake) reached Baba Deep Singh's ears. The leader of the Shaheedan Misl at once made preparations and asked his men to be ready. Driving the Afghans out of the holy city and restoring the temple was his resolve. With 500 men, he started for Amritsar. "May my head fall at the Darbar Sahib," uttered Baba Deep Singh at the onset of the march. On his way towards the holy city, many villagers joined him. By the time he reached Tarn Taran Sahib, several miles away from Amritsar, he had an army of 5,000 Sikhs armed with hatchets, swords, and spears. The warriors took a bath at the holy sarovara at Tarn Taran Sahib and marched towards the Golden Temple. Baba Naudh Singh, S. Dial Singh, and S. Balwant Singh, all valiant commanders armed with double-edged swords and riding their own horses, had joined Baba Deep Singh.

When Jahan Khan heard about the approaching Sikh warriors towards Amritsar, he immediately set out with his forces to stop the

Sikhs from advancing further. Both the armies met at Gohlwarh, few miles away from Amritsar. Baba Deep Singh was an excellent war strategist. He divided his army into four parts. He entrusted one group each to Baba Naudh Singh and advised to attack the Afghan forces on the right and S. Dial Singh to attack from the left. He and S. Balwant Singh, with their respective groups, strategized to attack after the breakage of entanglement of the Afghan forces. The Sikh army fiercely fell upon the Afghan forces. The battlefield ground was not limited to one place. As both the forces fought, they advanced towards Amritsar.

During the battle, Balwant Singh with a heavy blow of his sword killed Zabardast Khan, a commander of the Afghan forces. Baba Naudh Singh attained martyrdom while killing Rustam Khan, another Afghan commander. Baba Deep Singh moved towards General Jamal Khan and sawed him and his horse. Furthermore, S. Dial Singh's arrow pierced the general's chest. Jamal Khan fell dead. A wounded Timur Shah fled from the battlefield. As the battle was about to end with the Sikhs winning, a sword of an Afghan hit Baba Deep Singh's neck and he fell to the ground.

Assisting himself, he held his head from falling off from his neck and stood up. A companion reminded him that he had vowed that his head should fall at Darbar Sahib, i.e., the Golden Temple. Meanwhile, as Timur Shah fled and a commander and a general were killed, the Afghan soldiers started fleeing from the battlefield. Baba Deep Singh rode fast towards the Golden Temple. His head fell in the temple. Baba Deep Singh thus kept his vow on 13th November 1757. At the place where Baba Deep Singh was cremated, stands the Gurdwara Shahid Ganj. The Golden Temple was rebuilt and the Amrit Sarovara was cleansed.

23

Dhan Singh Gurjar

His Role in the 1857 War of Independence in Meerut

1857. Meerut, UP. He was the *kotwal*, the chief police officer of Meerut, employed under the British. When the War of Independence started in that city on 9th May, he joined the freedom fighters along with his police forces. He motivated the sepoys and civilians to join hands in groups against the British. He allowed the native soldiers and civilians to attack the British and pillage British properties as well as offices. He set free not only the 85 Indian sepoys but also other native inmates imprisoned in Meerut jail, numbering over 800. He facilitated the inmates' movement towards Delhi to give shape to the freedom struggle activities the big way. He invited Gurjars from his village to the town to attack the British officers. The British caught him and hanged him to death on a tree on 4th July 1857. He was then 37 years old. He was one of the first to start the War of Independence of 1857 and the first police officer to do so. He was Kotwal Dhan Singh Gurjar, also known as Dhunna Sing in British records.

Much of the historical records available about the glories and victories of Indian warriors were destroyed by the British. This was to prove their superiority and show the later generations and the world that they were superior and that they civilized India. The Gurjars were very brutal against the British. Kalyan Singh Gurjar and his men attacked a group of 200 plus British soldiers when they were transporting British treasury from Jawalapur to Saharanpur in 1823. This warrior group butchered many British soldiers and looted their treasury. This continued for years. In return, the British confiscated their lands and branded them as 'dacoits' and 'criminals' under the Criminal Tribes Act. Their crime was they did not accept British suzerainty. Gurjars constituted the majority of the population in villages around Meerut. The British confiscated their lands, gifting the same against revenue payment to other natives who were loyal to them. During the War of Independence of 1857, the Gurjars of these villages participated in the freedom struggle under the leadership of Dhan Singh Gurjar.

Dhan Singh Gurjar was born on 27th November 1820 at Panchli Khurd village in Meerut. His father was Saligram and his mother was Manohari. He belonged to the Chaprana *gotra* (lineage) of the Gurjar community. Saligram was the *mukhiya* (headman) of his village. He was called a warrior by the village folks because of his strong stand against British policies and oppression. Dhan Singh Gurjar grew up in a patriotic atmosphere. Going by his skills, he was appointed as the *kotwal* (police officer) of Meerut. His jurisdiction covered from Dehradun to Sahibabad with an office at Sadar Bazaar in the heart of Meerut city.

The large military cantonment in Meerut, deemed to be holding one of the largest concentrations of British troops in India, had 2,038 British soldiers, 12 British-manned guns, and 2,357 Indian sepoys in 1857. According to British records, there were a total of 136,000 Indian troops in the entire Bengal Presidency in 1857; there were three presidencies–Bombay, Madras, and Bengal with a total count of

Indian sepoys at 300,000 and British sepoys at 50,000! Meerut served as the headquarters of the Bengal artillery, garrisoned by one light cavalry and two native infantry regiments. Hewitt was the Major General, Wilson the Brigadier General, Finnis, and Mackenzie–both Colonels, Smyth the Lieutenant Colonel, MacNabb and Gough, both Lieutenants, to name a few.

Meanwhile, rumors about the use of greased cartridges in the newly introduced Enfield rifle hurt the religious sentiments of both Hindu and Muslim sepoys. The grease was believed to be made from cows' and pigs' fat. The grease in the cartridge eased the process of loading; the cartridge required to be torn open with the teeth, which was objectionable to the native sepoys. A group of 85 Indian sepoys out of 90 at the Meerut regiment refused to open the cartridges of the Enfield Rifles when ordered by Lieutenant Colonel Smyth.

At 5 a.m., on 9th May 1857, the entire garrison was paraded to hear the sentences of those 85 sepoys, the names of whom were read out. These 85 sepoys were made to stand in a line in the middle with the other sepoys forming three sides of a square. While the British sepoys were armed with ammunition, the natives were without arms. It continued for more than an hour and while the sentence was being read, 85 sepoys were stripped of their uniforms and iron shackles were put on them one after another. The "felon shackles were being methodically and of necessity slowly hammered on the ankles of the wretched criminals" described MacNabb, as mentioned in *The Great Fear of 1857: Rumours, Conspiracies and the Making of the Indian Uprising* by Kim A. Wagner. The Indian sepoys were termed 'wretched criminals' only because they refused to use the cartridges because they opposed their British commanders. The 85 sepoys were imprisoned in Meerut jail. Out of the 85 sepoys, 74 were sentenced to 10 years imprisonment with hard labor and 11 to five years imprisonment. As

Dhan Singh Gurjar with 830 Indian released prisoners, all geared up to attack the British.

they were marched off to Meerut jail, they rebuked the other native soldiers for failing to support them–this was also one of the reasons why the sepoys did not wait any longer to attack the British the same day later.

By the afternoon of the same day, several native sepoys left for Delhi on their own to spread the news of the imprisonment of the 85 native soldiers. A few soldiers cut the telegraph line between Meerut and Delhi. The civilians of Meerut did not like the treatment meted out to the 85 native soldiers. In Sadar Bazaar, few prostitutes jeered at the other native soldiers walking down the street, saying thus: "Your brethren have been ornamented with these anklets and incarcerated; and for what? Because they would not swerve from their creed; and you, cowards as you are, sit still indifferent to their fate. If you had an atom of manhood in you, go and release them." The soldiers started realizing that they might meet the same fate–they would be forced to accept the cartridges, which was against their religion, or get imprisoned by the British at the point of the bayonet. The soldiers shot dead Colonel Finnis. They knew they had to stay together and their only goal was to defeat the British and kill all the officers. They then killed Captain Macdonald and Trepar, a British civilian. Meanwhile, British soldiers ran towards the heart of the Sadar Bazaar, seeking protection from a guard of sepoys in red uniform stationed there only to be shot at by them besides being pelted with stones and beaten with sticks by the native civilians. A group of soldiers set British properties, houses, and offices on fire.

Dhan Singh Gurjar, entrusted to maintain law and order in the city, did not perform his colonial duties. From 9th May onwards, he participated in the freedom struggle. He along with forces allowed the sepoys and locals to attack the British and their properties. He summoned the villagers, especially Gurjars, from Panchli village to come armed towards Sadar Bazaar. He also summoned thousands of more people from around 16 villages in and around Meerut to come armed to the city to fight against the British. The assembly of villagers at a single summon suggests that Dhan Singh was already mobilizing a big group besides spreading awareness about the cruel policies of the British. The villagers came armed with sticks and a few with swords.

Dhan Singh Gurjar, like the sepoys and the locals, did not like the British imprisoning the 85 soldiers. He and his police forces moved towards Meerut jail to set free the prisoners. Around 40 native soldiers, 'bare-headed, with drawn swords' including a few hundred villagers, the locals of the city, joined Dhan Singh Gurjar. They attacked the British officers posted there. They released around 830 Indian inmates including the 85 sepoys. The freedom fighters then attacked the British. Col. Mackenzie later described the scene that met them at the jail: "The prisoners were already swarming out of it; their shackles were being knocked off by blacksmiths before our eyes: and the jail guard of native infantry, on our riding up to it, answered our questions by firing at us, fortunately without hitting any of us…"

By the night of 9th May, all the villagers summoned by Dhan Singh Gurjar arrived in the city. To quote from Kim A. Wagner's *The Great Fear of 1857: Rumours, Conspiracies and the Making of the Indian Uprising:* "The Gujars made their first appearance here, although they were later to play a significant role in the uprising across the countryside… some of the rumours that flourished after the parade on 9th May referred to Goojurs of the neighbouring villages and had characters generally who were preparing to plunder Meerut by the thousands." From 9th to 10th May, rioting, loot, and plunder in British residences continued. The freedom fighters also attacked few native homes that fully enjoyed British favor. Many buildings of the British were set on fire. Several Britishers were killed. The freedom fighters also did not spare the loyal natives who came forward to support and save the British from being attacked.

The prisoners that Kotwal Dhan Singh Gurjar released in Meerut played an instrumental role in sparking the revolt in Delhi. Bahadur Shah Zafar, the then Mughal ruler, who only in name resided in Delhi, and the British controlled the city's finances and courts. Freedom fighters including the prisoners released by Dhan Singh Gurjar from Meerut laid siege of Delhi, started killing the British soldiers and officers, and looted their wealth. Dhan Singh played a leadership role for some time in creating strategies for the uprising until he was caught by the British.

A committee was formed by the British to identify people who participated in the freedom struggle movement on 9th and 10th May in Meerut. Upon investigation, they found that Dhan Singh Gurjar and the villagers of Panchli Khurd were the key people involved in the uprising. They attacked Panchli village with canons on the night of 3rd July 1857. They opened fire and plundered the whole village. Around 400 freedom fighters were killed during the action. It was a planned massacre! The British arrested the surviving male freedom fighters including the young and the old, numbering around 40 (according to few historians, the number is 80), and hanged them on trees in front of children and womenfolk on 4th July. Dhan Singh was executed the same day. Not even a single teenager or adult male of Panchli village was spared. All of Dhan Singh Gurjar's family members were executed, except the womenfolk and children. Those who survived were the ones who visited long-distance relatives during that time, far away from Panchli Khurd.

Had Dhan Singh Gurjar, in his role as the *kotwal* of Meerut, deployed his police forces to maintain law and order, had he not invited the villagers to the city, had he not led the freedom fighters to attack the jail, had he protected the British, the revolt would have been nipped in the bud at Meerut, the epicenter of the 1857 war. Under his leadership, even the native police forces joined the movement. Hence, the British consider Dhan Singh Gurjar as the one responsible for the spread of the revolt in the city and to other parts of the country.

Today, the trees where hundreds of freedom fighters were hanged, are still there, mutely narrating to every onlooker the gory cum valorous saga of the past, revealing how we breathe free today as a result of their resistance and sacrifices.

According to a 2018 *Statesman* (Kolkata-based English newspaper) report, a statue of Dhan Singh Gurjar was unveiled in Sadar Bazaar police station by O.P. Singh, DGP of UP in 2018. To quote from the newspaper: "Uttar Pradesh Director General of Police O.P. Singh unveiled the statue of Kotwal Dhan Singh Gurjar on the premises of the Sadar police station here on Tuesday. Dhan Singh was posted here 161 years ago during the First War of Independence in 1857, and is still remembered for his contribution to freedom struggle… The DGP also announced that a chapter of Dhan Singh Kotwal would be included in police training and a documentary made to take his inspiring story of bravery and martyrdom to the public."

24

Krishnadeva Raya

Defeated the Sultans of the Deccan

Krishnadeva Raya established Hindu supremacy in the south at a time when Islamic invaders were authoritative in various parts of the country. He led battles from the front. He defeated the Bahmani Sultanate including the Sultans of Bijapur, Bidar, Ahmednagar, and Golconda. As a warrior winning many battles and as a scholar, he earned the titles of *Mooru Rayara Ganda*, meaning 'King of Three Kings', *Andhra Bhoja*, meaning 'Andhra Scholar King', and *Kannada Rajya Rama Ramana*, meaning 'Lord of the Kannada Empire'. He was fluent in several languages. He was a scholar and an author of several books in Sanskrit and one in Telugu. He patronized Tamil literature. During the time when Mughal rule started in Delhi, Krishnadeva Raya had the most extensive empire in Bharat, several times bigger than the later Mughal dominion. He built several temples. He was one of the greatest and most powerful kings of India from the Vijayanagara Empire.

Here is a statement by Mukku Thimmana, a Telugu poet that well summarizes the warriorhood, power, and qualities of Krishnadeva Raya, as quoted in *Vijayanagara Voices Exploring South Indian History and Hindu Literature* by William J Jackson:

"O Krishnaraya, you Man-Lion.

You destroyed the Turks from far away with just your great name's power.

Oh Lord of the elephant king, just from seeing you the multitude of elephants ran away in horror."

Mukku Thimmana was one of the *Astadiggajas*, meaning eight elephants, in the court of Krishnadeva Raya. The emperor had a literary assembly at his court comprising of eight Telugu poets. They were regarded as the eight pillars and were known as *Astadiggajas.*

Krishnadeva Raya was born to Nagala Devi and Tuluva Narasa Nayaka on 16th February 1471 at Hampi, Karnataka. According to accounts of travelers, Krishnadeva Raya was of medium height, fair, and had a healthy physique. Wrestling was his passion. He became an expert in the art of warfare from a very young age. He was an excellent horse rider and an efficient swordsman.

Tuluva Narasa Nayaka was an army commander under Narasimha Deva Raya, the emperor of the Vijayanagara Empire from the Saluva dynasty. During his commandership, he won many battles and helped the king expand the boundaries of his empire. Few years after the death of his king Narasimha Deva Raya, Tuluva Narasa Nayaka laid the foundation for the Tuluva dynasty, the third of the four dynasties that ruled the Vijayanagara Empire. Krishnadeva Raya was the third Tuluva king, his predecessor being his elder brother Vira Narasimha Raya. He was married to Tirumala Devi, the princess of Srirangapatna, and Chinna Devi, the princess of Coorg. His daughters were Tirumalumba, married to Aliya Rama Raya, and Vengalamba, married to Tirumala Deva Raya. His son-in-law Aliya Rama Raya later became the founder of the Aravidu dynasty and ruled the Vijayanagara Empire. Aliya was succeeded by his brother Tirumala Deva Raya. Krishnadeva Raya's elder son was poisoned to death at the age of six.

When Krishnadeva Raya ascended the throne of the Vijayanagara Empire in 1509 at the age of 38, the boundaries of the kingdom had already shrunk over time with smaller chiefs and vassals claiming their sovereignty. Besides, there were several rival claimants. As soon as Krishnadeva Raya assumed rulership, he dealt with his rival claimants and secured his position free from all plots and intrigues. Soon after, in 1510, he built the eastern tower of Virupaksha temple at Hampi, signalizing his accession to power. Virupaksha temple was built by Lakkan Dandesha, a nayaka under Deva Raya II of the Sangama dynasty, though the shrine of Shiva existed beyond the seventh century. This temple was expanded and beautified over time. Thereafter, Krishnadeva Raya started claiming back the lost territories and expanded his empire. Several chiefs acknowledged their loyalty to the emperor. An expert in warfare and an excellent war strategist, he led battles from the front.

In 1510, Alfonzo Albuquerque, the Portuguese Viceroy to India, visited the court of Krishnadeva Raya for negotiations and to sign a treaty. By then, the Portuguese had gradually established their trading bases in the coastal areas in the South including Goa. Alfonzo Albuquerque offered to help Krishnadeva Raya deal with the enemies, especially the Muslim chiefs of neighboring kingdoms, and in return sought his approval to permit the Portuguese to set up a factory in any Vijayanagar port between Bhatkal and Mangalore (now Mangaluru). Krishnadeva Raya diplomatically turned down the proposal. In later years, the emperor entered into a treaty with the Portuguese for the supply of horses and Portuguese artillery.

During that time, several commanders and nobles under the Bahmani Sultanate declared their independence and stamped their suzerainty as Sultans, claiming territories. They were Qutb Shahi of Golconda, Nizamshahi of Ahmednagar, Adil Shahi of Bijapur, Barid

Shahi of Bidar, and Imad Shahi of Berar, collectively known as 'Deccan Sultanates'. During the reign of Krishnadeva Raya, Yusuf Adil Shah, also known as Adil Khan, was the Sultan of Bijapur (now Vijayapura) and Quli Qutb Mulk of Golconda. Both the Sultans led campaigns on the eastern frontiers of the Vijayanagara Empire. Krishnadeva Raya checked their advances.

Part of the territory of the Bahmani Sultanate was earlier under the Vijayanagara Empire. Krishnadeva Raya decided to recover the lost possessions from Adil Shah. He marched with his army towards the Bijapur frontier located in the north of his empire. On his way, he halted at Shivaganga and paid obeisance to Gangadhareswara, the presiding deity of the place. At Ikkeri, Sankanna Nayaka joined him with additional troops. At the news of the advancing big Vijayanagara army, many soldiers of Adil Shah fled from Bijapur, deserting their garrisons. Krishnadeva Raya captured parts of the Bijapur territory, especially the forts of Mudgal, Addanki, and Advani where he stationed his own troops and then marched towards Raichore (now Raichuru). He laid siege of Raichore Fort and in no time the army of Adil Shah surrendered in 1512.

In 1512, Quli Qutb Mulk had just declared independence from the Bahmani kingdom and established a base at Golconda. He was all geared up to expand his territory. He launched a surprise attack on Rajakonda (present Rachakonda) and imprisoned its ruler Venkatappa Nayaka. Quli Qutb then laid siege of Devarakonda where the Hindus offered resistance for several days until it fell into the enemy's hands. The Golconda Sultan destroyed the palaces and the temples in the city. This news reached Krishnadeva Raya. The Hindu emperor immediately set out towards Golconda with a huge army, comprising of 30,000 horses and 300,000-foot soldiers. By the time he reached the banks of the Krishna River, he captured most of the territories of Quli Qutb

Mulk. The Golconda Sultan marched ahead from his capital to prevent Krishnadeva Raya's further progress into his dominion. He reached the banks of river Krishna. The Sultans of Ahmednagar and Bijapur sent their respective contingents to Quli Qutb's aid. A fierce battle took place between the two sides on the banks of the Krishna. It was the summer of 1512 and the river was flooded. The Hindu soldiers displayed utmost gallantry. Thousands of Golconda soldiers were killed in combat against the Vijayanagara soldiers. One of the commanders of Krishnadeva Raya–Pemmasani Ramalinga Naidu, who was the Kanuna chief of the Gandikota family, entered 'the enemy's camp, cut their tent ropes and put everything into disorder'. When defeat was certain for Quli Qutb Mulk, his army fled the battlefield with many, while trying to swim across the Krishna, getting drowned. The Golconda army was defeated. Krishnadeva Raya then sent his army further inwards. They captured Pangal and Ganpura. Later, Quli Qutb regained Pangal. Following the advice of his ministers, Krishnadeva Raya proceeded towards Udayagiri from the banks of the Krishna.

By 1514 CE, i.e., after two years, the Bahmani Sultanate was restored in Bijapur. At the end of 1514, Krishnadeva Raya set out with a huge army including Portuguese horses to invade the Bijapur territories of the Bahmani Sultanate. When the Nizamshahi of Ahmednagar heard about it, he sent a large force under the commandment of Feroz Khan, Talit Khan, Sanjar Khan, Munial Khan, Dustoor Khan, Vagir Khan, Rabut Khan, and Bokka Singh to check the emperor's advances. They drew up near Jamkhandi. Krishnadeva Raya sent a part of his army under the commandment of Sadasiva Nayaka, the chieftain of Keladi, to Jamkhandi. Sadasiva Nayaka was known for gallantry in battles. At this battle of Jamkhandi, the Vijayanagara army won. While most of the commanders of the

Raja Krishnadeva Raya with his opponent in a wrestling match.

Muslim army were killed in battle and few fled, Bokka Singh was taken prisoner. Krishnadeva Raya further entrusted Sadasiva Nayaka to capture the Bijapur territories of Kalyani and Dhoolikota, and he proceeded towards Gulbarga (now Kalaburagi), which was then under the troops of Adil Shah. Again, Sadasiva Nayaka emerged victorious, Krishnadeva Raya conferred on him the titles of *Immadi*, meaning 'doubly gifted' and *Raja Nayaka*, meaning 'royal chieftain' for his gallantry. The vijayanagara forces also captured more parts of the Bijapur territories. Sadasiva Nayaka's troops then rejoined the Vijayanagara army near Gulbarga.

The battle of Gulbarga between the Vijayanagara and Adil Shahi armies took place for eight days. Krishna Deva Raya then changed his strategy; the Raya retired to his camp at Jamavadanakote and then sent his troops for a fresh attack under the commandments of Sadasiva Nayaka, Doddavasanta Nayaka, and Pemmasani Timma Nayaka. The Vijayanagara forces won and Gulbarga was taken. Krishnadeva Raya rewarded the commanders magnificently and further honored Sadasiva Nayaka with the title of *Kote Koldhala*, meaning 'Wrecker of Forts'. Entrusting the affairs of Gulbarga to Gujjari Kalyana Rao, the Tuluva emperor returned to his capital.

In 1516, Krishnadeva Raya again marched towards Golconda with his forces. He attacked from the eastern side. The Vijayanagara army emerged victorious with Indrakonda, Uralakonda, Aruvapalli, Jallepalli, Kondikonda, Kappulavayi, Nalagonda, Commomet Devarakonda, and Warangal being taken. The same year, Krishnadeva Raya sent Sadasiva Nayaka to Bidar and he joined the advance guard later. During this time, Amir Bareed was at the helm of affairs of the then Bahmani city. The battle between the Vijayanagara army and Amir Bareed's forces continued for several days. Krishnadeva Raya won the battle.

By 1516, Krishnadeva Raya had defeated the Sultans of Golconda, Bijapur, Bidar, and Ahmednagar. He, thereafter, marched towards the Gajapati kingdom. On the way, he encountered a local Muslim chief named Shitab Khan. The Vijayanagara armies were in a forest then when Shitab Khan laid a surprise attack, surrounding the Hindus on all sides with 60,000 archers. A terrible battle followed. After long-drawn combat, the Hindu army won.

Meanwhile, Adil Shah retook the fort of Raichore. Krishnadeva Raya made up his mind to recover the fort at any cost. Adil Shah strengthened his garrison at Raichore with all required army, artillery, and enough food supplies for five years. To quote from *The History of the Vijayanagara Empire* by M.H. Rama Sharma: "The garrison of this place consisted, at this time, of 8,000 foot, 400 horses, 20 elephants, and 30 catapults. But its power of resistance depended more upon the 200 heavy artillery and a good many smaller pieces, besides supplies enough to last for 5 years." In 1520 CE, Adil Shah sent additional reinforcements–a captain and some troops to Raichore Fort. Krishnadeva Raya's strength stood at 573,000 infantry, 28,600 cavalry, 586 elephants, 40 trained Portuguese artillery men including 12,000 water carriers. The most distinguished Vijayanagara generals in that expedition were Kama Naik, Thimmappa Naik, Adeppa Naik, Triambaka Raya, Kondama Reddy, Baluva Govinda Raja, and Kumara Veerayya. The chiefs of Dambar and Bankapur along with their forces joined Krishnadeva Raya. The Vijayanagara army camped at Malliabad near Raichore.

For three months, the siege of Raichore fort continued. Adil Shah marched towards Raichore with 120,000-foot soldiers, 18,000 horses, and 150 elephants, and very strong artillery. He encamped on the northern bank of the Krishna River, creating a snare for the Vijayanagara army to attack him. But Krishnadeva Raya knew the enemy's motives and waited for Adil Shah to move towards where he camped. When Adil Shah realized that his plan failed, he crossed the Krishna with his troops and encamped within three leagues of the Vijayanagara camp. Adil Shah's advantage was his strong artillery which Krishnadeva Raya lacked. Learning about Adil Shah's change of position, Krishnadeva Raya advanced a league more and strengthened his position by 'digging trenches and mounting guns'. A night passed and then the war began. The Tuluva emperor ordered two of his forward divisions of 30,000 men to attack Adil Shah. The enemy forces, all armed, opened fire with their whole artillery upon the 30,000 men, who were taken unawares followed by the charging of the cavalrymen. The Vijayanagara ranks were thrown into disorder, experiencing major damage due to the artillery shots. The surviving soldiers started fleeing and were pursued by the enemy forces for half a league.

At this critical juncture, Krishnadeva Raya himself got ready to lead the army from the front with a fresh attack. Before starting, he gave to his attendant the ring he wore on his finger to be delivered to his queens as a token of his death. He then motivated his soldiers with a fiery stirring speech, who were kindled like fire to fight and die for the motherland. The emperor also ordered the slaughter of all those who fled from the battlefield. And they marched forward. No artilleries could stop them or throw them into disorder. They fell upon their enemies like beasts on their prey. The defeated Adil Shahi army started fleeing from the battlefield and in an attempt to cross the Krishna, many were drowned. Thousands of the enemy soldiers were slain. While Adil Shah and several of his commanders escaped, Mirza Jehangir was killed and five commanders including the most distinguished of them all–Salabut Khan–were imprisoned. With the war on the banks of the Krishna being over, the Vijayanagara army rested at Adil Shah's tents. The spoils of the war included 400 heavy canons, smaller artilleries, 100 elephants, horses, oxen, and more including women prisoners. Krishnadeva Raya ordered the release of the women captives (Islamic invaders did exactly the opposite of the rules of Dharma followed by Hindu warriors at war. They not only raped women but also took them as sex slaves. This was the reason why when Hindu warriors attained martyrdom on the battlefield, their women performed *ffect*–immolating themselves to save their honor). About 16,000 soldiers including Sungut Ray, a commander, from the Vijayanagara army attained martyrdom. Commanding the dead to be cremated following rituals, Krishnadeva Raya with his soldiers marched towards Raichore fort. After 20 days of siege, the Vijayanagara army captured the fort with the commander slain and Adil Shahi army having surrendered. Krishnadeva Raya ordered his soldiers not to harm the civilians or loot their property. He further emphasized that they were all secure under the Vijayanagara Empire. Those who wanted to leave Raichore were allowed to go.

In another battle in 1521, Krishnadeva Raya razed the Gulbarga fortress to the ground. Gulbarga was the early capital of the Bahmani Sultanate. After Raya's siege of the fort in 1514, it was retaken by Adil Shah. Krishnadeva Raya sacked Sagar and killed the majority of the Muslim soldiers who offered resistance there. Another battle against the Adil Shahi army followed at Kembavi. Adil Shah's forces faced a crushing defeat. That was followed by another battle at Gobbur, where Krishnadeva Raya emerged victorious again.

Few reasons why Krishnadeva Raya won almost all the battles he led were the upgradation of his military infrastructure, the inclusion of the latest weapons, a well-maintained army, and recognition of soldiers for their gallantry. Krishnadeva Raya himself led several wars from the front. He would motivate his soldiers ready for battle. An excellent battle strategist, he often changed battle plans abruptly and turned a losing battle into victory.

In 1524, Krishnadeva Raya abdicated his throne, placing his six-year-old son Tirumala as the crown prince and king. He appointed himself as Tirumala's minister. In a few months, Tirumala fell ill and died, rumored to be poisoned to death. Krishnadeva Raya punished the offender and his family and continued with his emperorship.

Krishnadeva Raya valued work more than anything else. He was just, kind, chivalrous, and generous. He recognized every talent from every field in his kingdom and patronized art and culture. He was an efficient ruler and always looked after the welfare of his subjects. A Vaishnavite, Krishnadeva Raya worshipped all the deities in the Hindu pantheon and built several temples. He often went on pilgrimages, visiting temples across his kingdom. His Rajaguru was Vyasatirtha, also called Vyasaraja or Chandrikacharya, a saint from the Dvaita order of Vedanta from Sadh Vaishnava Sampradaya. A scholar, Krishnadeva Raya was proficient in several languages including Sanskrit, Tamil, and Telugu. He was the author of several books in Sanskrit–*Jambavati Kalyana, Rasamanjari, Satyavadu Parinaya,* and *Madalasa Charita*. He patronized Tamil literature. He composed *Amuktamalyada*, an epic poem in Telugu. He invited scholars and philosophers from other parts of the country to his court and was involved in discourses.

Krishnadeva Raya had a galaxy of eight Telugu poets in his court. The period of his reign is known as the golden age of Telugu literature. His courtiers also included scholars with knowledge of the ancient scriptures including Astronomy, Astrology, Theology, and Law. Foreign travelers in their travelogues praised the emperor and wrote about the prosperity of the people of Vijayanagara during his reign. Duarte Barbosa, a Portuguese writer, and an officer who was in India between 1500 and 1516 and visited the Vijayanagara Empire wrote thus about the kingdom: “Bijanagar is on a level ground surrounded by a very good wall on one side, a river on the other and a mountain on the third. It is very large and populous. There are many large and handsome palaces and wide streets and squares.” Domingos Paes, another Portuguese traveler who visited Vijayanagara in 1520 wrote: “These dominions are well cultivated and very fertile... The land has plenty of rice and Indian corn, grains, beans, and other kinds of crops which are now sown in our parts; also an infinity of cotton... There are temples in every street...”

In 1529, while preparing for an attack on Belgaum, Krishnadeva Raya fell seriously ill. He knew his end was near. But as his son then was only 18 months old, he nominated his brother Achyuta Deva Raya as his successor. He asked his brother to lead the Belgaum expedition. Soon after, Krishnadeva Raya breathed his last in 1529, aged 45 years.

25

Krishna Bahadur Mukhia

Netaji Subhas Bose's Bodyguard in Burma Jungles

The Azad Hind Fauz comprised of soldiers not only from across the country including the north-east but also of Indians settled abroad across other countries of Asia. After the failed 1942 Quit India Movement of Mohandas Karamchand Gandhi, it was Netaji Subhash Chandra Bose's Azad Hind Fauz that created panic in the minds of the British. Netaji Bose and his Azad Hind Fauz (INA) were the primary catalysts that inspired the military revolts that ultimately forced the British to quit. The truth about Netaji Bose and the sacrifices he made for India have been wiped out from history, so were the sacrifices of Azad Hind Fauz soldiers. An Azad Hind Fauz soldier from the north-east of the Sikkim-Darjeeling region was Captain Krishna Bahadur Mukhia. He was the personal bodyguard and driver of Netaji Bose at a time when war between the British and Azad Hind Fauz soldiers took place in the jungles of Burma around 1943-44. He fought in battles against the British in the frontline.

Krishna Bahadur Mukhia was born on 12th May 1921 at Bannockburn Tea Estate, a tea garden located in the west of Darjeeling Hills. Bannockburn Tea Estate happens to be one of the first tea gardens created by the British in the 1850s. This hill hamlet is a paradise on earth with spectacular views of snow-capped mountains of the Himalayas, waterfalls, and greenery spread across acres. Mukhia was an excellent boxer right from a young age. He worked as a mechanic. Awestruck by his boxing skills, the British recruited him to the Gorkha Regiment in 1941 from Ghoom Army depot in then Bengal. Krishna Bahadur Mukhia was then aged 20 years. Not much detailed information is available on Krishna Bahadur Mukhia, except his role in India's freedom struggle.

During World War II, the British, who were part of the Allied Nations, sent over 2.5 million Indian soldiers to fight against the Axis powers in Asia, Europe, and Africa. The soldiers served in divisions of infantry, armory, and the Air Force. The bulk of them, which also included Krishna Bahadur Mukhia, fought against the Japanese Army. Around 40,000 Indian soldiers were captured with the fall of Singapore in 1942. Krishna Bahadur Mukhia became a POW on 15th February 1942, in Malaya.

Meanwhile, on 1st September 1942, Rash Behari Bose formed the Indian National Army (INA) as the military wing of his organization called the Indian Independence League in Tokyo. Japan supported his initiative. The captured prisoners of war (POWs), i.e., the Indian soldiers were given a choice, either to join the INA and fight for the independence of India or stay imprisoned. About 30,000 of them joined the INA; the rest who refused were transported to New Guinea as POWs. Krishna Bahadur Mukhia too joined the INA. Rash Behari Bose ideated the concept of the INA in March end of 1942 in Tokyo. Anand Mohan Sahay and military officer Mohan Singh were the key people who helped Bose form it. Rash Behari's Japanese citizenship after marrying Toshiko Soma (daughter of a Japanese entrepreneur couple and social/ right-wing activists) eased his process of establishing a firm base in Japan with Japanese support. The key objective behind the establishment of the Indian Independence League and INA was to free India.

In June 1942, Rash Behari Bose declared that Netaji Subhash Chandra Bose should take the lead of INA as President. In 1940, at the age of 43, Netaji Bose had escaped from India to seek help from other countries and from Indians settled and working overseas for the country's freedom. Netaji accepted Rash Behari's offer and he further expanded the INA as Azad Hind Fauz and established the Azad Hind Govt on 21st October 1943 in Singapore. This Provisional Government of Free India, i.e., Azad Hind Govt., was recognized by 11 countries. Netaji's cause for the freedom of India was funded by Imperial Japan monetarily, militarily, and politically. Many Indians donated huge amounts of money for the formation of the Azad Hind Fauz and themselves became part of the army. Netaji delivered speeches in several parts of Asia where his tagline '*Tum mujhe khoon do, mei tumhe azadi dunga*' (you give me your blood and I will give you freedom) became popular drawing the participation of thousands of supporters. The total count of Azad Hind Fauz soldiers then numbered over 60,000.

After the alliance with Japan, the Azad Hind Fauz won several battles in Burma and the north-east. Captain Krishna Bahadur Mukhia worked as a spy as well as a soldier in combat. He gathered intelligence, scrutinized areas that he would visit, and fight in the frontline. One of the soldiers who also underwent training as a nurse for treating wounded soldiers of Azad Hind Fauz in the frontline was Lt. Rama Mehta. She worked for a brief period in Burma in the make-shift hospitals in the frontline. In this Burma expedition, Krishna Bahadur Mukhia served as one of the personal bodyguards and driver of Netaji Subash Chandra Bose. Netaji chose Mukhia as his driver because the latter was also a mechanic.

Captain Krishna Bahadur Mukhia, in the jungles of Burma, checking the jeep after repairing a glitch in the engine; Netaji Bose and few Azad Hind Fauz soldiers wait.

The Azad Hind Fauz hoisted the National Flag in the Andamans and Manipur. After Japan surrendered on 15th August 1945, Azad Hind Fauz's support of Japan ended. By then 26,000 Azad Hind Fauz soldiers died in action for the freedom of India. Japan saw no other option than to surrender, as the nuclear bombing of Nagasaki and Hiroshima by the US on 6th and 9th August had already paralyzed the island country, and not surrendering would have led to further bombings, which could have had a devastating effect. With Japan's withdrawal, its support to the Azad Hind Fauz ended. Many INA soldiers were taken as prisoners of war. And the INA operations stopped.

Krishna Bahadur Mukhia was wounded while fighting in the frontline in Burma. Lt. Rama Mehta, in an interview done by me, recollected how at times, the hospitals used to be filled up with many wounded soldiers and the nurses did not even have time for food. And due to unfavorable conditions, many of the wounded soldiers died of malaria. Also, the badly wounded soldiers attained martyrdom in the hospitals. Krishna Bahadur Mukhia recalled, as quoted from a 2012 *Hindustan Times* report by Amitava Banerjee: "We are the ones who turned days into nights and nights into days in the jungles of Burma, fighting alongside Netaji. We used to sleep the whole day in the jungles and attack the British at night. The British used to light up the jungle with flares and open fire with machine guns. We charged them with bayonets and *khukuris*. *Dilli Chalo* was the slogan that wrung fear into the hearts of the Goras."

Krishna Bahadur Mukhia was captured by the British on 31st January 1944. He was imprisoned in Burma for six months and then transported to a prison in Bangladesh. He was released in 1946. The same year, he returned to his hometown Darjeeling.

Why did the British leave India? Was it because of Mohandas Karamchand Gandhi's *ahimsa* as projected in history textbooks or

Netaji's Azad Hind Fauz? If Gandhi was a true follower of *ahimsa* why did he ask Indians to join the World War on behalf of the British? Out of the 2.5 million Indian soldiers sent to war, over 87,000 died, 34,354 were wounded, and 67,340 became POWs! To quote from Dr. Kalyan De's *NETAJI: India's Independence and British Archives*, a book based on authentic documents from the British archives, declassified in 1971: "These documents are in the form of carefully selected letters, reports and minutes exchanged between the main protagonists of the British Raj in India–the Viceroy Field Marshal Viscount Wavell, the Commander-in-Chief of the British Indian Army General Sir Claude Achinlek and other functionaries, such as the Governors of various states and the Intelligence Department on the one hand and Secretary of State for India, Lord Pethick Lawrence and other functionaries of the British administration in London on the other, leading to their ultimate decision to leave India as early as possible. These documents are especially important as the proof of the INA's impact comes from top British authorities, who were directly concerned with the decision. They also describe in detail the irony of British unpreparedness and inability to deal with the situation arising out of their decision to try the three senior most commanders of the INA–Shah Nawaz, Gurbaksh Singh Dhillon, and Prem Sehgal on charges of war crimes and betrayal of the oath of allegiance to the British Crown. These documents thus provide a ring side view of the decision making process for their early exit from India to avoid having to face 1857 like situations jeopardizing the lives of 43,000 European people on the sub-continent at the time."

Thousands of Azad Hind Fauz soldiers lived in oblivion in penury after Independence. Only a few were recognized during their middle/old age and few received freedom fighters' pensions. The son of an INA veteran recalls: "My father joined Netaji Bose's INA from Singapore. He donated a huge amount for forming of INA. Due to this, after freedom, our family was under severe poverty, and my father could not send me to school. I was brought up illiterate. I have seen some of my father's friends who were INA soldiers. They all perished in poverty and their families have vanished."

After independence, Krishna Bahadur Mukhia got a job in the district school board in Darjeeling. He followed Netaji's ideals throughout his life. He was invited to various platforms to deliver speeches on the freedom struggle movement, his experience in the Azad Hind Fauz, and on Netaji. He used to say thus in these functions, as quoted from the aforementioned 2012 *Hindustan Times* report by Amitava Banerjee: "Materialistic happiness is important but it is not everything. Values are more long lasting and give greater happiness. Walk on the path that Netaji showed and nothing can go wrong."

Krishna Bahadur Mukhia retired in 1986. He breathed his last on 13th September 2012.

26

Sangolli Rayanna

Mobilized Masses and Attacked British from 1824-1830

He was the commander of the army of Rani Chennamma of Kittur, Karnataka. Rani Chennamma considered him her deputy. With his guerrilla force, comprising mainly of villagers who he trained, he attacked the British several times. He was one of the earliest freedom fighters of India, who created terror in the minds of the British. When the rebellion of 1824 started in the northern part of the country, he gave shape to it in the south. He intercepted British troops and was involved in combat with them. The British could never defeat him. He burnt British Government offices and plundered their treasuries. Using treachery, the British caught him and hanged him to death. He was then 34 years old. He was Sangolli Rayanna!

Sangolli Rayanna was born as Rayanna Bharamappa Rogannavar on 15th August 1796 at Sangolli village in Bailahongal taluka of Belagavi, Karnataka. He belonged to the *Kuruba* (shepherd) community from a family of warriors who were loyal to the Kittur rulers. His father was Dodda Baramappa Balappa Rogannavar. He got the name of his village Sangolli prefixed to his name. His height was around seven feet and he had a well-built physique like that of a bodybuilder.

Two wooden weights used by Rayanna for bodybuilding adorn the two sides of his statue at Nandagad, the place where he was hanged by the British. Being from a family of warriors, Sangolli Rayanna became an expert in warfare from a very young age. He also became proficient in guerilla tactics. By dint of his skills and expertise, Sangolli Rayanna became the *Shesanadi*, the chief of the army, of Kittur under Rani Chennamma. He was then aged around 26 years.

From a very young age, Sangolli Rayanna had been witness to the cruel policies of the British. He nurtured the dream of driving away the British from his motherland, hence he trained the masses including villagers in the art of warfare.

Long before the Doctrine of Lapse came into full effect under Lord Dalhousie, the British East India Company imposed a rule wherein if a ruler had no son, he couldn't declare an adopted child as his heir. After the ruler's death, the rights to the throne including treasury, administration, and everything pertaining to the kingdom would fall into the hands of the British. Raja Mallasarja of the Desai family was the Raja of Kittur, a princely state in Karnataka. Rani Chennamma, who was trained in battlefield skills right from childhood, was his second queen. They had a son, who died at a very young age. Shivalingarudra was Mallasarja's son by the elder queen. Raja Mallasarja died in 1824 and was succeeded by Shivalingarudra. The same year Shivalingarudra died without an heir. Before his death, he adopted Shivalingappa, a minor and a relative. Anticipating interference from the British on the adoption and also foreseeing his end, Shivalingarudra had already sent a letter dated 10th July 1824 to John Thackeray, Collector and Political Agent of the British East India Company at Dharwar (now Dharwad) about the same. It was a predated letter and the king was already postponing the adoption process then. Thackeray received the letter on the 12th September. Shivalingarudra died on 11th

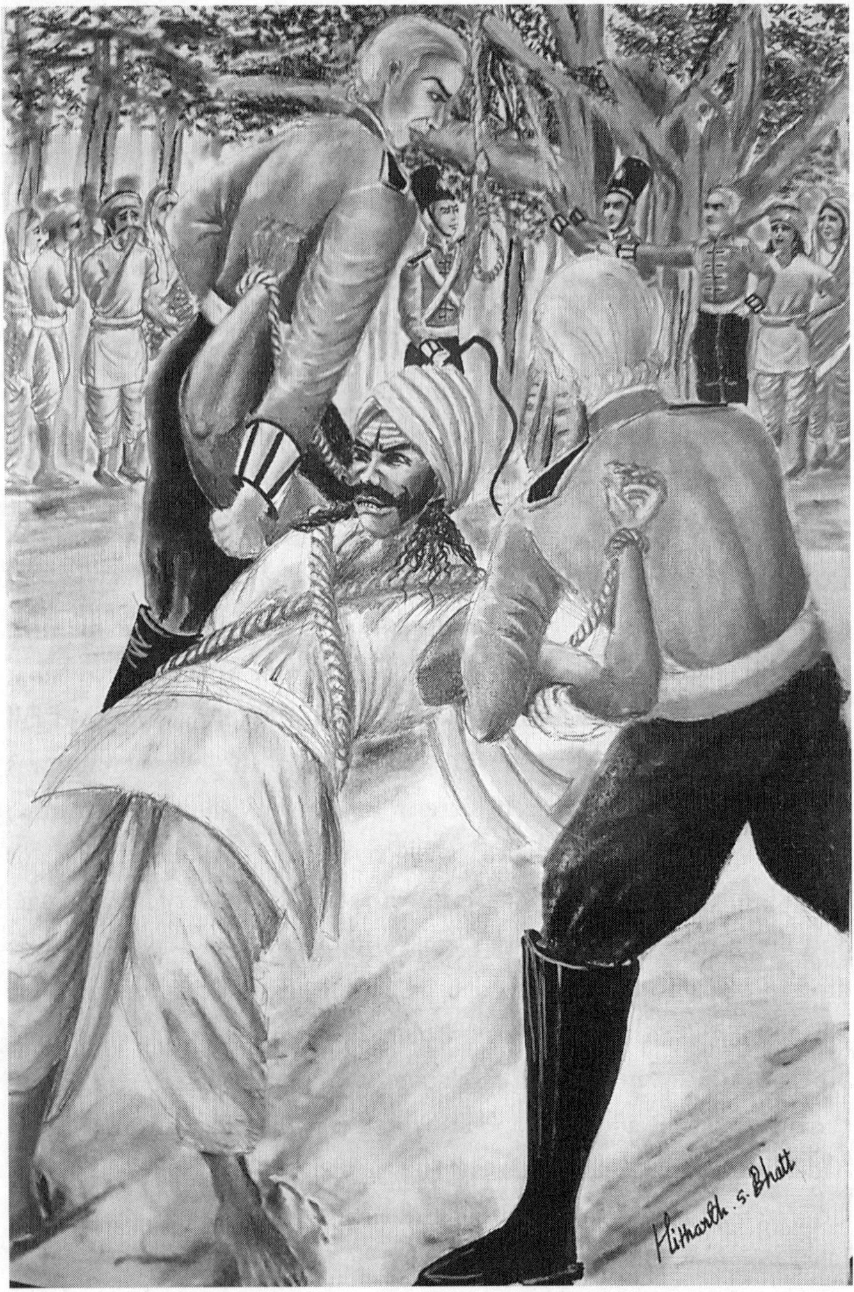

British police dragging Sangolli Rayanna towards the banyan tree on the outskirts of Nandagad village.

September. Rani Chennamma became the Queen Regent of Kittur. Sangolli Rayanna and Gurusiddappa were the queen's close aides.

Thackeray had his eyes on the treasury of Kittur and he wanted the princely state to be annexed to the British dominion fast. Venkat Rao and Mallappa, two officers from the Kittur court, became traitors. They collaborated with Thackeray, providing him information about the internal affairs of the kingdom. Venkat Rao and Mallappa wanted a share from the treasury to which Thackeray agreed. Thackeray along with Chaplain, the British Commissioner of Deccan, reported to the higher authorities of the British East India Company, stating the adopted boy Shivalingappa was not related to the deceased king of Kittur. Besides, they forged the letter written by Shivalingarudra, proving the king died without an heir and that the minor was not adopted by him. The British then declared Shivalingappa's adoption invalid and ordered the annexation of Kittur.

Meanwhile, Rani Chennamma took the administration of her kingdom into her hands. She took into confidence several nobles anticipating intervention from the British. Thackeray, on the other hand, started preparing accounts of the treasure. He introduced certain administrative measures, thus interfering in the affairs of the kingdom of Kittur. Thackeray tried to confiscate the treasure and jewels of Kittur, valued at around 1.5 million rupees but in vain due to resistance by Rani Chennamma. To avoid war, as a first option, the Rani sent letters to Chaplain and also to Mountstuart Elphinstone, the Governor of Bombay (now Mumbai) about Shivalingappa's right to the throne. Elphinstone turned down the petition. Rani Chennamma consulted with Sangolli Rayanna and the other officers. And the queen declared war against the British.

In October 1824, the first battle between the Kittur army and the British took place. The Kittur army of 12,000 men was commanded by Rani Chennamma, Sangolli Rayanna, Amatur Balappa, Gurusiddappa, amongst other warriors. The British force of 20,797 men and 437 guns was commanded by Thackeray including Walter Elliot, Stevenson, and other officers. A fierce battle ensued. The British forces faced a crushing defeat. John Thackeray was killed by Amatur Balappa and the two officers, Walter Elliot and Stevenson, were taken prisoners.

Chennamma sent word to Chaplain that she would release the two prisoners on the condition that the British should no longer interfere in the affairs of her kingdom. Chaplain agreed and Chennamma released the prisoners. But the British did not keep up their words; treachery and deception had been on their agenda ever since they started colonization in India. The British under Chaplain started preparations for war again. The battle between the two forces took place in December 1824. That time the British, who were superior in numbers and artillery, won. Rani Chennamma and other Kittur nobles including Sangolli Rayanna were taken prisoners. The queen was imprisoned at Bailhongal Fort. Sangolli Rayanna was later released.

Soon after his release, Sangolli Rayanna pledged to free his motherland, put Shivalingappa on the throne, and free Rani Chennamma from prison. The British had annexed Kittur. Sangolli Rayanna remained in hiding and started mobilizing forces. Meanwhile, the rich landlords under the British in Kittur started exploiting the poor farmers. The British imposed heavy taxes, confiscated lands of many nobles and the common people. They also confiscated the land and properties of Sangolli Rayanna.

Sangolli Rayanna moved from village to village and secretly trained the youth in the art of guerilla warfare. With his small army, he started attacking British troops in transit. He was never defeated. He looted the treasury of the British and destroyed the colonial buildings, also destroying revenue records. He looted the wealth of the rich landlords, who were loyal to the British, and distributed it amongst the needy. He pounced on garrisons from behind with his band of brave fighters. The colonial powers feared every now and then of an attack by Rayanna. Such was the terror that the Shesanadi of Kittur created in the minds of the British! And all their efforts to subdue or capture Rayanna proved futile.

Rani Chennamma died in prison on 2nd February 1829 (a few records mention February 21). Sangolli Rayanna tried to install Shivalingappa as the king of Kittur but in vain. He mobilized the masses and was all ready for war when the British laid a trap for him. The British convinced and bribed Rayanna's uncle Lakshmana to their side. It has been rightly said that it was because of traitors that foreigners could rule Bharat for a long time. Lakshmana informed the British about Rayanna's whereabouts. While Rayanna was taking a bath in a stream, leaving his sword at the hands of Lakshmana, the British overpowered him and caught him. Rayanna kept pleading to his uncle for his sword but the latter gave it to the British. It was April 1930, Rayanna was imprisoned in Bailhongal prison, tried, and sentenced to death.

Rayanna was hanged from a banyan tree on the outskirts of Nandagad village on 26th January 1831. *Gee gee padas*, i.e. native folk songs, ballads, historical folklore of Karnataka, profusely glorify Rayanna. According to one of these ballads, Rayanna's last words before he was hanged was–"I may die now but I will soon take birth again and come back to fight for my kingdom and the people until it is free from the clutches of British."

That's how Dharmic warriors pledged to be born again only to free the motherland from foreign clutches! Vande Mataram!!!

27

Velu Nachiyar

1st Queen in the History of India to Win a Battle against the British

There are names, the very utterance of whom will ship us to warriors' paradise! We will experience goosebumps!!! Their lionhearted endeavors inspired many to fight for India's independence. Amongst the unsung heroines of the Indian Independence Movement is Rani Velu Nachiyar, the queen of Sivagangai, presently a district in Tamil Nadu. She was the first queen in the history of India to wage a successful war against the British!

Velu Nachiyar was the daughter, the only child of Raja Chellamuthu Sethupathy and Rani Sakandhimuthal of Ramnad kingdom, Tamil Nadu. She was born on 3rd January 1730. A scholar of numerous languages, she was proficient in French, English, and Urdu. Velu Nachiyar was trained in martial arts, use of war weapons, archery, and horse riding. She became an expert in the use of *silambam* (fighting using a stick) and *valari* (a boomerang-shaped weapon; it can be hurled in the air at breakneck speed during hunting and war).

The princess was married to Muthuvaduganathaperiya Udaiyathevar, the king of Sivagangai. The couple was blessed with a daughter. Muthuvaduganathaperiya Udaiyathevar was killed in a battle against the combined forces of the British and Nawab of Arcot at Kalaiyar Koil on 25th June 1772. The invading British army plundered Kalaiyar Koil and collected jewels worth 50,000 pagodas.

Rani Velu Nachiyar fled with her daughter Vellacchi to Virupachi, a neighboring kingdom ruled by Palayakkarar Kopaala Nayakkar. She was all determined to take vengeance against the British. On her way to Virupachi on horseback with her daughter and followed by British forces, she came across a cowherdess named Udayal in Ariyakuruchi Kollangudi forest. A thirsty Velu asked Udayal for some water. Udayal knew she was the queen. She offered her water and asked her why she was in a hurry in the forest. The queen told her that she was being chased by the British forces. She immediately left. British forces reached the spot. They asked Udayal if she had seen the queen. Udayal bravely replied that she had seen her but would not tell them in which direction she went. The British first chopped off her left hand as punishment and asked her to tell them which way the queen went. Udayal remained adamant. She would rather sacrifice her life than say anything about her queen! The British forces then chopped off her right hand and finally beheaded her.

Later, Velu Nacchiyar came to know about Udayal's sacrifice. She remained in hiding at Virupachi near Dindigul for eight years under Kopaala Nayakkar. Dindigul was located at a distance of around 100 kms from Sivagangai. During the eight long years in hiding, she managed to arrange a huge army. Her army also included a big contingent of women warriors under the banner of Udayal Padai in memory of Udayal. This wing was commandeered by Kuyili. Velu Nachiyar trained them to perfection. Kuyili was a beauty with brains and was one of the ablest of the queen's commanders.

Periya Marudhu and Chinna Marudhu, two Marudhu Pandiyar brothers, helped Velu Nachiyar in arranging and training the army.

Muthuvaduganathaperiya Udaiyathevar had appointed them in the Sivagangai state army after hearing about their deeds of bravery. The two brothers had killed tigers that created havoc entering the residential area of the kingdom.

In 1780, Velu Nachiyar formed an alliance with few neighboring kingdoms and was all geared up for a war against the British. She marched with her allies and army towards Sivagangai. On the way, they encountered enemy troops at intervals. Their army first encountered Mallari Ryan, the supporting Palgar of the Nawab of Arcot at Madurai Kochadai. Within an hour, the queen and her forces killed all of the Nawab's soldiers including Ryan. At Thirubuvanam, Mallari Ryan's brother put up a resistance against Nachiyar's army led by the Marudhu brothers. Mallari Ryan's brother was also easily defeated.

The rani and her army then encountered the combined forces of the Nawab of Arcot and the British under the command of Captain Martins at Manamadurai. A fierce battle ensued. The colonial alliance retreated when many of their soldiers were slain and when they saw that defeat was certain. After this, Velu Nachiyar reached Kalaiyar Koil, the place where her husband breathed his last, fighting on the battlefield. Here she encountered British captain Joseph Smith. He was one of the British soldiers who slaughtered her husband. The queen's army defeated the British forces led by Joseph Smith.

The British stationed at Sivagangai were alerted of the approaching army of Velu Nachiyar. Meanwhile, the queen and her army continued their march towards Sivagangai to recapture the fort and drive away the British from the city. The queen had stationed spies in Sivagangai so that she was alerted on possible strategies and tactics to be employed by the British. The spies rushed towards the queen and advised her not to march towards Sivagangai at that moment as British troops were all

Kuyili pouring ghee over herself at the Raja Rajeswari temple to lit herself and destroy British ammunition stored nearby.

ready with heavy guns and ammunition including cannon barrels at several places at distances of a kilometer each in and around Sivagangai.

The enemy British forces were superior in terms of guns and ammunition using which they could kill their opponents from a long distance. Rani Velu Nachiyar wished that the enemy's ammunition and guns were destroyed so that she could successfully lead the battle against them. The spies also informed that the British stored the guns and ammunition at a warehouse inside the Raja Rajeswari temple at Sivagangai palace.

During ancient and medieval times, and to this day, devotees on particular festive occasions walk several miles to visit their favorite places of worship. Kuyili, the commander of the Udayal Padai women's wing, saw a group of women walking towards the route to Sivagangai. She asked them where they were heading to. They replied that the next day was Vijayadashami. It was only on Vijayadashami day that the British allowed entry of women to the Raja Rajeswari temple at Sivagangai palace for worship.

Kuyili immediately devised a plan for the queen. She undertook complete responsibility by volunteering for the task. She chose Vijayadashami as the day for executing her plan. Kuyili divided the Udayal Padai wing into groups. They all disguised as worshippers and hid weapons tucked into their sarees. Velu Nachiyar, also disguised, mingled in the group. And the groups, one after another, headed towards the temple. Three rounds of worship were to be carried out at the temple, which the queen and the women army were well familiar with. They strategized to strike after the third round after the general devotees would leave.

As decided, after the third round of worship after maximum devotees left, Velu Nachiyar and her women army attacked the British. Captain Benjour and the entire British troop were taken unawares. In a short while, many British soldiers were slain. British sepoys rushed towards the warehouse in the temple to bring ammunition. Kuyili immediately rushed towards the deity where a large ghee oil lamp was burning. Two British sepoys shot at her. The wounded Kuyili moved forward. There was a pot of ghee oil nearby. Kuyili poured the ghee from the pot and emptied it over herself. Holding the ghee oil lamp, she rushed towards the warehouse. British sepoys rushing towards the warehouse suddenly stopped as they realized what was going to happen. In no time, the warehouse exploded. Kuyili had lit herself in the warehouse! She perished and turned into ashes in no time. But her sacrifice led to the destruction of guns and ammunition of the British forces.

A fierce face-to-face battle ensued between the British and Rani Velu Nachiyar. The British stood no chance before the queen's mighty warriors. They were defeated. Captain Benjour surrendered. He pleaded for his life at the same time promising that the British would never interfere in the affairs of the Sivagangai kingdom in the future. Velu Nachiyar spared the captain's life and let him free.

Queen Velu Nachiyar regained her kingdom. She ruled for 10 years and later vested the administrative powers of her kingdom to Periya Marudhu and Chinna Marudhu, who were experts in their respective roles. She built a temple in the name of Udayal at Ariyakuruchi. This temple is known as the Vettu Udayal Kali temple. Velu Nacchiyar died on 25the December 1796 after anointing her daughter Vellacchi as her successor.

28

How Khen Rulers of Assam Defeated Islamic Invaders in 13th-14th Century

Assam was known as Pragjyotishpura in ancient times, Kamarupa in the early and late medieval period, and Kamrud or Kamata or Kamtah in records of medieval Muslim historians. The antiquity of this region dates back thousands of years. Pragjyotishpura finds mention in the Ramayana, Mahabharata, *Harivamsa, Vishnupurana, Brahmandapurana*, and more ancient texts. Kamarupa, which finds mention in the *Kalika Purana* and other records, draws its name from Kamadeva and also from Goddess Kamakhya. According to legend, it was at a small hillock called Bhasmachal in the middle of the Brahmaputra River in Guwahati that Kamadeva interrupted Shiva's meditation many thousands of years ago. Shiva burnt Kamadeva to ashes with his anger. This hillock is also known as Peacock Island–the world's smallest inhabited river island. The *Kalika Purana* describes the location of *Kamakhya Pitha*, one of the 51 Shaktipithas dedicated to Goddess Kamakhya, at the heart of the kingdom. According to the *Vishnu Purana*, this region had a radius of one hundred Yojanas with Kamakhya Pitha at its center. One Yojana is equivalent to approximately

13 kms. The *Yogini Tantra* mentions the geographical length of ancient Assam at one hundred Yojanas and breadth at 'thrice ten Yojanas' with Kunjagiri on the north, Lakshya and Brahmaputra on the south, Dikrong and the Dikhow on the east, and Karatoya on the west. Kamarupa also finds mention in Samudragupta's inscriptions.

Besides the main dynasties that ruled Assam in ancient and medieval times, there were several feudatories and small independent neighboring kingdoms. At times, the feudatories ruled as independent rulers. Though the feudatory chiefs often involved in conflicts with the central ruler, during times of emergency, such as foreign invasion, they united against the common foe, providing military aid to the Maharaja. The first Islamic invasion of Assam took place in 1206 under Bakhtiyar Khilji, a Turkish general. The 13th century Persian historian, Minhaj-i-Siraj, in his book *Tabaqat-i-Nasiri,* documented Bakhtiyar Khilji's battlefield exploits, loot, and plunder in India. This book contains a detailed account of Khilji's attack on Kamarupa and his defeat. The Kanai Borasi rock inscription of Kamarupa describes the utter rout of the Muslim army in 1206 CE. Khilji had, by then, destroyed several universities including Nalanda, and conquered major parts of Bihar, Bengal, and Orissa. But he met with a crushing defeat at the hands of Prithu, also called Vishwa Sundaradeva, the then Raja of Assam from the Khen dynasty. Few historians also identify Prithu as Jalpesvar and as Niladhwaj. He is mentioned as Bartu by Minhaj-i-Siraj, going by differences in pronunciation. Thousands of Khilji's soldiers were slain by the Kamarupi forces. The defeat of the powerful Khilji corroborates Prithu's expertise in military tactics. In this battle, Prithu received military support from the feudatory chiefs and the rulers of the neighboring small independent kingdoms. Worth mentioning here were the Koch Rajbongshi, Bodo, and Keot tribes and later the Baro Bhuyans.

Tabaqat-i-Nasiri describes the prosperity and temple culture of Assam through the eyes of Bakhtiyar Khilji. Fleeing from the battlefield, Bakhtiyar Khilji and few hundreds of his soldiers reached the Barnadi River, but could not find the bridge, which they used for entering Kamarupa. It was destroyed by Prithu's forces so that the enemies could not cross the river. Khilji sought refuge at an ancient temple located near Barnadi till the time his soldiers built boats/ rafts for crossing the waters. *Moortis* (statues or idols) in most ancient temples across India were made of gold and silver. Not only Islamic invaders but also the British looted these Moortis. The Moortis of this temple in Assam were made of gold and silver. Minhaj-i-Siraj gives a detailed description of the temple. To quote from Raverty's translation of *Tabaqat-i-Nasiri*: "...an idol temple in the vicinity of that place [where they then were] of exceeding height, strength, and sublimity, and very handsome, and in it, numerous idols both of gold and silver were deposited, and one great idol so [large] that its weight was by conjecture upwards of two or 'three thousand mans' of beaten gold." Prithu and his forces soon reached the spot. Khilji and his men fled from there, trying to cross the river riding on their horses. Hundreds of soldiers perished in the waters and the hands of Prithu's forces. Only a heavily wounded Khilji and few men crossed the river and then out of Assam. Khilji could no longer commit any loot or plunder after this failed Assam expedition and died bedridden, a few months later.

Ghiyas-ud-din Iwaz Shah, also known as Ghiyath ad-Din Iwaz Khalji, was the Governor of Bengal from 1208 to 1210 CE and again from 1212 to 1227. He attempted the second invasion of Kamarupa in 1227 CE. During Bakhtiyar's conquest of parts of Bihar, Bengal, and Odisha, including the destruction of universities, Ghiyas-ud-din Iwaz Shah was his deputy commander. His successful exploits drew the attention of Bakhtiyar and the latter granted him the *jagir* of Kangori in Bengal. Ghiyas-ud-din hailed from Afghanistan and worked as a donkey's driver carrying loads to distant places until he came to India at the advice of Muslim saints. He came with Bakhtiyar Khilji to India in 1195 CE. After Khilji died in 1206, he became the Governor of Bengal two years later, i.e., in 1208.

During Ghiyas-ud-din's attack of Assam with an enormous army following the same route as Bakhtiyar, Raja Prithu was still the ruler of Kamarupa. After the first Islamic invasion of Assam, Prithu had fortified the boundaries of his kingdom, especially the cities of Rangpur and Jalpaiguri on the western frontier, located near the territory of Lakhnawati, then under the Bengal Sultanate. It was one of the reasons why later Muslim armies under the Bengal Sultanate and then the Mughals could not directly and easily enter the boundaries of Assam through the western frontier.

Ghiyas-ud-din and his army faced stiff resistance from Prithu in the west due to which they followed another route. He reached up to Nagaon. The Nowgong Gachtal inscription of Vishwa Sundaradeva mentions Ghiyas-ud-din's advance to that place. Ghiyas-ud-din's army destroyed temples that they came across. The inscription also records Prithu's order to Chandrakanta to repair the damage done by the Muslims to the temple of Shiva located in that area. Ghiyas-ud-din Iwaz Shah faced a crumbling defeat at the hands of Prithu. A great number of the Muslim soldiers were slain and captured. A defeated and wounded Ghiyas-ud-din retreated from the Hindu territory only to be attacked and killed by Nasiruddin Mahmud Shah, son of Iltutmish, the Sultan of Delhi.

The Baro Bhuyans, who extended their military support to Prithu, played an instrumental role in subjugating Ghiyas-ud-din. Who were the Baro Bhuyans? While the term Baro means '12', Bhuyan indicates *bhumi*, meaning land. Baro Bhuyans thus mean 12 warrior landlords in the context of Assam. In earlier times, kings of Assam often appointed 12 governors or chiefs or ministers of states for the administration and protection of the kingdom. According to accounts by Vaishnavite saint Sankardev of Assam, the Baro Bhuyans initially consisted of 14 leaders comprising each of seven Kayasthas and seven Brahmins in the 13th century. The Kayastha leaders were Chandibar, Sridhar, Hari, Srihari, Sripati, Chidananda and Sadananda. The Brahmin leaders were Krishna, Raghupati, Rambar, Lohar, Baran, Dharam, and Mathura. They assumed the title of Bhuyan and later they came to be known as the Baro Bhuyans, each Bhuyan assuming power as the chief of a principality. Their principalities were located towards the east of Kamarupa. Sankardev was a descendant of Chandibar Bhuyan. Bengal also had a legacy of Baro Bhuyans.

Attacks by Muslim invaders were constant. After Ghiyas-ud-din, Nasiruddin Mahmud Shah attacked Kamarupa in 1228 CE. Raja Prithu attained martyrdom on the battlefield. The Muslim army settled in Assam for some time until Raja Sandhya, the son of Prithu drove them out of his territory the same year.

Further attacks stopped until 1257 CE. Raja Sandhya was then the ruler of Kamarupa. Ikhtiyaruddin Yuzbak Tughrilkhan, also known as Malik Ikhtiyaruddin Yuzbak, attacked Kamarupa in 1257 CE. He was the Sultan of North Bengal with capital at Lakhnauti; prior to his rulership, he was the Governor of Bengal from 1251 CE to 1255 CE under the Delhi Sultanate. As Sultan, he assumed the title of Sultan Mughithuddin Abul Muzaffar Iuzbak, making coins in his own name. Before he attacked Kamarupa, he conquered Bihar and Awadh from the Delhi Sultanate. Ikhtiyaruddin had a robust army and owned war boats. With his strong forces and war boats, he initially emerged successful at the entry point in Kamarupa. He looted the wealth of a small area and the accumulated treasure he possessed 'cannot be contained within the area of record', which suggests that Kamarupa was very prosperous and rich in the 13th century. Raja Sandhya employed effective military strategies in the next battle. In the second battle, Ikhtiyaruddin faced a crushing defeat at the hands of Raja Sandhya. The Kamarupi forces, also supported by the Baro Bhuyans, fiercely fell upon the forces of the Bengal Sultanate killing them all. Ikhtiyaruddin was taken captive and executed at the orders of Raja Sandhya.

After this victory against Ikhtiyaruddin, Raja Sandhya shifted his capital from Kamarupa Nagar to Kamatapur in the west. He further fortified the boundaries of his kingdom, following his father Prithu's policies on military infrastructure. Thenceforth, the rulers were called Kamateshwar. At Kamarupa, the kings were called Kameshwar. Raja Sandhya also made preparations to invade the territories of the Bengal Sultanate to avenge their previous invasions of Kamarupa. But he could not give shape to his plan due to his death in 1260, three years after he defeated ikhtiyaruddin.

There was another Muhammadan invasion under Muhammad Shah in 1337 CE. Raja Durlabh Narayan, the descendant of Raja Prithu, was then the ruler of Kamarupa. The 100,000 well-equipped horsemen sent by Shah were so badly defeated that all of them perished.

Assam remained one of the regions in India where Islamic invaders attacked several times, right from the beginning of the 13th century till the time of Aurangzeb, i.e., 17th century but every time they were defeated. Whatever little success they could achieve was very short-lived due to which they could never establish their rule. One of the reasons why Assam could resist the attacks was because, in times of war, all the inhabitants of the kingdom irrespective of whether they wished or not had to go to battle. For example, in 1532, when Ahom commander Phrasengmung Borgohain attained *Veergati* on the battlefield against the Bengal Sultanate army, his wife Mula Gabharu marched immediately towards the battlefield riding on a horse with a flashing sword in hand like Goddess Chandi. The demotivated soldiers, seeing the woman who never participated in the battle fight like a seasoned soldier, fought with renewed energy. She killed dozens of Muslim soldiers, including two commanders before attaining martyrdom. The Ahom army won this battle. Historian Shihabuddin Talish, who accompanied Aurangzeb's forces to Assam, wrote about the Assamese warriors in his book *Fathiya-i-Ibriyya* thus: "No invader on former times was successful in his enterprise of Assam… Invaders who entered Assam could hardly go back alive… A small number of Assamese people could checkmate thousands in battle… The Assamese commanders prayed in a body to Kamakhya to 'eat up the foreigners and protect our own people'." According to the same historian, weapons used by the Assamese warriors were 'matchlocks, cannon, arrows with or without iron heads, short swords, spears, long bows, and crossbows'. Aurangzeb's forces were defeated by Ahom commander Lachit Barphukan in the Battle of Saraighat. As Guwahati was the entrance, the defeated enemies could never penetrate the interiors of Kamarupa and the neighboring kingdoms that now constitute the north-east.

29

Raja Ganesha

Re-established Hindu Supremacy in Bengal in the 15th Century

Think of the world's largest delta formation–the Ganga-Brahmaputra delta system and we will be transported to the terrain of Bengal. This region, once known as Gangaridai, had extensive trade networks and shipping links with ancient Greece, Arabia, and other international cities. Bengal has been a sea-faring region since antiquity and home to several major *janapadas* (kingdoms). Ancient kingdoms of Pundra, Magadha, Suhma, Anga, Vanga, Samatata, and Harikela wove sagas of glory here, so did the Mauryas and Guptas. Shashanka, a local Bengali ruler, united the kingdoms of Bengal for the first time after the Gupta rule only to collapse and get reunited again under Gopala. The region remained under the Pala Empire followed by Chandra, Sena, and Deva dynasties. Hindu Maharajas of Chandradwip and Cooch Behar established their supremacy for some time until the Bengal Sultanate took over.

Muslim rule in Bengal started in 1204 CE with Bakhtiyar Khilji plundering and capturing the region. The Khilji dynasty survived till 1227 until it fell under the Mamluk Sultanate with Nasiruddin Mahmud as the founder. This was followed by the Balban dynasty of

Muslims from 1281 to 1324. Ghiasuddin Tughlaq conquered Bengal in 1324. The region was then administered by the Governors of the Tughlaq Sultanate till 1339. From 1338 to 1332, independent Sultans ruled Bengal. That was followed by the establishment of supremacy by the Illyas Shahi dynasty founded by Shamsuddin Ilyas Shah in 1352. Raja Ganesha re-established Hindu supremacy in Bengal in 1414, seizing the throne from the Illyas Shahis.

Who was Raja Ganesha? How did he capture the throne of Bengal? How did he establish his superiority and Hindu dominion in a region dominated by the Muslims for over 200 years?

Raja Ganesha was a direct descendant of the Deva dynasty of Bengal, whose families had been landlords since the time of the Palas and the Senas, spanning 400 years. He was also known as Danujamardanadeva. 'He wielded effective control over the rich lands running along the Ganges between modern Rajshahi and Pabna.'

Muslim rulers sought the cooperation of elite Hindu landlords in administrative affairs. Ganesha was appointed by the Illyas Shahis in the Sultanate court as an officer of Pandua (now located in Malda).

Sufi saints of the Chisti and Firdausi orders, who championed a reformed and purified Islam, objected to the appointment of Hindus in administration. They insisted that the state's foreign and Islamic identity should not be diluted by admitting Hindu Bengalis to the ruling class. Maulana Mujaffar Shams Balkhi, a Sufi of the Firdausi order, complained in a letter highlighting the issue addressed to the then Sultan Ghiyasuddin Azam Shah, also called Ghiyath-al-Din. In this letter, the Sufi Maulana termed the Hindus as 'vanquished unbelievers', especially targeting Ganesha for exercising political authority over the Muslims in Bengal. Ideologically, the Bengal Sultans aligned with the Middle East, but they did bank upon the local elite Hindus for political gains.

After the death of Ghiyath-al-Din in 1410, tensions between the Muslims and the Bengali Hindus intensified. Ghiyath-al-Din was succeeded by Saifuddin Hamza Shah, who ruled for a few months and was succeeded by Shihab-al-Din, also known as Shihabuddin Bayazid Shah. During Shihab-al-Din's tenure, the situation only worsened. According to an account by 16th century Persian historian Muhammad Qasim Firishta, Ganesha 'attained to great power and predominance' and became the 'master of the treasury and the kingdom'. Firishta further wrote that after the death of the Sultan, Ganesha, 'raising aloft the banner of kingship, seized the throne and ruled for three years and several months'. It was 1414 and the Arab chroniclers mention him as Raja Kans.

The book *Riyaz-us-Salatin*, a chronicle written in the Persian language by Ghulam Husain Salim Zaidpuri in 1788 on the complete history of the Muslim rule in Bengal gives a slightly different account of how nobleman Ganesha of the Bengal Sultan rose to power as the king. According to this account, Ganesha killed Shihabuddin and seized the throne.

Though Firishta wrote about Ganesha as a just ruler, who did not harm the Muslims of his kingdom, *Riyaz-us-Salatin* portrays the opposite. According to this book, Raja Ganesha oppressed the Muslims of Bengal and slew a number of them. This led Chishti Shaikh Nur Qutb-ul-Alam to write a letter to Ibrahim Shah Sharqi, the Sultan of Jaunpur, appealing to him to invade Bengal and overthrow the Hindu king. A purport of this letter is found in Jaunpur.

With rising Muslim influence, Ganesha installed his 12-year-old son Jadu to the throne of Bengal and himself became his Regent. In his absence in the court, Jadu exerted influence supported by other Bengali Hindu nobles. Ganesha was alerted of the possible invasion of Bengal by Ibrahim Shah. He approached Sivasimha, the king of Mithila for help. The combined army of Sivasimha and Ganesha tried to check the advancing army of Ibrahim Shah but in vain. This alliance of the two Hindu kings is proven by an account by Mulla Taqyya, a courtier of Akbar and Jahangir.

When Ibrahim Shah's army was about to reach Bengal, Ganesha pretended to seek pardon from Chishti Shaikh Nur Qutb-ul-Alam. At this juncture, the Chishti grabbed the opportunity of converting the Raja's son Jadu to Islam. He converted him and renamed him Jalaluddin Muhammad Shah.

Contemporary Arakanese accounts have recorded a completely different angle to the battle story. According to this account, Raja Ganesha defeated Ibrahim in battle. The king had given refuge to an Arakan ruler in his kingdom after the latter's defeat by a Burman monarch. This Arakan ruler gave military advice to Raja Ganesha following which he defeated the Sultan of Jaunpur. Probably, during his absence from the court, Shaikh Nur Qutb-ul-Alam grabbed the opportunity of converting his minor son Jadu to Islam.

The Arakan version of Raja ganesha winning a battle against Ibrahim is justified. It was true that Ibrahim attacked Bengal following a request by Shaikh Nur Qutb-ul-Alam to overthrow the Hindu king. Had Ibrahim not been defeated, Alam would have sought his help to imprison or execute Raja Ganesha. But that didn't happen. Alam would not harm Ganesha's son or object to his claim to the Bengal Sultanate as he had been converted to Islam by him.

Raja Ganesha despised this act of the Chishti and no longer wished that his converted son continue the kingship. Hence, he declared himself as the king of Bengal. Going by the Arakanese account, the declaration seems null and void as he was already the king of Bengal. Unfortunately, few servants of his converted son assassinated the king soon after. Jalaluddin Muhammad Shah, also known as Jalal-al-Din, was then restored to the throne.

Raja Ganesha ruled for nearly four years and re-established Hindu supremacy in Bengal. Muslim scholars eulogize Shaikh Nur Qutb-ul-Alam for his act of inviting the Sultan of Jaunpur thus playing an instrumental role in rescuing Bengal from Kans. According to another account, Kans, i.e. Raja Ganesha executed Nur Qutb-ul-Alam's son Ulama Shaikh Anwar. The incident has been described as 'unjustly persecuted and executed by Raja Kans'. As per Muslim chronicles, 'Qutb-ul-Alam who thus can be said to have saved Islam at a critical moment in its history in Bengal; but for his intervention, it might have met with the same fate as Islam in the Iberian peninsula in Europe'. This statement well corroborates the influence of Raja Ganesha in Bengal during his rule and how the Muslims dreaded the Hindu king's supremacy.

Sultan Jalal-al-Din, the son of Raja Ganesha, who minted and distributed coins of lion motif as a vehicle of Goddess Chandi described himself of his paternity in Arabic letters as Bin Kans Rao, 'son of Raja Ganesh', thus proclaiming himself as a sovereign who was the son of a Hindu king.

Nalini Kanta Bhattasali in his book *Coins and Chronology of the Early Independent Sultans of Bengal* assumes that Danujamardanadeva was Raja Ganesha. According to his account, Danujamardanadeva minted silver coins in 1416–18 devoted to the feet of Goddess Chandi in Bengali script on the reverse. He also mentions that Ganesha's converted son reconverted to Hinduism under the title of Mahendradeva. He maintained this title till he converted to Islam again for the second time.

According to Historian Jadunath Sarkar, after the death of Raja Ganesha, the Hindu Bengali nobles of Bengal raised the king's second son to the throne under the title Mahendradeva. Jalal-al-Din soon ousted his younger brother to become the Sultan of Bengal. Raja Ganesha's descendants ruled Bengal till 1435.

30

Lalitaditya Muktapida

Defeated Arabs and Subjugated Turks in Eighth Century

Lalitaditya Muktapida! He was one of the bravest kings of India, who resisted attacks by Arabs. Junaid, the Arab governor of Sindh, attacked Kashmir following the orders of Caliph Hisham. Lalitaditya defeated Junaid and thus the Arab attempt of plundering Kashmir failed. He subjugated the Turks by attacking their territories. He also defeated the Tibetans, who were then very strong. He built the famous Martand Sun temple. This temple is the only surviving structure that speaks volumes about this great emperor from Kashmir.

Do you know Lalitaditya Muktapida had one of the biggest empires in world history? But it was short-lived. It was more of a military expedition. He was able to subjugate kings of regions ranging from Afghanistan and Punjab, major parts of Haryana and Uttar Pradesh to Bengal, Bihar, and Orissa in the east. In the south, he helped Rashtrakuta queen Ratta also known as Bhavagana, the mother of Dantidurga, with an army to maintain her supremacy from rivals. It was Ratta who sought Lalitaditya's help and thus started friendly relations between the two regions of the north and south. In the west,

Lalitaditya invaded Kathiawad. He also defeated Momin of Bukhara (Uzbekistan) and subdued the Turks and Tibetans. Lalitaditya's empire shrank after his death.

Lalitaditya Muktapida was the most powerful ruler of the Kartoka dynasty. According to the chronicled account of Kashmiri historian Kalhana's *Rajatarangini*, Lalitaditya's rule lasted for 36 years, seven months, and 11 days. *Rajatarangini,* which consists of 7,826 verses in eight parts (books) in Sanskrit, happens to be the only major source of chronicle of the rulers of Kashmir and its neighbors in the north-western parts of India preceding the 12th century. Later historians and ethnographers rely on this book for details of Kashmiri kings and their times. *Rajatarangini* contains a detailed account of Lalitaditya Muktapida. Durlabhvardhana, a contemporary of Raja Harsha of the Vardhana dynasty, founded the Kartoka dynasty in 625 CE. Lalitaditya Muktapida, contemporary of Yashovarman, was the fifth Kartoka king and the great-grandson of Durlabhvardhana.

Lalitaditya Muktapida was born as the youngest son to Raja Durlabhaka, who was also known as Pratapaditya and Rani Narendraprabha. Before he ascended the throne of Kashmir, his elder brothers Vajraditya, also known as Chandrapida, and Udayaditya, also known as Tarapida, were kings respectively. According to *Rajatarangini*, Lalitaditya ruled from 700 to 736 CE. Modern historians date his reign from 724 to 760 CE. The dating may differ by a few years but the events are true.

A German art historian Hermann Goetz from the 20th century has claimed that events described in *Rajatarangini* by Kalhana about Lalitaditya Muktapida are true. Contemporary historian André Wink supports Goetz's statement. Marc Aurel Stein, a Hungarian-born British archaeologist, from the later 19th and early 20th centuries, first translated the *Rajatarangini* into English.

Our focus in this chapter is not on Lalitaditya's military expeditions in other kingdoms of Bharat but his expeditions and victories against foreigners, especially Tibetans, Arab forces, and Turkish Muslims. Indian kings did involve in wars against one another for the expansion of empire and supremacy. But they followed rules of Dharma in warfare contrary to what Islamic invaders followed. Indian kings avoided fighting with an opponent already engaged in a fight with another. They avoided stabbing from behind or hitting below the navel. They took care of the injured at the end of the day. They considered women, prisoners of war, and farmers as sacred. They never pillaged the land or destroyed standing structures in enemy lands. They were merciful if enemies asked for pardon.

But Islamic invaders did the opposite of these very rules of Dharma followed by Hindu kings in warfare. They followed the tactics of treachery, deception, and cruelty. They plundered kingdoms, pillaged the land, killed the weak and innocent, raped women and took them as slaves, stabbed warriors from behind, destroyed standing structures and temples, and what not! Converting the defeated people to Islam was one of their key strategies. They did this wherever they set their foot in India.

Lalitaditya Muktapida had a strong army. It was because of his military strength that he was able to subjugate many kings from across the country and in foreign lands. He recruited his soldiers and generals from neighboring kingdoms as well as from foreign lands. Regarding this, P.N.K. Bamzai wrote in his book *Culture and Political History of Kashmir*, Volume 1: "It seems that his army was mainly recruited from the north and most of his generals, including his commander-in-chief, Cankunya, also came from the same region. It appears that due to the decline of the Tang rule, the Kashmir ruler attracted many an adventurer and Lalitaditya was not slow in taking advantage of their

Lalitaditya Muktapida heading for war after paying obeisance to Suryadev in the temple.

experience and martial abilities. For instance, it is clear that Cankunya must have acquired fame as a military commander even before he joined the services of Lalitaditya since he bore the Chinese title of Cankiun-General."

The Kashmir king drove the Tibetans from Baltistan. Ladakh and some western provinces, which were under the Tibetans then, were subjugated by him. Lalitaditya Muktapida sought the help of the Chinese to completely subjugate the Tibetans, who were then a threat to his rule. Chinese chronicles find mention of that meeting. P.N.K. Bamzai wrote: "It was due to his intention to completely subjugate the Tibetans that Lalitaditya sent his famous embassy to the Chinese court. The Chinese Annals mention that U-li-to, the ambassador of Mo-to-pi (Mu ktaph da) the king of Kashmir, came to the Chinese court to seek aid from the Emperor against the common enemy, the Tibetans. That Lalitaditya should have endeavoured to enlist the friendship of the powerful Chinese king Yuen Tsun is natural enough seeing that the Tibetan expansion threatened the Chinese kingdom too."

The Chinese emperor was then busy quelling a rebellion, hence the proposal wasn't accepted. Lalitaditya single-handedly subjugated the Tibetans. According to Kalhana, Kashmiris annually celebrated Lalitaditya's victories. As per Alberuni, one of the greatest scholars of the medieval Islamic period, Kashmiris observed the second of Chaitra (April 14 as per Hindu almanacs) as a day of Lalitaditya's victory over the Tibetans.

According to Goetz, Lalitaditya's contemporary kingdoms in the region had been weakened by foreign invasions and wars. Those regions were mostly parts of Afghanistan, Pakistan, Punjab, and beyond where Hindu rulers were being gradually subjugated by Islamic invaders. Lalitaditya Muktapida subjugated Dardistan and

Tukharistan. In the words of P.N.K. Bamzai: "We know that Arab invasion was threatening the Kabul valley already from the commencement of the eighth century and that simultaneously the Muhammadan power in Sind was making efforts to advance northwards! While the Shahi rule in Kabul and Gandhara was exposed to these attacks, Lalitaditya may well have found an opportunity to extend his authority in the direction of the Indus. He led a victorious army through the Dard Desha (Dardistan) to the Tukhara country (Tukharistan of the later historians). The whole region was then thoroughly imbued with the Kashmiri traditions and learning, thanks to the efforts of the numerous Kashmiri monks and the Kashmiri settlements in the various Central Asian cities. It cannot, therefore, be difficult to understand that the Kashmir armies under Lalitaditya gained an easy victory there."

Junaid, the Arab governor of Sindh, attacked Kashmir following the orders of Umayyad Caliph Hisham. After the death of Muhammad, four major caliphates were established. Umayyad was the second of the Caliphates; they hailed from Mecca. Hisham was the 10th Umayyad Caliph. The Arabs had established their rule over the Hindu regions of Sindh after Muhammad bin Qasim led an Umayyad force and defeated Raja Dahir in 711. Thereafter, Hindu chiefs rose in rebellion in Sindh. Hisham sent armies to end the Hindu rebellion, and he was successful. The Umayyads reasserted their rule over major portions in Sindh and lower Punjab, which were once ruled by Hindus. Muhammad bin Qasim was also on an expedition of attacking Kashmir. Lalitaditya's elder brother Chandrapida was then the ruler of Kashmir. Chandrapida sought military aid from the Chinese but did not receive any help. Fortunately, the Umayyad Caliph called back Qasim to Damascus. Hence, during Lalitaditya's reign, the Umayyad Caliph sent armies to attack Kashmir again.

Lalitaditya Muktapida defeated Junaid and thus the Arab attempt of plundering Kashmir failed. Junaid also attacked North India but failed in this expedition. Besides, Lalitaditya Muktapida defeated Momin of Bukhara (Uzbekistan), the heart of the Persian civilization, located on the Silk Route and expanded his territory near the banks of the Caspian Sea.

The Kashmir king was never satisfied with his conquests and victories. He wanted to subjugate more territories. It was during one of his new expeditions that he lost his life. According to Kalhana, it was a distant expedition on the north that brought his end. According to one version, Lalitaditya perished because of excessive snow in Afghanistan.

Lalitaditya Muktapida is counted among the greatest kings of Kashmir. He not only protected his subjects but also patronized art and crafts and different branches of learning. He looked after the welfare of his subjects. He was the first Kashmiri king to clear the bed of the Baramulla River of rocks and silt to control recurring floods. Swamps and other uncultivated lands were reclaimed for purposes of cultivation. He facilitated irrigation. Kashmir thus prospered under him though he went on regular military expeditions. According to Kalhana, Parihasapura city became Lalitaditya's residence for a brief period, while Srinagar continued to serve as the other capital.

There are three major ancient sun temples in India–Modhera Sun Temple built by Raja Bhima I of the Chalukya Dynasty in the 11th century, Konark Sun Temple built by Raja Narasimhadeva I of the Eastern Ganga Dynasty in the 13th century, and Martand Sun Temple built by Raja Lalitaditya Muktapida in the eighth century. The Martand Sun Temple, with a primary shrine in its center surrounded by 84 smaller shrines, is the oldest of the shrines dedicated to *Surya Dev*.

Lalitaditya Muktapida also built several other temples and learning centers in Kashmir. But those could not withstand the destruction by Islamic invaders and the ravages of time. Under the orders of Sikandar Butshikan, the Martand temple was destroyed completely. Such was the grandeur and strength of the temple that it took two years for Butshikan's men to destroy it! Sadly this 1300 plus-year-old temple is still in ruins today!

31

Uyyalawada Narasimha Reddy

Led 5000+ Farmers against British in 1846; Hanged

Uyyalawada Narasimha Reddy! He was one of the earliest freedom fighters who challenged British supremacy. He led a war and several skirmishes against the British. He led over 5,000 farmers against the ryotwari system in particular introduced by the East India Company and against heavy taxation policy in general. U. Narasimha Reddy was supported by Vadde Obanna, whom he appointed commander-in-chief. For his brave act. Reddy was hanged in public by the British.

Uyyalawada Narasimha Reddy was born to Seethamma and Mallareddy on 24th November 1806 at Rupanagudi village, Kurnool in the Rayalaseema region. He belonged to a Telugu family related to Nayakars. His father was a Polygar, a feudal chief. He hated the British since his childhood. Farmers in his region led a comfortable life and earned revenue from their crop yields. The British started looting them in the name of taxes that soon resulted in the latter's impoverishment. Besides, the British also appropriated land rights of many not only in that region but also across the country.

Rayalaseema region, the hub where Uyyalawada Narasimha Reddy gave shape to war and a number of skirmishes against the British, was then under Madras Presidency. It started in July 1846. What was the immediate cause of the revolt? By then, ryotwari, a land revenue system introduced by the British, had already taken a toll on the life and livelihood of farmers in not only Rayalaseema but also other parts of India. Ryotwari system was first administered in the Baramahal area (the present-day Dharamapuri District of Tamil Nadu which was then under the Mysore kingdom) of Mysore (now Mysuru) by British Captain Alexander Read. It was then introduced by Thomas Munro, the Governor of Madras Presidency, in 1820.

The British had introduced three key land revenue collection systems pertaining to farmers–Zaminidari, Ryotwari, and Mahalwari. The Ryotwari system, which also included features implemented by the Mughals, was applicable to farmers–the cultivators of agricultural land. The land revenue was imposed directly on the farmers, termed as ryots.

To quote R.C. Dutt from *The Economic History of India Under Early British Rule*. Vol. I: "The land-tax assessed on each holding is fixed at the discretion of revenue officers at each recurring settlement. The Madras Ryot has no fixity of rental, no security against enhancements, no adequate motive for improvements. The uncertainty of the land-tax hangs like the sword of Damocles on his head." After the East India Company was abolished and colonial rule in India taken over by the British crown, the farmers were made to pay half a share 'of the rent as Land Tax', which 'is a very high rate'. 'In practice, even this high limit is exceeded; and what is realised as Land Tax in Madras often sweeps away the whole of the economic rent.'

The ryot tax was levied based on the soil potential not on produce. As there was no fixed revenue, at times the farmers were forced to pay more than 50 percent of their gross revenue. Thomas Munro gradually reduced the revenue from the rate of taxation from one-half to one-third of the gross produce. But even the collection of one-third of revenue by the British affected the farmers. R.C. Dutt in *The Economic History of India Under Early British Rule*. Vol. I quotes and describes an account by Bishop Heber on the land revenue system implemented by the British. Heber toured the country and interviewed the people in different provinces which he compiled in the form of a journal book and private letters.

To quote R.C. Dutt on Heber's feedback: "What created the saddest impression on him was the poverty of the people, and the heavy Land Tax which was levied by the East India Company in their dominions."

Besides, the Ryotwari system implemented by the British directed at maximizing revenue not only affected farmers, leaving them impoverished, but also deprived landholders of their land rights and as revenue collectors. Many Polygars in the region were deprived of their authoritative positions and possessions and awarded paltry pensions. Polygars who revolted against the British were denied pension. The Polygar concept was introduced by Viswanatha Nayaka in the 16th century wherein he organized the quasi-feudal organization of Polygars into 72 palayams or provinces with each palayam ruled by a chieftain, also termed Palaiyakkarar or Polygar. The Polygars were entrusted with the role of administering their respective territories, collecting taxes, running the local judiciary, and maintaining an army for the Nayaka rulers. Each Polygar was also entrusted with controlling one of the 72 strongholds of the Madurai fortifications. Reddy was a Polygar of Uyyalawada in Koilkuntla taluk.

Narahari Venkatakrishnamaiah Chetty in *The Manual of Kurnool District in the Presidency of Madras* describes Uyyalawada Narasimha

Reddy thus as reported by The East India Company in their district manual of 1886: "Since 1839 nothing of political importance has occurred, unless we mention the disturbance in 1847 caused by Narasimha Reddy, a pensioned Poligar of Uyyalavada in Koilkuntla Taluk, then part of Cuddapah district. He was in receipt of a pension of Rs. 11 a month. As a grandson of Jayaram Reddy, the last powerful Zamindar of Nossam, he was sorely disappointed when the Government refused to pay him any portion of the lapsed pension of that family. Just before this time the question of resuming Kattubadi Inams has been brought under the consideration of the Government, which made the Kattubadis discontented. Narasimha Reddy collected these men and attacked the Koilkuntla treasury. He moved from place to place and sheltered himself in Thepi hill forts of the Erramalas and Nallamalas, and though pursued by troops from Cuddapah and Kurnool, he continued to commit his ravages in Koilkuntla and Cumbum. At Giddalur, he gave battle to Lieutenant Watson and killed the Tahsildar of Cumbum."

Uyyalawada Narasimha Reddy with Vadde Obanna and their group of farmers killed many Britishers. They attacked British posts and reclaimed part of the treasury (which the British looted from Indians). This was followed by a battle against the British near Kotakota and more regions over a period of few months.

Around 200 freedom fighters from Kurnool attained martyrdom in this battle. Uyyalawada Narasimha Reddy and his followers retreated to the Nallamala Hills where skirmishes against the British continued. More farmers rose in rebellion in adjoining areas. Facing defeats, the British sent added reinforcements. Around 50 more freedom fighters attained martyrdom fighting against the British in Nallamala Hills. There, Uyyalawada Narasimha Reddy and 90 more freedom fighters were caught.

Thereafter, many more freedom fighters involved in the rebellion were caught and another 112 convicted. Uyyalawada Narasimha Reddy was awarded a death sentence. He was hanged in public in front of a crowd of 2,000 people on 22nd February 1847 in Koilkuntla at the age of 41. To terrorize the people in the region so that they didn't rise in rebellion, the brutal British kept Uyyalawada's head on the Koilkuntla fort wall in public view for 30 long years until 1877. But did this barbaric act of the British dampen the spirit of the freedom fighters in the region? No! For the next many decades, thousands of freedom fighters rose in rebellion until 1947!

Uyyalawada Narasimha Reddy raised his voice against the British. In a short period of time, over 5,000 farmers joined him. They got trained in the art of warfare led by Uyyalawada Narasimha's right-hand man Vadde Obanna. And then the series of incidents against the British happened from July 1846 until February 1847.

This is how freedom fighters in each and every part of India challenged the British rule from the very beginning, which ultimately forced them to leave India. This is how many freedom fighters sacrificed their lives over a period of time for the freedom we enjoy today. Vande Mataram!

32

Bhama Shah

Funded Rana Pratap Restore Army, Regain Mewari Area from Mughals

The Battle of Haldighati of 1576 between Maharana Pratap of Mewar and Akbar's Mughal forces was a stalemate. Neither party won. One of the most memorable scenes (depicted in many old artworks and made immortal by bards and poets) from this battle that froze the blood in the veins of the onlookers was Maharana Pratap vertically cutting Mughal commander Behlol Khan into two pieces along with his helmet, armor and even his horse! Many historians have distorted this battle story to show Akbar's victory and this distorted version is portrayed in history textbooks. Rana Pratap involved in wars with Mughals later and regained most of the Mewari territory. This could happen because of Rana's firm determination to regain the territories of his kingdom and because of the wealth donated by Bhama Shah and his brother Tarachand.

Who was Bhama Shah? Not many of us, except from Rajasthan, know about this brave general, trader, minister, and adviser of the royal court of Mewar. Many are driven by the notion that Jains strictly follow the tenets of non-violence. But when it comes to Raj Dharma, of defending the motherland, they have been at the forefront. Bhama Shah was a Jain but he not only donated almost all his wealth but also led the Mewari army to battlefields and helped restore Mewari territory from the Mughals.

Bhama Shah's younger brother Tarachand was also a minister and warrior in the Mewari army and administration. He also led several Mewari battles to victory. He was generous and loyal like his brother. He too donated the maximum of his wealth to Maharana Pratap to maintain the Mewari army and regain lost territories. Even after donating their wealth, both Bhama Shah and Tarachand intruded into Mughal territories, defeated the Mughal armies, and brought wealth from those regions, which were then used for maintaining the Mewari army, especially after the battle of Haldighati when Maharana Pratap was exhausted of resources. Here is a proverb from the *Manusmriti*:

धर्म एव हतो हन्ति धर्मो रक्षति रक्षितः।
तस्माद्धर्मो न हन्तव्यो मा नो धर्मो हतोऽवधीत्।।

(Dharm Eva Hato Hanti, Dharmo Rakshati Rakshitah!
Tasma Dharmo Na Hantvyo, Ma No Dharmo Hato-Vadhit!!)

The meaning of the above *shloka* is:

Dharma destroys those who destroy it, Dharma protects those who protect it.

Dharma does not destroy and cannot be destroyed.

In short, the essence and meaning of this *shloka* are 'Dharma protects the protector', which holds true for Bhama Shah and Tarachand.

Bhama Shah was born in 1542 in an Oswal Jain family. He belonged to the *Kavadia* gotra. His father Bharmal Kavadia worked under Rana Sanga (grandfather of Maharana Pratap) as Qiledar of

Ranthambore Fort and then as Prime Minister under Maharana Udai Singh (father of Rana Pratap). Tarachand was Bhama Shah's only brother, younger to him by four years.

Bhama Shah and his brother Tarachand got trained in warfare as they grew up. The elder brother soon rose to the position of a general. Besides undertaking military responsibilities of the Mewari kingdom, Bhama Shah was in-charge of administrative responsibilities in the role of a minister in the court of Maharana Pratap. Additionally, he looked after the treasury. He was an adviser and close aide of the Maharana. Tarachand was also a commander of the Mewari army.

Akbar always looked for opportunities to use Indians against Indians in battles to create further divisions between them. While most kingdoms surrendered to his supremacy and became vassal rulers, Maharana Pratap neither recognized Mughal supremacy nor agreed to any meetings or alliances. To quote from *Saffron Swords* Vol. 1, Akbar "sent Man Singh as his emissary to Mewar. He wanted Rana Pratap to acknowledge him as the emperor and wanted Pratap to be his vassal, just like Man Singh. Maharana Pratap did not pay heed to any of the logic and schemes put forward by Man Singh. The mission failed; then something happened which brought war to the gates of Mewar even earlier than predicted.

"During his stay in Mewar, Man Singh was invited to a royal dinner. Maharana Pratap refused to join him on the pretext that kings dine only with kings and Man Singh was just a crown prince and that too, of a vassal state of the Mughals. Pratap sent his son Amar Singh for the dinner. Man Singh considered this to be an insult and left. He started advising Akbar to attack and depose Maharana and capture Mewar. Akbar was already looking for a moment like this. He quickly ordered an attack on Maharana Pratap. Akbar himself did not lead the army. He entrusted the task to Syed Hashim of Barrha along with his brothers and Man Singh."

In 1576, in the Mughal Army, Man Singh himself was a commander ranking 5,000 horses and other ancillaries. Syed Hashim was another commander matching him in stature. The Mughal army was also supplemented by the Kachchwaha forces. Rao Lunkaran of Sambhar brought his Rajputs to the Mughal fold too. Gazi Khan of central Asian provinces joined Akbar. And the kinsmen of the famous Salim Chishti of Fatehpur Sikri were also present there with their followers.

Mewari forces were heavily outnumbered compared to the Mughals. The Mewar army was commandeered by Maharana Pratap Singh along with lieutenant Ram Das Rathore, commanders Ram Shah Tanwar of Gwalior, his sons, Shaliwahan, Hakim Khan Sur, Bhama Shah and his brother Tarachand, Bhim Singh of Dodia, Rao Punja, the Bhil commander, and Jhala Maan, to name a few.

Rana Pratap organized his army with himself commanding the center. Bhama Shah and his brother Tarachand were on the right flank. In the battle that ensued, a river of blood flowed soon after. Ultimately, the battle turned out to be a stalemate with neither party winning. A wounded Chetak, Maharana Pratap's horse, took his master to the hills facilitated by Jhala Man Singh and succumbed to injuries. Gogunda, Kumbhalagarh, Udaipur, and more Mewari territories fell into the hands of Akbar.

Maharana Pratap with his army stayed hiding in the jungles. In a few months, the Mewari Raja used guerrilla warfare techniques and regained parts of the Mewari territory. But the Maharana was exhausted of resources, which proved a deterrent in maintaining, arranging, and expanding his army for further bigger battles. Meanwhile, during this time Bhama Shah and his brother Tarachand intruded into the Mughal territories of the Malwa region and looted the Mughal treasury.

Returning from the Malwa expedition, Bhama Shah not only donated his wealth to Maharana Pratap but also the amount looted from the Malwa expedition. So did Tarachand! According to the book *Maharana Pratap* by Bhawan Singh Rana, Bhama Shah and his brother presented to Maharana Pratap 20,000 gold coins and Rs. 2,500,000. Gopi Nath Sharma and M.N. Mathur in their book *Maharana Pratap and His Times* describe how the wealth donated by Bhama Shah and Tarachand was equivalent to the maintenance of 25,000 men for a period of 12 years!

Had Bhama Shah been selfish and greedy, he would not have donated his wealth. And Tarachand always followed his brother's footsteps in loyalty, generosity, and duties towards the motherland. Furthermore, Bhama Shah and Tarachand, if they wished, could have kept the looted Mughal wealth for themselves. Few historians have drawn critical conclusions that Bhama Shah did not donate his wealth but only the looted amount. And few more historians are of the opinion that he looted villages that were under the dominion of a Hindu king Rao Durga of Ram Pura of the Malwa region, which is again completely false and baseless. Bhama Shah and Tarachand looted only those regions of Malwa which were under the Mughal rule of Akbar. Another group of historians is of the opinion that as Bhama Shah looked after the Mewari assets, he only gave Maharana Pratap wealth from the Mewar royal treasury. But there are no evidences that Bhama Shah gave Maharana Pratap the royal treasury as the king was already depleted of resources.

Bhama Shah and Tarachand attacked more Mughal camps and brought in more looted wealth which they again donated to Maharana Pratap for maintaining and adding to the strength of the Mewari army so that all the Mewari territories from Mughals could be regained. An overwhelmed Maharana Pratap promoted Bhama Shah to the post of prime minister and appointed Tarachand as governor of the Godwad region. Tarachand was also bestowed the title of *Thakur*.

The wealth donated by Bhama Shah and Tarachand helped Maharana Pratap arrange a huge army. At the same time, he became free from financial stress. Maharana Pratap then launched an attack against Sultan Khan of the Mughals at Dewair near Kumbhalgarh on 16th September 1582. The Mewari Rajput army was divided into two groups, one led by the Maharana and the other by his eldest son Amar Singh. In the battle, Amar Singh killed Mughal commander Sultan Khan. About 36,000 Mughal soldiers surrendered to Maharana Pratap. Thirty-six garrisons and 84 more posts were captured by Maharana Pratap, with most of the Mewari territory thus regained.

Bhama Shah also served under Maharana Amar Singh as in-charge of Mewar's treasury. He breathed his last in 1600.

33

Rani Abbakka Chowta

Successfully Resisted Portuguese Attacks for 40+ Years

She is known as Abhaya Rani, meaning the fearless queen. She was an expert in sword fight, archery, and horse-riding. She was one of the first Indians to successfully resist colonial rule. She defended her kingdom from the Portuguese for over 40 years. She was the first Tuluva queen to fight the Portuguese, defeating them in battle not once but several times. She had a robust army and an equally formidable naval force. Her persistent courage and indomitable spirit inspired later freedom fighters to bravely resist colonial rule. She is Abbakka Chowta, also called Abbakka Mahadevi, the Rani of Ullal, from the Chowta dynasty.

Tirumalaraya Chowta I founded the Chowta dynasty in Tulu Nadu around the mid-12th century. The Chowtas were Digambara Jains from the Bunt community with a feudal and martial heritage. They followed the Aliyasantana custom of matrilineal inheritance for succession to the throne with preference to the sister's son's lineage. This practice was similar to Marumakkathayam, a traditional system that gave women liberty and the right to property. Brothers generally managed the matrilineal family land on behalf of the sister. The Tulu

Nadu kingdom of the Chowta dynasty initially comprised 200 villages with the capital at Ullal, an international port and trading center. Later, another capital at Puthige was added. Abbakka Chowta was crowned queen of Ullal by her uncle and predecessor of the Chowta dynasty–Tirumala Raya Chowta III. It was Tirumala, who further trained Abbakka in statecraft, military strategies, and warfare.

Abbakka is described as dark and beautiful in local historical folklores. Right from her childhood, encouraged by her father, she practiced sword fighting, horse-riding, archery, and the use of various weapons. She was also proficient in the use of *agnivaan* (fire-arrow) and happens to be the last woman warrior to use it in battle. It is said that no one in the Tulu Nadu kingdom could match her in military science and warfare. She wore simple clothes right from her childhood, which she continued even after she was crowned queen. She looked more like a simple common village woman rather than a queen. Soon after she ascended the throne of the Tulu Nadu kingdom, she ensured the well-being of her people. Riding on her horse, she regularly visited all parts of her kingdom to enquire about her subjects and to stay updated about administrative affairs.

Tirumala, being the male head of the family as per Aliyasantana custom, looked for a strategic marriage alliance–a suitable groom for Abbakka. He got her married to Lakshmappa Banga Arasa, the king of Banga, a principality near Mangalore. Banga Arasas were a royal clan, claiming descent from the ancient Alupas, who ruled coastal Karnataka. Pandyastha Banga was the first king of the Banga Arasa dynasty, his rulership in 1224 was conferred by Raja Vira Narasimha of the Hoysala Empire. Since then, rulers from this lineage continued to rule. Lakshmappa Banga Arasa was the 18th king of this dynasty.

The Portuguese were initially involved in commercial activities, exporting spices from the South Indian coastal regions. They started using military power to capture parts of the Indian territories. On 25th March 1505, Francisco de Almeida, appointed the first Viceroy of the Portuguese territory in India, came with a troop of 1,500 Portuguese soldiers. Soon the colonial power occupied three *talukas* of Goa–Bardesh, Matagram, and Tiswadi from the Sultan of Bijapur in 1510. They increased their military strength further. The Portuguese had their eyes on Ullal, as this region was a strategic trading point and an international port.

Meanwhile, Abbakka's marital relationship with her husband Lakshmappa Banga Arasa started turning sour. Differences cropped up between the two, which ultimately culminated in Abbakka's permanent return to Ullal with her three children. A patriot to the core, Abbakka did not like Lakshmappa's idea of maintaining friendly relations with the Portuguese. By that time, the Portuguese had started extracting taxes from a few kingdoms. Lakshmappa agreed to pay the subsidy demanded by the Portuguese to which Abbakka resisted but in vain. Abbakka returned the jewelry that she received from her husband and in-laws. Later, as a gesture of revenge, Lakshmappa collaborated with the Portuguese, providing them secret information pertaining to Ullal and the combined army planned to attack the port city of the queen.

Though a Digambara Jain, Rani Abbakka Chowta ensured that her court had ministers belonging to all other faiths. Her army consisted of people from all sects including Mogaveeras, a fisherfolk community. Her naval force also consisted of men from the Byari (also known as Beary) community. She forged friendly ties with neighboring kings including Raja Venkatappanayaka of Bidnur. She also trained her daughters in military warfare and they took part in later battles against the Portuguese. Abakka strengthened her military infrastructure and base. She never compromised on the welfare of her people. For dispensing justice, she worked till late at night. Under her patronage, nine lakes were constructed to meet the water needs of her people and to facilitate irrigation of fields of farmers. She always remained alert and stayed prepared against any attacks by the enemies. She built a dam in Malali in Bagalkot (now Bagalakote) area, herself personally supervising its construction. She also built several temples, including a majestic Shiva Temple and the Rudra Rock at Ullal.

Ullal, the Chowta capital, is located at a distance of 10 kms from Mangalore. Abbakka's Ullal Fort, located on the shores of the Arabian Sea near the ancient Someshwara temple on an elevated spot of the Western Ghats, was built of clay bricks. The Portuguese attacked Mangalore port and destroyed it in 1526. Rani Abbakka, noticing the enemies very near to her territory, anticipated war and started making preparations for it. The Portuguese, aware of her preparations, did not advance further. But later, they sent messengers to her court, asking for tributes against her sovereignty. But Abbakka turned down their proposals and demands.

The first Portuguese attack of Ullal took place in 1556 under Admiral Don Alvaro de Silveira. Rani Abbakka, leading from the front, defeated them and drove them out of her territories. The Portuguese attacked again in 1558 destroying to some extent the Ullal fort, temples, and the city. Rani Abbakka defeated them once again with military support from neighboring chiefs. The next attack took place 10 years later, i.e., in 1568, unexpectedly. That time, the Portuguese under the command of Joao Peixoto, came with a larger force. They captured the city of Ullal, including the queen's royal palace. Rani Abbakka, who remained in hiding to gather her forces, attacked the Portuguese with 200 brave loyal soldiers. In the battle that followed, Rani Abbakka defeated the Portuguese forces, besides killing General Joao Peixoto. About 70 enemy soldiers were taken prisoners. The surviving Portuguese soldiers fled from her kingdom. More battles followed in later years. In one of the battles, she along with her forces killed Admiral Mascarenhas. Rani Abbakka also drove the Portuguese away from Mangalore fort.

Rani Abbakka's brave exploits of victory against the Portuguese became the talk of neighboring kingdoms. They started drawing inspiration from her. Fearing revolt from the kingdoms from where they collected taxes and anticipating attacks by their enemies, the Portuguese passed edicts warning against any alliance with the queen. They also threatened to burn the principality of Banga, if Lakshmappa provided her any aid. But the warning measures in no way affected the queen.

Italian traveler and historian Pietro Della Valle heard a lot about Rani Abbakka Chowta. He was so fascinated by her bravery and warriorhood that he wanted to meet her but all his attempts of seeking permission for a meeting failed. He even roamed the *bazaars* and streets of Ullal to somehow catch a glimpse of the queen. His efforts ultimately met with success when he, by coincidence, saw her in a *bazaar*. Abakka Chowta, seeing a foreigner, enquired about his presence in her city. With the help of an interpreter, courtesies were exchanged and the queen invited her to her royal court. Abbakka was then around 40 years old. Pietro Della Valle described her as 'dark-complexioned and with an elegant figure', wearing a simple 'loincloth' like a common woman.

In 1581, the Portuguese under the command of D. Luís de Ataíde, the Portuguese Viceroy of Goa, attacked Ullal at pre-dawn. Their strength comprised well-armed 3,000 Portuguese soldiers supported by an armada of battleships. Lakshmappa also collaborated in this attack. Rani Abbakka, who was returning from a visit to her family temple, was taken by surprise, as she never thought of being attacked at pre-dawn. She instantaneously mounted her horse, raised her battle cry motivating her soldiers, and rode into the battle, leading her troops. A fierce battle followed. Using the *agnivaan*, Abakka and her soldiers set fire to many of the ships in the Portuguese armada. As Lakshmappa familiarized the Portuguese with her battle tactics and strategies, the Portuguese overpowered the old wounded queen. It is said, few of Abbakka's officers sided with the Portuguese, which led to her capture. Rani Abbakka Chowta was imprisoned and she breathed her last in captivity.

Had the Portuguese not laid a surprise attack at pre-dawn, had her estranged husband not disclosed to her enemies her battlefield strategies, had her officers not turned traitors, Rani Abbakka Chowta would have won that battle too. The treachery of the Portuguese and few of her own people led to her subjugation in the end. It is rightly said, traitors did more harm to the motherland than foreigners!

34

Shivappa Nayaka

Defeated the Portuguese and the Bijapur Sultanate

This king of the Keladi kingdom was the greatest and the ablest of the rulers of his dynasty. He conquered Dharwad from the Bijapur Sultanate. He defeated the Portuguese several times and captured their colonized territories. He built several forts and captured all the Portuguese forts in the coastal Kanara region. He expanded his kingdom through conquests. He regularly performed Vedic rituals and patronized Advaita philosophy. He built several temples. Art and literature saw a boom under his reign. He worked for the welfare of his people. He was Shivappa Nayaka, the eighth ruler of the Keladi Nayaka dynasty.

Most South Indian kingdoms were subdivided into *palayams* or regions with each region under the chieftainship of a Nayaka. The Nayakas were generally military governors. They were entrusted with the role of administering their respective territories, collecting taxes, running the local judiciary, and maintaining an army for the key king under whose aegis the principalities were run. The concept of a kingdom where a ruler shared sovereignty with his carefully selected set of subordinates was a paradigm associated with the Kakatiyas during the 12th to 14th centuries. During the reign of Kakatiya king Prataparudra, there were 75 Nayakas. Under the Vijayanagara Empire, the number of Nayakas was reduced and they ruled as vassal chiefs. After the gradual decline of the Vijayanagara Empire following the battle of Talikota in 1565, several independent Nayaka dynasties emerged.

The Nayakas of Keladi initially ruled as a vassal under the Vijayanagara Empire from 1499 with Chaudappa Nayaka as the first king. After asserting independence in 1565, the Keladi Nayaka territory included significant parts of the Malnad region of the Western Ghats, central plains along the Tungabhadra River, parts of northern Kerala, Malabar, and most of the coastal regions of Karnataka. Keladi, in the present-day Shimoga (now Shivamogga) district of Karnataka, was their main capital. Ikkeri and Bidanur were their other capitals. Keladi Nayakas were also known as Ikkeri Nayakas and Nayakas of Bednore. Shivappa Nayaka, also known as Sistina Nayaka, is considered the greatest of the Keladi Nayaka rulers.

Not much information is available about the childhood of Shivappa Nayaka. He was the uncle of Virabhadra Nayaka, the seventh ruler of the Keladi Nayaka dynasty. Virabhadra was a weak ruler. During his reign, the Bijapur Sultan plundered Ikkeri and various rival chieftains tried to annex part of the Keladi territory. Considering the situation, Shivappa Nayaka, a brave warrior, deposed his nephew and ascended the throne of Keladi in 1645.

Three years before Shivappa Nayaka became a king, Shriranga Raya III was the emperor of the Vijayanagara Empire. He was a great-grandson of Aliya Rama Raya, the founder of the Aravidu dynasty of this empire. Two years after his ascension, Shriranga Raya III defeated the Golconda Sultanate. Drawing inspiration from his victory, he increased the strength of his army and started collecting tributes from

Shivappa Nayaka worshipping Mahadev.

a few Nayakas. Several battles against the Bijapur and Golconda Sultanates followed until he lost most of his territory and was left only with Vellore Fort by 1652. The Golconda Sultan ultimately seized Vellore Fort and Shriranga Raya III was left without an empire and a home. Shivappa Nayaka gave him refuge. The last ruler of the Vijayanagara Empire from the Aravidu dynasty spent his last years with the support of Shivappa Nayaka and the later Keladi king until he breathed his last.

Within five years of his reign, i.e., by 1650, Shivappa Nayaka built several forts and renovated a few, thus strengthening his military base. A few of the forts he constructed were Chandragiri Fort, Bekal Fort which is the largest in Kerala, and Mangalore Fort, to name a few. He annexed Kasargod to the Keladi kingdom and installed a pillar of victory at Nileshvara.

The Portuguese were always 'on the go' of interfering in the affairs of the kingdoms in the south, setting up factories and forts, collecting taxes, and annexing territories through battles. They attacked the Keladi kingdom several times but Shivappa Nayaka successfully repulsed each attack. The Portuguese were utterly routed by 1653 and the Keladi king acquired the ports of Mangalore, Kundapura, and Honnavar from them.

In 1498, the Portuguese had captured the Kanara region and established their political power. This region comprised of present Uttara Kannada, Udupi, and Dakshina Kannada on the west coast of India by the Arabian Sea. Shivappa Nayaka defeated the Portuguese in the Kanara region and captured all their forts in this area. He thus emerged as a powerful ruler in no time.

During this time, the Dharwad region, a place of strategic importance, was under the Bijapur Sultanate. Dharwad was under the Chalukyas in the 12th century, which later fell into the hands of the

Bahmani Sultanate in the 14th century. The Vijayanagara kings further annexed it to the Vijayanagara Empire and they built a fort during the start of the 15th century. In 1573, Adil Shah, the Sultan of Bijapur captured the city and the fort and annexed it to the Bijapur Sultanate territory. Shivappa Nayaka was all geared up to reclaim what was once part of the Vijayanagara Empire. He defeated the Bijapur Sultanate army and annexed part of the Dharwad territory to the Keladi kingdom. Shivappa Nayaka was never defeated!

Shivappa Nayaka introduced several schemes for the welfare and prosperity of his subjects. One was a revenue scheme called the 'Sist' due to which he was also called Sistina Nayaka. The scheme was highly favorable to farmers. According to the scheme, depending on available irrigation facilities and type of soil, lands were divided into five types. The tax was levied according to the irrigation facility available including fertility of the soil and yields. As a result, no discrimination in terms of revenue existed between the farmers. More subjects joined farming as a result of the scheme and the Keladi region soon expanded its agrarian wealth. To ensure that businesses flourished in his kingdom, Shivappa Nayaka encouraged the business community besides helping the *Komatis* and *Konkanis* (communities that focused on trade and business activities) to settle down and set up their businesses in his jurisdiction.

Shivappa Nayaka was highly religious but he was equally tolerant to other religions. The Keladi Nayakas were Shaivite Hindus and Shivappa also patronized the Advaita Vedanta philosophy of Sringeri, the first mutt of which was established by Adi Shankaracharya many centuries ago. Advaita Vedanta, a school of Hindu philosophy, emphasizes seeking spiritual liberation through knowledge of the identity of the self as Atman, which is the same as Brahman, the highest metaphysical reality. Advaita Vedantins believe the soul is not ffectrent from Brahman. Shivappa Nayaka also performed Vedic rituals regularly. He built several temples.

Shivappa Nayaka ruled until 1660. He was succeeded by his younger brother Chikka Venkatappa Nayaka.

Naman (bow) to Shivappa Nayaka! Vande Mataram!!!

35

Vigraharaja IV

Defeated Ghaznavid Rulers Bahram Shah, Khusrau Malik in 12th Century

The initial Muslim conquest of the northern parts of the country and surrounding regions, from the eighth century to the 12th century, saw little success. Whatever success the invaders could achieve was temporary and they could not establish their rule. This was because of the continuous resistance offered by the Indian kings, one after another, decade after decade, and century after century. Here is one ruler of north-western India who successfully resisted the attacks of Turkish Muslim invaders. He defeated Ghaznavid rulers Bahram Shah and Khusrau Malik. The Delhi-Shivalik pillar inscription describes him as the destroyer of *mlechchhas* (foreigners). He is also described as the 'the conqueror of Muslims' in the *Prabandha Kosha*, a collection of legendary biographical narratives in Sanskrit, compiled by Rajashekhara Suri, a Jain scholar in 1349 CE. He is Vigraharaja IV–one of the greatest kings of the Shakambhari Chahamana dynasty.

Vigraharaja IV was the son of Raja Arnoraja of the Shakambhari Chahamana dynasty. The dynasty, started in the 6th century CE, ruled the Sapadalaksha kingdom that comprised parts of Rajasthan and north-western India with Vasudeva as the earliest ruler. From the eighth to the 10th centuries, they served as vassal rulers under the Gurjar Pratihars and became sovereigns once again. Raja Arnoraja, who ruled from 1135 to 1150 CE, repulsed a Ghaznavid invasion from the west. Vigraharaja IV continued the legacy of valor of his ancestors in repulsing foreign attacks. He ascended the throne of the Sapadalaksha kingdom in 1150 CE after dethroning his brother Jagaddeva, who had killed their father Raja Arnoraja for the throne.

During the reign of Vigraharaja IV, the Sapadalaksha kingdom expanded further through conquests. His sovereignty was acknowledged in much of today's Haryana, Delhi, and Rajasthan. To quote from Cynthia Talbot's *The Last Hindu Emperor: Prithviraj Chauhan and the Indian Past, 1200–2000:* "In an inscription issued by Vigraharaja himself in 1164, which was originally situated in the Himalayan foothills about 150 miles north of Delhi, the king is said to have subjugated the entire tent, from the Vindhya mountains in the south to the Himalayas in the north." Vigraharaja IV was the uncle of Prithviraj Chauhan.

Bahram Shah, a Turkish Muslim and a Sultan of the Ghaznavid Empire, who ruled from 1117 to 1152, was a contemporary of Vigraharaja IV and his father Arnoraja. Shah's grandson Khusrau Malik was the last Sultan of the Ghaznavid Empire; he ruled from 1157 to 1160 and was a contemporary of Vigraharaja IV. Historian Peter Jackson, citing from several sources, wrote that Bahram Shah and his grandson Khusrau Malik led several expeditions to India. To quote from his book *The Delhi Sultanate: A Political and Military History*: "Bahram Shah is said to have conducted holy wars (*ghazuha*) in India, and his grandson Khusraw Malik appears to have fought against Hindu powers not long before the truncated Ghaznawid Sultanate was finally overwhelmed by the Ghurids."

Historian R.B. Singh, citing 13th century Persian historian Minhaj-i-Siraj, claims Bahram Shah conducted several expeditions to India but was defeated. There are literary evidences that Arnoraja defeated Bahram Shah. Besides, both inscriptions and literary evidences suggest Vigraharaja IV emerging victorious against *mlechchhas*, i.e., foreign invaders. The Delhi-Shivalik pillar inscription finds mention about his defeating the *mlechchhas.* Jain scholar Rajashekhara Suri authored the *Prabandha Kosha*, also known as *Chaturvinshati Prabandh*, a collection of 24 legendary biographical narratives, in Sanskrit. In this book, Rajashekhara hails Vigraharaja IV as 'the conqueror of Muslims'. Going by the records of R.B. Singh, Minhaj-i-Siraj, and Rajashekhara Suri, the defeat that the Ghaznavid rulers Bahram Shah and Khusraw Malik faced in India was in the hands of Vigraharaja IV and his father Arnoraja.

The Sanskrit play *Lalita Vigraharaja Nataka*, also called *Harakeli Nataka*, was written by Vigraharaja IV in the style of 6th-century poet Bharavi's epic poem *Kirātārjunīya.* It is also attributed to his court poet Somadeva. Part of this play is available in the inscribed form in the ruined Sanskrit college and Saraswati temple at Ajmer built by Vigraharaja IV. The temple and college were converted into the Adhai Din Ka Jhonpra mosque by Qutubuddin Aibak. Vigraharaja IV patronized art and literature during his reign and built temples and colleges. To quote from *The Last Hindu Emperor: Prithviraj Chauhan and the Indian Past, 1200–2000*: "In addition to his military successes, Vigraharaja is known for his patronage of the arts. He was most probably responsible for the construction of the building in Ajmer that was later transformed into the Adhai-din-ka-jhompra mosque, where the play about him titled *Lalita Vigraharaja* was inscribed." The Sanskrit college and Saraswati temple also have a *stuti* (prayer) inscribed in *kavya* form, invoking Hindu deities. Islamic invaders converted many temples into mosques and the temple built by Vigraharaja IV being turned into a mosque was no exception.

According to this play, Vigraharaja IV had a robust army that included one million men, 100,000 horses, and 1,000 elephants. *Lalita Vigraharaja Nataka* describes Vigraharaja's military preparations against a Turkish Muslim ruler described as Hammira. A Muslim general or chief was generally described as Hammira in early historical records and epigraphs. 'Hammira' denotes the pronunciation 'Emir' an Arabic term for a male king. Here, Hammira is identified with Khusrau by few historians. The play describes Hammira as a powerful adversary. Shridhara, Vigraharaja's minister, dissuades him from involving in the battle against the Turkish ruler. But the Shakambhari Chahamana king is all geared up for battle. He successfully repulses Hammira's invasion. This play also mentions Desaladevi, daughter of Raja Vasantapala of Indrapura, as Vigraharaja's beloved. Vigraharaja sends a messenger to her, informing her about the upcoming battle and that it would give him an opportunity to meet her.

Vigraharaja IV is described as 'a protector of the needy and the distressed' in the Bijolia rock inscription. He was not only a seasoned military warrior but also an able administrator committed to the welfare of his subjects. He was a devout Shaivite but several temples dedicated to various Hindu deities were built under his patronage. Most of these temples were destroyed by Islamic invaders. He also constructed the Bisaldeo temple dedicated to Shiva located beside the Bisalpur Dam on the Banas River in Tonk, Rajasthan. The temple is presently in good condition. Vigraharaja IV participated in Jain religious ceremonies and also had Jain scholars in his court. He patronized many scholars and is described by poet Jayanaka, in *Prithviraja Vijaya* as *kavi bandhava*, meaning 'the friend of the poets'. As a poet, he composed in Sanskrit and patronized this ancient language in his court. He built several lakes and cities.

Vigraharaja IV ruled till 1164 CE. He was succeeded by his son Amaragangeya.

36

Govindachandra

Defeated Ghaznavid Forces of Mas'ud III in Early 12th Century

Raja Govindachandra! This king from the Gahadavala dynasty repulsed several Turkish Muslim attacks. He is also known as the Raja of Kashi. He defeated the Ghaznavid forces several times when he was a prince and the last when he was a king. The Vishnu-Hari inscription found in the Babri mosque debris was actually the remnants of a temple he constructed at the birthplace of Shri Ram. Many more inscriptions attributed to Raja Govindachandra have been found in UP and also in Kannauj. He built many temples. He was renowned for generosity. Out of the numerous copper grants recovered, around 42 are ascribed to Raja Govindachandra for village, house, land, and estate grants/ donations. He expanded his kingdom through conquests and maintained diplomatic relations with several kingdoms.

Govindachandra was born to Rani Ralha Devi and Raja Madanapala, his predecessor. He was the third king of the Gahadavala dynasty. The dynasty was founded by Raja Chandradeva, who ruled from 1089 to 1103. Initially, Gahadavalas served as vassals under the Kalachuris of Tripuri. Chandradeva declared independence around 1089 CE. The Chandrawati inscriptions of 1093 CE and 1100 CE describe the occupation of Kannauj (then known as Kanyakubja) by the Gahadavalas. The region ruled by the dynasty was known as Antarvedi that comprised of present Uttar Pradesh and parts of Madhya Pradesh with boundaries stretching to Burhi-Ghandak River in the north-east, Etawah in the north-west, Munger further east, and Yamuna River in the south. Kashi (Varanasi) was their capital with Kannauj as another capital. According to a few historians, Gahadavalas belonged to a branch of the Rashtrakutas. Kannauj was also known as Gadhipur in ancient times. Roma Niyogi in *The History of the Gāhaḍavāla Dynasty* claims Gahadavala is derived from 'Gadhipur', which a ruler of this dynasty conquered. Copper grants of Govindachandra describe the Gahadavalas as *Paramamaheshvaram* meaning Shaivites. Govindachandra ascended the throne of Antarvedi in 1114 CE.

Copper plates and inscriptions reveal a lot of facts about rulers though not of any particular dynasty. These are inscribed in history. Around 70 copper grants and inscriptions mention the Gahadavalas as 'Suryavamshis'. These have been found majorly in UP and also in Kannauj. Out of these, three inscriptions issued by Govindachandra, when he was a prince, find mention of the Gahadavala dynasty. Besides, the inscription of Kumaradevi, wife of Govindachandra, also mentions the king as a Gahadavala. Govindachandra was married to Nayanakelidevi, Gosaladevi, and Vasantadevi. Out of the total 70 copper grants and inscriptions aforementioned, 42 copper plates and two inscriptions are from the timeline of Govindachandra's reign. Twenty-one of these copper grants were found near Kashi. The 17th grant, dating 1123 CE, describes this Gahadavala king's decoration as 'Ashvapati', 'Gajapati, 'Narapati', 'Rajatrayadhipati',

'Vividhavidyavicharavachaspati', and more titles. The 41st copper grant describes a charitable grant made by Gosaladevi, one of his queens. It also mentions all the honors of the kingdom enjoyed by her. The Kamauli grant of Govindachandra records a gift made by Rani Nayanakelidevi. Only a powerful and generous king could issue such a vast number of grants. The majority of these copper plates were records of village, house, land, and estate grants/ donations made by Govindachandra. This is the reason why Govindachandra is considered the greatest ruler of this dynasty.

Govindachandra's father Madanapala minted silver coins. But Govindachandra issued hundreds and thousands of gold coins, which corroborated the economic prosperity of his kingdom during his 41 years of reign. In 1887, during the construction of the Bengal-North-West Railway in Bahraich in Oudh, around 800 gold coins and a large number of copper coins, minted during Govindachandra's rule, were discovered. More gold, silver, and copper coins have been discovered in other parts of Uttar Pradesh and Bihar including Kannauj. All of these coins bear the name of Govindachandra in the obverse (commonly referred to as the head of a coin). The reverse (tail) of these coins depicts an image of Goddess Lakshmi.

Kumaradevi's inscription, undated, was found at Sarnath. She was a Buddhist. Another of Govindachandra's queen Vasantadevi was a Mahayana Buddhist. Kumaradevi was the daughter of Raja Devarakshita of the Chikkora dynasty of Pithi (Magadha), a vassal ruler under the Palas. Devarakshita and Govindachandra's father Madanapala were friends, the marriage was probably conducted to further strengthen their friendly relations. The inscription also mentions Kumaradevi's Rashtrakuta connection. Her mother Shankaradevi was a daughter of Raja Mathandeva, a Rashtrakuta king of Anga, also a vassal ruler under the Palas. The inscription further mentions Kumaradevi's construction of a temple dedicated to Dharmachakra Jina.

Before ascension to the throne, Govindachandra was crowned the Prince Regent for some time by his father. During this time, he looked after the administration and led several battles to victory including a few against Ghaznavid forces. To quote historian Roma Niyogi from her book *The History of the Gāhaḍavāla Dynasty*: "As a prince, this king had already fought some successful defensive battles during his father's reign, and the grants issued by him at that time clearly say that he was 'endowed with all the royal prerogatives'..." For a successful king concerned about the safety of the people, maintaining a robust army and a strong defense on the boundaries were important. As a king, Govindachandra guarded the frontiers as a mark of safety from invasions by foreigners and neighboring kingdoms. To further quote Niyogi: "It was quite in the fitness of things that Govindachandra would take all possible precautions to guard this frontier."

Govindachandra maintained a large army consisting of both cavalry and elephant corps. His eighth copper grant, dating 1117 CE, describes an army of his elephants. His titles of 'Ashvapati', 'Gajapati' described in his 17th grant, dating 1123 CE, suggest he had many horses and elephants for battles.

Mas'ud III was a Sultan of the Ghaznavid Empire in Afghanistan; he ruled from 1099 to 1114. According to an account described in the book *Diwan-i-Salman* by Muslim historian Jamal-ud-Din Muhammad Salman, as cited by Niyogi, Mas'ud III sent a huge force under commander Hajib Tughatigin to attack Hindustan in Vikram Samvat 1161-62, corresponding to 1104-05 CE. Mas'ud III's forces advanced as far as Kannauj. Niyogi further cites from Minhaj-i-Siraj's *Tabaqat-i-Nasiri* that mentions Hajib Tughatigin crossing the river Ganga in order to carry on a holy war in Hindustan. In the attack, Madanapala was taken prisoner, who was later released against a ransom. The Ghaznavid forces could only temporarily hold siege of Kannauj. Govindachandra attacked the Mohammedan forces in Kannauj with a

Raja Govindachandra inspecting his war elephants.

huge army in 1105 CE. He was then the Prince Regent (*Maharajaputra*) of the Gahadavala kingdom. He emerged victorious in the battle. After his triumph, he issued a copper grant from his 'victorious camp' at Visnupura by the Ganga, granting a village in the vicinity of Kannauj to commemorate his victory over the Muslim army. To quote Niyogi: "It thus appears that an army of the Ghazni Sultan Mas'ud III, led by Hajib Tughatigin, advanced as far as Kanyakubja by V.S. 1161-62, defeated and, if Salman is to be believed, captured the second Gahadavala king Madanapala who was compelled to ransom his person; the valiant Maharajaputra Govindacandra, however, was fighting the enemies as early as V.S. 1162 when from his 'victorious camp' at Visnupura he made the grant of a village in the vicinity of Kanyakubja."

A Muslim general or chief was generally described as Hammira in early historical records and epigraphs. 'Hammira' denotes the pronunciation 'Emir', an Arabic term for a male king. According to the Rahan inscription, dated 1109 CE, Govindachandra fought several battles against 'Hammira'. Here, Hammira refers to Hajib Tughatigin. The defeated Hammira thus signed a peace treaty with Govindachandra, who was still the Maharajaputra and had not yet ascended the throne. The inscription mentions thus: '*Hammlrarh nyasta-vairam muhur-asama-rana-krtdaya yo vidhatte*', meaning 'again and again by the play of his matchless fighting makes the Hammira lay aside his enmity'.

The Rahan inscription also describes an announcement made by Govindachandra of a land grant made by Ranaka Lavarapravaha, an elderly minister in the court of Madanapala. Before donating, Lavarapravaha worshipped Mahadev with five-fold offerings, suggestive of rituals followed by donors before giving gifts in the ancient and medieval era. Land grants or village grants were generally made on an auspicious occasion or after a victory in a battle against an enemy or for the maintenance of temples. The land grant, which Lavarapravaha did on behalf of Raja Madanapala, is suggestive of Govindachandra's victory against Hajib Tughatigin.

After Govindachandra became king, he encountered another battle against the Hammira in Varanasi. Govindachandra's court poet and minister Mahasandhivigrahika Lakshmidhara in his book *Krtyakalpataru* describes an attack of the Gahadavala by the Hammira. This book describes Hammira as heroic and a 'paragon of valor', which suggests him to be very powerful and leading an equally powerful force. According to the book, Govindachandra defeated the Muslim forces and killed the Hammira. The undated Kumaradevi's inscription of Sarnath that mentions the restoration of a Buddhist shrine also describes the protection of Varanasi by Govindachandra against the 'Turuska' forces. Turuska here means the 'Turkish' or 'Muslim' army. To quote from Niyogi on what is mentioned exactly in the inscription, translated thus: "Hari, who had been commissioned by Hara in order to protect Varanasi from the wicked Turuska warrior, as the only one able to protect the earth, was again born from him, his name being renowned as Govindacandra."

Few of the Muslims stayed back and settled in the Gahadavala kingdom. Govindachandra imposed heavy taxes on them so that they do not become economically prosperous. Termed *turushkadanda*, this was similar to the *jijya* tax imposed by the later Muslim rulers on Hindus. This taxation was imposed after Govindachandra as a prince defeated the Muslim army in Kannauj. Madanapala was the ruler. *Turushkadanda* taxation finds mention in the Basahi copper grant of 3rd March 1116 issued by Govindachandra. Pandit Bisheshwar Nath Reu in his book *History of the Rashtrakutas* writes: "We learn from the copper grant... of Govindachandra, found at Basahi, that it was Chandradeva of the Gahadavala branch of the Rashtrakuta family... It also refers that Govindachandra had granted in charity the village of Basahi together with the 'Turushkadanda', (cess levied upon the Mohmmedans), which shows that just as the Mohammedan kings levied 'Jaziya' upon the non-Mohammedans, in the like manner, Madanapala levied a tax upon the Muslims."

Govindachandra patronized art and literature including different branches of learning in his kingdom. He was himself a scholar and a poet. His title of 'Vividhavidyavicharavachaspati', mentioned in his 17th copper grant, suggests his scholarly attributes. He also facilitated scholarly exchanges between kingdoms. While *Rajatarangini* by Kalhana describes the friendly relations between Kashmir King Jayasimha and Govindachandra, *Shrikantha-Charita* authored by Jayasimha's courtier Mankha depicts the organizing of an assembly of scholars by Alamkara, another Kashmiri minister. *Shrikantha-Charita* describes Suhala's attendance in the assembly. Suhala was a scholar in the court of Raja Govindachandra. Like Chanakya, whose *Arthashastra* describes certain laws enacted for the welfare of the people, Govindachandra enacted laws, which was compiled in the form of a book titled *Vyavaharakalpataru* by Lakshmidhara.

Govindachandra built several temples during his reign. A temple he built at the Ram Janambhoomi site was later destroyed by Babur's Mughal forces. The Mughals erected the Babri Masjid over the temple remnants. The Vishnu-Hari inscription, found in the Babri mosque debris in the lower portion of a wall, was the remnant of this temple constructed by Govindachandra. The inscription available in 20 lines is composed in high-flown Sanskrit verse, in Nagari script, with a very small portion in prose, dating to the 12th century. During the 12th century, the present Uttar Pradesh region was ruled by the Gahadavala dynasty with Govindachandra ruling for 41 years. Gahadavalas ruled from 1089 to 1197. Hence, though there are several other claims pertaining to the attribution of the Vishnu-Hari inscription, the timeline, and the place suggests its probable credit to the Gahadavalas.

The Ram Janambhoomi site remained disputed for many decades. It was in 1853 that two groups of Hindus and Muslims clashed over this site of worship in Ayodhya. A series of lawsuits were filed, the first by Raghubar Das. After the independence of India, the first lawsuit was filed after 1949. Nirmohi Akhara, in the year 1959, claimed the disputed site by filing a lawsuit. In 1961, the Uttar Pradesh Waqf Board also filed a case in court seeking possession of Babri Masjid. It was on 30th September 2010 that the Allahabad Court distributed the disputed land into three parts, giving each to Ramlalla Virajman, Nirmohi Akhara sect, and the Sunni Central Wakf Board, UP. But on May 9th, 2011, this order was challenged before the Supreme Court and the verdict was stayed. After a 40-day hearing, on November 9th, 2019, the Constitution Bench of the Supreme Court of India awarded the entire disputed area in Ayodhya to the Hindus. The verdict included offering an alternative land of five acres in Ayodhya to the Sunni Central Waqf Board for the construction of a mosque.

Govindachandra ruled until 1155 CE. He was succeeded by his son Vijayachandra.

37

Kalyani Das and Nameless Women Freedom Fighters in Jail in the 1930s

Like thousands of unsung freedom fighters, her name is in oblivion in the pages of History. She is Kalyani Das Bhattacharjee. Almost all her family members actively participated in India's freedom struggle. They were jailed and tortured. Her younger sister Bina Das attempted to assassinate Stanley Jackson, the Governor of Bengal in the Convocation Hall of the University of Calcutta in 1932. She fired five shots but failed to assassinate the Governor. She was captured and sentenced to nine years of rigorous imprisonment. The news hit the headlines in India and Britain related to this incident. Both sisters were members of Chhatri Sangha (Girl Students' Association) and later of Jugantar Party.

Kalyani Das was born on 28th May 1907 to Beni Madhab Das and Sarala Devi at Krishnanagar in then Bengal Presidency. Beni Madhab Das was a scholar, teacher, and freedom fighter. During his stint as a teacher at Ravenshaw Collegiate School in Cuttack, Netaji Subhash Chandra Bose was his student. Beni Madhab Das motivated and mentored Bose and left an indelible mark in the latter's mind, creating a future leader in him. Sarala Devi was a social worker. Kalyani Das thus grew up in a patriotic atmosphere.

While in school, Kalyani Das served as the Secretary of Chhatri Sangha. It was Santi Ghosh, then aged 15, who co-founded Chhatri Sangha and was its secretary before Kalyani Das. Another Chhatri Sangha member Suniti Choudhury became an expert in the use of the dagger, sword, and *lathi*. She was recruited as the in-charge of training female members of the Chhatri Sangha on the use of weapons. She was also selected as the 'custodian of firearms'. Both Santi and Suniti jointly assassinated Charles Geoffrey Buckland Stevens, a British bureaucrat and the District Magistrate of Comilla on 14th December 1931. They were sentenced to life imprisonment.

Chhatri Sangha was closely associated with the Jugantar Party, a secret group that masterminded the assassination of many British officers. Both Chhatri Sangha and Jugantar Party believed in the use of arms to drive the British out of India. Many members of the Jugantar Party caught by the British were arrested, hanged, or deported for life to *Kala Pani*, the Cellular Jail in the Andaman Islands. Training in the use of arms including pistols and the *lathi* continued in both the groups. The arrest of members of the Chhatri Sangha, Jugantar Party, and other groups of Bengal was a regular affair.

Thanks to a first-hand account of the many unsung heroes and heroines by Kalyani Das Bhattacharjee in her book *Jeebon Adhyayan* in Bengali, which was translated to English by Dhira Dhar titled *A Study of Life* and published by her son Jayabrata Bhattacharjee. Most of the stories were related to her experiences in jail as well as about the life and role of many freedom fighters she came across during her imprisonment. Hundreds of freedom fighters from all age groups including teenagers and the old were sent to jail with or without trial. Many were tortured to death while many were hanged and hundreds deported to Kala Pani.

Dr. Kalidas Nag, who has written a preface to *Jeebon Adhyayan,* describes thus: "Kalyani Das (Bhattacharjee) is the elder sister of Bina Das. But that is not her only identity. The two daughters of Acharya Beni Madhab Das were in the forefront of the freedom movement when women first realized that they too must pay the price for freedom. Why should only men make sacrifices? Women too have the same right. Did they learn of this 'mantra' of equality from the teachings of Brahmananda Keshub Chandra Sen, who was going round the city chanting songs of divine glory? They were schoolgirls at the time of the 1921 movement. But as they entered college, they emerged as true partners of men in the fiery battle for freedom. Kalyani passed through so many trials and tribulations, along with her younger sister... In Kalyani's book, we find new matters for thought. The contribution of the very ordinary and uneducated women was not negligible at all. I was filled with wonder by the profiles of so many women …from different social strata, brought into sharp focus against the background of the jails."

In the words of Kalyani Das Bhattacharjee: "Deshabandhu Chittaranjan had described India, under British rule, as one vast prison, where everyone was a prisoner. Heartless rules and regulations are like iron walls that block off all the light and fresh air outside."

Kalyani Das and other freedom fighters in jail were subjected to extreme torture. But they could never complain as this would subject them to harsher punishments. Regarding this, she wrote: "As rebels against the Government, we had no inclination to complain about our suffering in prison." She also wrote: "The Presidency Jail was infested with mosquitoes and it was a hard task to sleep at night." On winters, she along with fellow inmates in jail shivered 'as the chill seeped from the damp floor through the thin blanket'. Kalyani Das was first imprisoned in Presidency Jail and after a few months shifted to Hijli Jail. Why? Because she influenced few freedom fighters to raise their heads in protest and taught other convicts to be politically conscious. The jail authorities thought it would be dangerous to keep her in the same jail.

In the words of Kalyani Das from her book: "The first thoughts to cross my mind as I entered the jail were 'humanity has never been so humiliated and outraged as it is in prison'. Here, every moment a person is being degraded and insulted. The worst criminal has to be treated with human dignity. Only then is there hope for redemption. In our country, jails are there for human torture, where thousands of prisoners are being sacrificed every day. No wonder, we hear of numerous prisoners killing themselves in order to escape from the inhuman treatment meted out to them in prisons. From the pages of *Nirbasiter Atmakatha* (The Memoirs of an Exile), we learn how so many prisoners in the Andaman Cellular Jail went so far as to commit suicide in prison, in order to escape from the horrors of their prison life ...Inside prison, we found abysmal darkness and penury all around. Not the slightest smile on anyone's face, as if spring had never touched their souls. Only deadly dreariness all around. Nature in all her glory of blossoming flowers and moonlit nights pass them by as prisoners continue to live under the burdensome shroud of misery. They know neither laughter nor tears. Nor do they have the power to raise their voice in a storm of protest to shake the walls of prison. The prisoners are deaf, dumb, and blind."

Hijli Jail had a track record of the British sepoys shooting political prisoners to death. In Kalyani Das' words: "This shooting of helpless political prisoners was unprecedented in political history. There was a storm of protest all over the country, against this inhuman action."

Before Kalyani Das was imprisoned, she had come to Hijli jail along with her eldest brother Bimal Das after one such incident of shooting by the British. In author Kalyani Das' words: "We were not allowed to see the wounded prisoners, but we tried to gather information about them the whole day. One prisoner had his arm amputated but still, there was a smile on his face. Many were wounded by a baton charge. After the shooting, when the prisoners fell on the ground other prisoners came forward to help them but they were also wounded with bayonets…"

Kalyani Das mentioned in her book about Santosh Mitra and Tarakeswar Sengupta, who attained martyrdom in prison as a result of the shooting. Their dead bodies were taken to the burning *ghat* at Keoratala on the banks of the Ganga in a torch-light procession at night. To quote her further: "The stillness of the night was broken as the pallbearers cried out 'we want the blood of tyrants!' And the darkness was shattered by the flames of the burning pyres…

"Later, in a large meeting at the Ochterlony Monument in Calcutta (now Kolkata), the great patriot Rabindranath had recited these immortal and sonorous lines:

Jahara tomar bishayiche bayu, nibhaeyche tobo aalo,
Tumi ki taader koriacho ffec, besecho tumi ki bhaalo?

"Have you forgiven those who are poisoning your air and putting out your lights? Have you loved them, too?"

Here are accounts of few unsung freedom fighters described by Kalyani Das Bhattacharjee in her book. Few of these warriors are unknown.

Bibha

In 1930, Bibha was only 15 or 16 years old when she was imprisoned for 10 months in Presidency Jail. Kalyani Das, the author, was already imprisoned there then. For Bibha, it was love for the motherland that was greater than the bond of love she shared with her parents and siblings. She left home and joined the secret revolutionary groups of

Bengal. She was only a teenager then! She, like many other girls, joined the Civil Disobedience Movement.

Bibha addressed a citizens' meeting at Hazra Park in Calcutta urging her audience to disobey and act against the Government. She was warned by the police. She addressed a gathering again, not paying any heed to the warning given by the British police. They arrested her and sent her to Presidency Jail.

It was only a few days of prison life for Kalyani Das when Bibha came to jail. She easily adjusted herself cheerfully to her new prison environment. In the words of Kalyani Das: "When, like us, she was made to wear a frock, she laughed and said, 'This is wonderful! I don't think I'll ever wear a sari again'!"

A few months later, Kalyani Das was shifted to another jail. She learned that the matron had punished Bibha by making her clean the wards. She had forced her into a solitary cell on false charges of attacking her.

Shobha Rani

Freedom fighter Shobha Rani was Kalyani's close friend. They together participated in several movements against the British. During one movement, the police arrested her and tortured her in custody. Signs of torture were visible all over her body. So brutal was the torture inflicted on her that she became bedridden soon after and became paralyzed for life. Kalyani Das often went to meet her. She saw the country attaining freedom.

After India gained independence, Shobha Rani witnessed that families of many freedom fighters and martyrs were starving and dying in poverty. The British had confiscated the properties of many freedom fighters and martyrs, forcing their families to live without food and shelter. The independent Government failed to do anything for those families. Moreover, the youth started forgetting the sacrifices of the martyrs. One day, holding Kalyani's hands when she went to meet her, she said (as written by the author Kalyani Das): "Kalyani, so many young people gave up their lives in the quest for freedom; today their families are starving and dying in utter poverty. Our country is not doing anything for them. The young people of today do not know anything about these martyrs. Let me get well, and then both of us will write the history of their lives."

Later Shobha Rani succumbed to those tortures by the British police. With her death, her dreams of penning down the history of the freedom fighters were gone! But Kalyani Das kept her friend's words. And she wrote *Jeebon Adhyayan*.

Two grandmothers in coarse frocks grinding lentils in a dark cell in jail.

Two Unknown Grandmothers

Two grandmothers were also arrested and imprisoned in Presidency Jail when Kalyani Das was brought to jail. Hundreds of freedom fighters were already jailed in the dark dungeons of this jail. Not only teenagers but also mothers and grandmothers had participated in the freedom movement and were arrested and jailed. In a day or two, the inmates were generally made to wear the jail uniform, which was made of coarse material and was uncomfortable to wear. These were short frocks.

Kalyani Das saw the matron of the jail forcing the two grandmothers to wear the coarse frocks. She and her companions interfered but in vain. They gave up persuading because if they refused to wear the frocks, they would be wrapped in jute cloth and thrown into a dark cell, away from other inmates.

The grandmothers could not but obey the orders of the matron. Soon after they changed their attire, they were taken to a room for grinding lentils. They were completely out of breath after a short while at the grinding wheel.

An Unknown 50-Year-Old Married Lady

A fifty-year-old married lady was also arrested along with Kalyani Das Bhattacharjee. All were brought to Presidency Jail. Kalyani addressed her as an aunt. The author Kalyani Das describes the horrors of how she had to remove all signs of her marriage.

To quote Kalyani: "She accepted the jail dress without any protest. She was married at 10, and all these years she proudly wore the gold-coated iron bangle along with the vermillion mark on her hair. She took off all her other ornaments but prayed for permission to keep the iron bangle on. The matron was most insistent to take it off her hand but even after a lot of struggle, it would not come off. She had put it on when she was only ten and it had never been taken off."

From the age of 10 since her marriage till the age of 50, the iron bangle adorned her wrist. To quote Kalyani Das further: "How could the matron slip it off her wrist when she was 50? When, finally, the matron got a pair of clippers and cut through the iron bangle, the lady broke down in tears, because she believed she wore the bangles for her husband's welfare. She had come to prison prepared to give up everything but she had not expected to be deprived of her iron bangle and vermilion mark…"

This account is only the tip of the iceberg, we know about the sacrifices of freedom fighters of all age groups. The freedom we enjoy today is a result of the sacrifices and martyrdom of thousands and lakhs of freedom fighters and Dharmic warriors. *Naman* to all the warriors! Jai Hind!!!

38

Avanijanashraya Pulakeshin

Defeated Arabs in Gujarat in 737 CE

Avanijanashraya Pulakeshin! Except in Gujarat and few parts of south India, the name of this brave son of Bharat Mata is in oblivion. He is one of the earliest feudatory chiefs from Gujarat, who bravely repulsed attacks by Arabs. He defeated the Arabs in a fierce battle in Navsari around 737 CE. This victory of Pulakeshin finds mention in the Navsari inscription. Had the inscription not been discovered, this victorious event would have remained hidden!

The Gujarat region's ancient settlements are corroborated by archaeological evidence confirming the existence of a prosperous city dating back to many thousands of years. This was Krishna's Dwarka. Besides, there are numerous archaeological substantiations of Stone Age settlements in this region. And who isn't familiar with the Indus Valley excavations in this area. Ancient ports here served as national and international trading centers. Nandas, Mauryas, Satavahanas, Guptas followed by Maitrakas, Gurjar Pratiharas, Rashtrakutas, Palas, and Solanki Chalukyas ruled the region.

The Chalukyas of parts of Gujarat and Maharashtra were vassals under the Chalukyas of Vatapi. They established their capital at

Navasarika (modern Navsari) during the seventh and eighth centuries. Prior to that, these kingdoms in southern Gujarat were subdued by a force sent by a Vatapi Chalukyan king. Numerous Chalukyan records and inscriptions find mention of the conquest. But those records find no mention of the defeated king. Durga Prasad Dikshit's *Political History of the Chālukyas of Badami* finds mention of the Chalukya conquests and inscriptions: "Vinayaditya also appears to have made an attempt to invade northern India. The inscriptions belonging to the reigns of Vijayaditya, Vikramaditya II, and Kirttivarman II refer to his victory over a ruler of all the regions of Uttarapatha, i.e., northern India... The earliest inscription which speaks of this conquest of Vinayaditya is the Kasar-Sirasi Plates dated in the Saka year 619 falling in the 1st regnal year of Vijayaditya, son of Vinayaditya... Several Chalukyan records confirm Vinayaditya's conquest of north India and the defeat of an unnamed paramount ruler." It was after the north Indian region relapsed into political instability immediately after Harsha's death that the early Chalukyas of Gujarat established their rule here. They were different from the later Solanki Chalukyas.

In the late mid-seventh century, Vikramaditya I, the Chalukya king of Vatapi appointed his brother Dharashraya Jayasimhavarman as the chief of the Gujarat region including Nashik and northern Konkan. The regions were located in the north-western part of the Vatapi kingdom. The Nashik inscription in Sanskrit of Dharashraya, dated 685 CE, records the grant of Dhondhaka village in Nashik to a Brahmin named Trivikrama. This suggests Dharashraya was appointed the governor several years before 685. The inscription also suggests the king's liberty to take independent decisions like making grants. As he was also a Vatapi Chalukyan prince, being the son of Raja Pulakeshin II, he exercised powers as that of an independent king of the regions entrusted to him. Dharashraya Jayasimhavarman had three sons–Shryashraya Shiladitya, Jayashraya Mangalarasa, and Avanijanashraya

Pulakeshin, the youngest. Shryashraya Shiladitya died when Dharashraya was still the ruler. He was succeeded by Jayashraya Mangalarasa, who was further succeeded by Avanijanashraya Pulakeshin. There is inscriptional evidence of all three rulers. But there are no records of what happened to the early Chalukyas after the three rulers.

Avanijanashraya Pulakeshin ascended the throne of Gujarat in 731 CE. Evidence about his reign is attested by the Navsari inscription in Sanskrit. This inscription was found by a resident of Satem village in Navsari and he gave it to the Epigraphical Society of India. The inscription is dated 490 of the Kalachuri era corresponding to 1st November 738 of the Gregorian calendar. Another estimated date is 21st October 739 CE.

Prior to and during the reign of Avanijanashraya Pulakeshin, the Umayyad Caliphate emerged powerful in the Arabian region. After the death of Muhammad, four major caliphates were established. Umayyad was the second of the caliphates. Their empire, after conquests, stretched from Spain in the west to Afghanistan and Pakistan in the east. To further expand their empire and to add to their wealth, they marched towards India and advanced up to Navsari. When the Vatapi king Vikramaditya II heard about the advancing Arabs, he sent a force under Rashtrakuta prince Dantidurga II to support Avanijanashraya.

The power of the arab forces can be well speculated by the fact that the same troops plundered Sindh, Kutch, Saurashtra, Chavolakas, Maurya, and Gurjara kingdoms by then, though later most of the rulers united and the combined army defeated the Arabs in the north. The strength of Dantidurga is noticeable by his later victories and the establishment of the Rashtrakuta Empire in the south. Both the warriors were valiant, fearless, and well-trained in the art of warfare. Both excelled in battle strategies. The combined forces of

Avanijanashraya Pulakeshin and Dantidurga II confronted the huge Arab forces in Navsari. The Arab forces were severely defeated. The terrible defeat dampened the spirits of the Arabs to such an extent that they dropped their idea of intruding into the southern kingdoms of India. This fierce battle is described in the Navsari inscription. Going by the inscription of Navsari, the battle between the Chalukyas and Arabs might have taken place in 737 or 738 CE.

To quote Durga Prasad Dikshit from his book about description of the battle and victory evidenced by the Navsari inscription: "During the reign of Vikramaditya II, the north-western limits of the Chalukyan empire were threatened by the inroads of Arab intruders. The dynastic records do not refer to this outstanding event but fortunately the details concerning this event are preserved in the Naysari Plates of Chalukya Pulakesiraja, a son of Dharasraya Jayasimha, dated in Kalachuri year 490 = A.D. 739. This record vividly describes the Arab invasion and the fierce fight that took place at Naysari. Further, it refers to the Mika army (Arab forces), which had plundered the Saindhavas (Sindhu kingdom). Kachchhelas (Cutch), Saurashtra (Kathiawada), Chavotakas, Mauryas, Gujaras, and other kings invading the Naysari vishaya during the course of its campaign for conquering all the southern kings… Avanijanasraya Pulakesiraja gave him a fierce fight somewhere near his headquarters in which he emerged victorious."

In recognition of that victory in the battle against the Arabs, Vikramaditya II mentioned as Vallabha Narendra in the inscription, bestowed upon Avanijanashraya Pulakeshin the following titles:

1. 'Dakshinapathasadhara', which means 'solid pillar of Dakshinapatha'.
2. 'Challukikulalathkara' meaning 'ornament of the Chalukya family'.
3. 'Prithivivallabha' connoting 'beloved of the earth'.

4. 'Anivartakanivartayitri', which means 'repeller of the unrepellable'.

The Arabs made several more attempts to conquer India. It was the stiff resistance offered by individual rulers as well as the unity of Indian rulers from north and south that helped in checking their advances and driving them out of the Indian soil. Junaid, the Arab governor of Sindh, attacked Kashmir following the orders of Caliph Hisham. Lalitaditya Muktapida, the then king of Kashmir, defeated Junaid, and thus the Arab attempt of plundering Kashmir failed. A confederacy of north and south Indian rulers under the leadership of Nagbhat I, the Gurjar Partihar, king defeated the Arab forces in Rajasthan during the eighth century. Had the stiff resistances not been offered, India would have been under Islamic rule right from the eighth century!

39

Lt. Rama Mehta who Joined Netaji Bose's Azad Hind Fauz at Age 17

Lt Rama Mehta as an Azad Hind Fauz soldier

Lt. Rama Mehta Khandwala! She was a freedom fighter. She was the Second Lieutenant, Platoon Commander, and also Guard of Honor in Azad Hind Fauz (INA). She had joined the INA at the age of 17 as an ordinary sepoy in 1943. She also worked as a nurse, treating and taking care of battle-wounded soldiers of Azad Hind Fauz. After Independence, she was offered a post in the Congress party by Sardar Vallabhbhai Patel, which she refused. She chose to be a tourist guide. She worked for 50 plus years in this capacity. She was India's oldest tourist guide. She was honored with the 'Best Tourist Guide' Award in 2017 conferred by President Ram Nath Kovind at the National Tourism Awards. She was also a speaker; delivered a TEDx talk in 2019. Lt. Rama Mehta Khandwala served the nation from the age of 17.

Netaji Bose's motivating speech *Tum mujhe khoon do me tumhe azadi dunga* inspired many Indians settled abroad to join the fight for the freedom of India. And it was after listening to Netaji's speech in Rangoon that Rama Mehta immediately joined the Azad Hind Fauz. Lt. Rama Mehtra breathed her last on October 28, 2021.

Here is an excerpt of an interview of Lt. Rama Mehta Khandwala done by me.

Manoshi Sinha: Please tell us about your childhood and your journey in Azad Hind Fauz.

Lt. Rama Mehta Khandwala: I was born in Rangoon, Burma, on December 1st 1926. I was a student in school then when World War II happened. Subhash Chandra Bose had arrived in this part of Asia and organized the Indian National Army (INA)–the Azad Hind Fauz, garnering supporters from Indonesia, Thailand, Malaysia, Singapore, and more countries, starting with Japan. He also established the Rani Jhansi Regiment for women soldiers. Dr. Lakshmi Sehgal was the head of the women's wing.

Around 1,000 women joined the Rani Jhansi Regiment in Rangoon then. I and my sister Neelam Mehta joined too. It was 1943. I was then 17 years old. My mother Major Leelavati Mehta joined as a Recruiting Officer. She was also entrusted to seek and collect donations for the Azad Hind Fauz. We were seven siblings; three of our elder sisters were then already married. One of our brothers was involved in errands to and from India for the Azad Hind Fauz. My sister-in-law Lt. Rama Mehta was also a soldier in the Azad Hind Fauz.

We underwent training for around eight months. We learned the use of sten guns, machine guns, rifles, and other war weapons. We attended lectures on warfare and were involved in mock practices. I also underwent training as a nurse for treating wounded soldiers of Azad Hind Fauz in the frontline. I had worked for a brief period in Myanmar in a hospital on the frontline. We were given uniforms and good food. All of us had the same food. In the mornings, we often used to have boiled *chana*.

Those who cleared the training well and performed well were promoted. I joined as an ordinary sepoy. Owing to my skills and performance I was promoted to second lieutenant, platoon commander, and also Guard of Honor.

As Guards of Honor, we were present in most of the meetings and gatherings where Netaji delivered talks. 'Give me blood and I will give you freedom'–this famous statement of Netaji inspired and motivated many Indians settled in Asia to join the fight for the freedom of India. Another slogan by Netaji Bose–'*Chalo Dilli*'–further motivated us all to fight against the British and march towards Delhi.

We had the full military and also the financial support of Japan in our fight for independence. After Japan lost in the war, it withdrew support to INA. We had to stop our operations. Netaji sent us all to Rangoon from the camps. It was 1945.

Manoshi Sinha: Your inspiration behind joining the Azad Hind Fauz at such a young age?

Lt. Rama Mehta Khandwala: I wanted to do something for my country. I wanted to participate in the fight for the freedom of our motherland. Patriotism and love for India run in our family veins. My family members have been freedom fighters. My grandfather donated a huge amount of money to Mahatma Gandhi for India's freedom. He was Gandhi's very good friend.

Most of the leaders like Gandhi, Nehru visited our home when they came to Rangoon. The atmosphere in Rangoon was already charged up with many Indians settled there ready to join the fight for India's independence. And then Netaji Subhash Chandra Bose came. And then many of us joined the Azad Hind Fauz.

Manoshi Sinha: Your mother Major Leelavati Mehta collected donations for the Azad Hind Fauz. Did she face any challenge in collecting funds or donations in kind?

Lt. Rama Mehta Khandwala: Indians settled in Malaysia, Singapore, Japan, Burma, Thailand, and more countries of Asia not only donated in cash and kind but also many joined the Azad Hind Fauz as soldiers. They were all ready to sacrifice their lives to free India. My mother was based in Rangoon, and she traveled across these countries to collect donations and to encourage people to join as soldiers.

Organizing a huge army of 75,000 soldiers is no easy task. But Netaji Bose did it. And my mother also played an active role in increasing the strength of Azad Hind Fauz.

Manoshi Sinha: How did the idea about forming the Rani Jhansi Regiment crop up in Netaji's mind?

Lt. Rama Mehta Khandwala: Netaji Bose opined that women should not be left behind. They should also come forward and play an active role in fighting for India's freedom. He believed in *Nari Shakti*, women power, and women empowerment. Yes, women can also dare and do– Netaji had said. That's how the Rani Jhansi Regiment came into existence.

All women recruited in this wing were aggressively trained following Netaji's guidance. And Netaji was very strict in terms of the safety and security of women soldiers. He ensured that we always remained safe and regularly inquired about our health and well-being.

We were not allowed to move out at certain hours. We followed a disciplined life in the camps. Netaji took good care of us. Once a week, he used to visit our camps and we all used to sing the national song together.

Netaji also advised and suggested that in battle, the women wing would be commissioned on the frontline only when the need arose. First, the men would be fighting on the frontline. But we served in the frontline hospitals treating and taking care of the battle-wounded Azad Hind Fauz soldiers. Such was the spirit and *josh* in the wounded soldiers that they would request us to hurry up so that they would return fast to the battlefield and continue fighting. I still remember how one Azad Hind Fauz soldier lost a leg in battle and he was all ready to go back fast to the frontline to resume fighting. That was how the sons of Bharat Mata were ready to sacrifice their lives for Her freedom.

At times, the hospitals used to be filled with many wounded soldiers and we did not even have time to have food. And due to unfavorable conditions, many of our wounded soldiers died of malaria. Also, the badly wounded soldiers attained martyrdom in the hospitals.

Manoshi Sinha: Your description of and views on Netaji Bose.

Lt. Rama Mehta Khandwala: Netaji was a dynamic leader. I have never in my life seen someone so patriotic and so much in love for the motherland. He was so full of *josh*. He used to tell us all, "You are here to fight for our country's freedom. You are here ready to sacrifice your lives for the cause. Together we can do it."

Netaji treated everyone equally. He used to wake up early. He loved singing. He hummed Bengali tunes most of the time. He was dynamic but also a human being like us all. I heard him sing several times. In Hindi, he used to sing *Kadam kadam barhaye jaa* individually and also with us.

Netaji was married when he was steering the Azad Hind Fauz. It was a love marriage with his secretary Emilie Schenkl in Germany. But while organizing and fighting for the country's freedom, he did not utter anything about her. I came across a few of his love letters addressed to his beloved. Most of the content of these letters was more about familiarizing Emilie Schenkl with Hinduism and Hindu culture. I have written about this in my book *Jai Hind*. The letters are published in this book.

They have a daughter Anita Bose, who is now married. She often visits India with her children. Emilie Schenkl never visited India. She wanted to visit India with Netaji. And her wish remained unfulfilled.

Manoshi Sinha: Please tell us a few words about your personal interaction with Netaji Bose.

Lt. Rama Mehta Khandwala: I interacted with Netaji Bose many times. All of the women soldiers of the Rani Jhansi Regiment did all types of duties on a rotation basis in the camps. This included cooking, cleaning, and guarding. The camp where I was stationed was spread across seven acres. Once I was allotted the job of a sentry of guarding the seven-acre camp. I strolled around at night within the camp premise with my rifle. Suddenly I slipped into a hole in the dark and I was badly injured in the leg. I was hospitalized for few days. During those days, in our camp hospital, there was no penicillin or antibiotics. It was only dressing wounds and applying medicine.

Netaji Bose came to meet me in the hospital. I cried at the very sight of him. He said to me "Now the war for the freedom of India has not started yet. You will be there in the frontline fighting. If you start crying like this how will you fight? Be bold and be brave. Do not cry.

Just think about attaining our country's freedom." These words motivated me and filled me with so much *josh* that I forgot my pain. And I felt more determined to be ready to fight for the freedom of my country.

As Guards of Honor, I and my fellow soldiers used to stand for over three hours at a stretch when Netaji Bose delivered talks in meetings and gatherings. Once the meeting was over Netaji Bose used to come and ask us, "Everything alright? Have you had tea and snacks? Are you facing any problems?" He cared for all of us a lot.

The very remembrance of Netaji Bose brings tears to my eyes always and also keeps me motivated. I will never ever forget my Azad Hind Fauz days.

Manoshi Sinha: Netaji Bose spoke in which language?

Lt. Rama Mehta Khandwala: Netaji spoke mostly in Hindi. He also spoke in English. He encouraged non-Hindi speaking Indians of the Azad Hind Fauz to learn Hindi. He taught Hindi to most of the Indian soldiers of Azad Hind Fauz from Malaysia, Thailand, Japan, Singapore, and other regions of Asia. The training happened in Hindi too.

Manoshi Sinha: I have read and also heard that after Independence the Azad Hind Fauz soldiers were not inducted into the Indian Army at the orders of Nehru. Is it true?

Lt. Rama Mehta Khandwala: Yes. Politics have spoiled everything. Nehru did not like Subhash Chandra Bose and Azad Hind Fauz. Had Sardar Patel been the Prime Minister instead of Nehru, India would have been a better nation today. Mahatma Gandhi liked Nehru, so he facilitated Nehru's prime ministership sidelining Sardar Patel though the majority wanted Patel to hold the post.

Nehru did nothing for the surviving Azad Hind Fauz soldiers. Later, Shahnawaz Khan joined politics and became Railway Minister. He was from the Azad Hind Fauz. It was under his initiative that a few of the INA soldiers started getting pensions.

Manoshi Sinha: Did we gain freedom by the *ahimsa* of Mohandas Gandhi?

Lt. Rama Mehta Khandwala: This is what I have been telling that it was because of the sacrifice of so many freedom fighters that we got freedom. Netaji Bose and the Azad Hind Fauz soldiers played an instrumental role in attaining freedom. It is politics that has let the wrong narrative spread.

Netaji Bose did so much for the freedom of the country but he did not get the recognition and honor he deserved. At the national level, Netaji is hardly celebrated except in small meetings and gatherings in few places across the country by Netaji fans like us. I would like to appeal that the song of Azad Hind Fauz–*Kadam kadam barhaye jaa* should also be included as a national song.

Manoshi Sinha: Please tell us about your journey as a tourist guide after Independence.

Lt. Rama Mehta Khandwala: After independence, Sardar Patel met me in Mumbai. He wanted to know from me in detail about Netaji Bose, the INA, and the Rani Jhansi Regiment. We talked for over two hours. Sardar Patel offered me a post, asking me to join the Congress. I refused the offer. Because I never liked politics.

I chose to become a tourist guide. I worked as a tour guide for 50 years. I have also trained tourist guides. I always tell them, "Always put the country first. Never do anything against the country. Never put the country's name at stake. You should always do things that would bring a name to our country. And for this, you need to work hard and do everything that is right. We should always feel proud of our country."

As a tourist guide, I also used to narrate the historicity of the sites. At times I used to narrate about Netaji and Azad Hind Fauz. I guide more tourists from Japan. And most tourists from Japan prefer me to be their tourist guide. I have a good name in the Japanese circle. I have received a number of letters of appreciation. As a tour guide, I was considered an asset.

I am now aged 94. I have worked till the age of 92. I deliver talks on Netaji and Azad Hind Fauz at places where I am invited. I can also deliver talks or give training on weapons used during our days and compare the same with that of the present used in the Indian Army.

Manoshi Sinha: Your views on Indian History portrayed in our history textbooks.

Lt. Rama Mehta Khandwala: It is all a result of politics that we don't get to read about true history in our history textbooks. Even Narendra Modi had praised and recognized the role played by Netaji Bose and the Azad Hind Fauz. But this is not there in the textbooks.

Today the situation is very bad. What will children who watch cartoon channels and spend time on mobile phones learn about history? The situation should change for the better.

Manoshi Sinha: Your message to readers.

Lt. Rama Mehta Khandwala: Please also think and do something for the country. We all do everything for the self, for the family. We should also dedicate ourselves to the country too. I feel so sad that not many citizens think for the nation. Only a counted few people cannot bring glory to a nation. It has to be a collective effort.

Many political leaders have looted the country and created vast wealth for themselves. There are counted few leaders who are honest, transparent and work for the benefit of the nation. We have attained freedom since long but real work for the country has only started now.

Please do not get swayed by the "divide and rule" policy adopted by political leaders. When we were in the Azad Hind Fauz, Netaji taught us one thing thus–"Bharat is our country and we are *Bharatiyas* [Indians]. Address or introduce yourself as a Bharatiya, not as *Gujarati*, *Bengali*, or *Punjabi*."

And it is also an appeal to control anger, as anger does more harm than good.

Manoshi Sinha: Any appeal to the Government?

Lt. Rama Mehta Khandwala: The pension amount we receive is very meager. It is not sufficient to meet the cost of our medicines and meet other basic necessities of life at this old age. I would like to request the Government to increase our pension amount. We are only a counted few freedom fighters surviving today and I hope the Government can do this for us all.

Note: This interview of Lt. Rama Mehta Khandwala, done in December 2019, was facilitated by Shubham Sharma, great-grandson of Maj K.P. Sharma, who led a mass revolt against the British in Jabalpur following INA trials in Red Fort. Shubham's forefathers were in Azad Hind Fauz. He is a close associate of Padma Bhushan Col. Gurbaksh Singh Dhillon's family. Col. Dhillon was tried in Red Fort, famous as INA Trials.

(Lt Rama Mehta breathed her last on 28 October, 2021.)

40

Hadi Rani

Gifted Head to Husband to Motivate Him to Go to War against Mughals

Hadi Rani! She is a familiar name in Mewar in particular and Rajasthan in general but unknown to the rest of India. Mewar, the south-central region of Rajasthan, was home to a few of the most chivalrous Rajput warriors of medieval India–Rana Sanga, who defeated the Delhi Sultan in the Battle of Khatoli, Rana Pratap who regained most of the Mewari territory from Akbar, Amar Singh, who defeated the Mughal forces, and the list goes on. Hadi Rani was the wife of Rao Ratan Singh, a Chundawat chieftain of Salumber (now a municipality in Udaipur) in Mewar. Rao Ratan Singh served as a commander in the Mewari army of Maharana Raj Singh I. During that time Aurangzeb was the Mughal ruler.

Few books and many web write-ups on Hadi Rani deem her as a folk heroine, and her story, a folk tale, which is wrong. If the term 'folklore' or 'folktale' is to be used, the prefix 'historical' should be added. Historical folklore or historical folktales are real stories that rarely find description or mention in historical accounts. These historical stories stay alive as oral narrations passed down from one generation to another. The chivalrous story of Hadi Rani is real and is part of a historical chronicle.

The book *Kshatrya Rajput Caste* by T. Bahadar Singh describes Chundawat Sisodias as descendants of Chunda, the first son of Lakha, further divided into 10 branches. Lakha ruled Mewar in the early 15th century. The Chundawat chiefs of Salumber played an instrumental role in the administrative affairs of Mewar besides offering resistance to invaders. Chundawat chieftain Rao Ratan Singh thus carried a legacy of chivalry and valor.

Hadi Rani was the daughter of a Hada Chauhan Rajput, who was the chieftain of Bundi, a region bounded on the west by Mewar. According to an account described in the book *The Rajputs of Rajputana: A Glimpse of Medieval Rajasthan* by V.P. Malik and M.S. Naravane, the Hada Chauhans were descendants of Anuraj, ruler of Hansi (parts of modern Haryana), who defeated Sabuktigin (Abu Mansur Nasir al-Din Sabuktigin)–father of Mahmud of Ghazni, who plundered India several times. Their ancestors also served in the army of Prithviraj Chauhan. Hadi Rani, thus, carried a legacy of chivalry and heroism too.

Indian Poetry: Modernism and After: A Seminar edited by K. Satchidanandan finds mention of Hadi Rani in a description about Rajasthani poetry and how poets chose subjects that were 'already popular with the masses'. That was how poets resorted to composing historical poetry, drawing popular characters from History. This book cites the example of how poet Meghraj Mukul composed a historical poem titled *'Sainani'* on Hadi Rani and rose to fame. Mukul had based this poem on the famous story of Hadi Rani who is believed to have cut her head and sent it to her husband who was leaving for a battle and who had asked her for a *Satnani*, a token of her memory.

For kings, commanders, and soldiers, motherland always came first. Ever since antiquity, there have been thousands of examples of how warriors left for the battlefield irrespective of what personal situations they were in. The beautiful Hadi Rani and Rao Ratan Singh were newly married. It was only a day past their marriage when Maharana Raj Singh I sent a messenger to Rao Ratan Singh, ordering him to join a battle against Aurangzeb's Mughal forces. That dampened the Chundawat chieftain's spirits as he was in no mood to leave his wife and go to the battlefield.

What led to war between Maharana Raj Singh I and Aurangzeb? *Folk Tales of Rajasthan* by Dina Nath Dube presents a detailed account of Hadi Rani. When the marriage between the Hada Chauhan princess and Chundawat chieftain took place, Charumati (also called Prabhavati), the Rajput princess of Roop Nagar, sent word to Maharana Raj Singh I seeking help. Mughal rulers, since the time of Babur, married several times. Whenever they heard about beautiful princesses, they entered into marriage alliances or forcibly married them. Rulers of several kingdoms were allowed rulership against certain terms and conditions including marriage. Aurangzeb entered into a marriage alliance with the Rajput ruler Rup Singh of Roop Nagar. Despite her father's request, Charumati refused to marry Aurangzeb. Instead, she expressed her interest to marry Maharana Raj Singh I of Mewar. Charumati was known far and wide for her beauty. The Deobari inscription finds mention of Rup Singh promising to give the hand of her daughter Charumati to Aurangzeb.

Aurangzeb started his march towards Roop Nagar with a huge army to marry Charumati. Maharana Raj Singh I had left for Roop Nagar too, ready to marry Charumati before Aurangzeb's arrival. It was the honeymoon night for the newly married Hadi Rani and Rao Ratan Singh when a lady messenger knocked at their door and delivered the urgent message from the king of Mewar, ordering the groom to rush towards the approaching Mughal army of Aurangzeb, commandeered by General Dilawar Khan and check their advancement.

Hadi Rani overheard the conversation between the messenger and Rao Ratan Singh in bits and parts. When the messenger left, waiting outside to receive the reply from the commander, she asked her husband about the matter. Rao Ratan Singh narrated the incident. A worried Hadi Rani soon cheered up. As she grew up, her mother had narrated to her many tales of Rajput valor. She had also heard how valorous her ancestors were. Hence, she would not let her husband get distracted only because they were newly married. She immediately asked him to leave for the battlefield. But Rao Ratan Singh hesitated.

The chivalrous Hadi Rani took a decision. She sent word to the messenger that Rao Ratan Singh ffecd immediately leave with the Mewari army to check the Mughal forces. An aggrieved and frustrated Singh caught hold of his bride by her shoulders, shaking her and asking her if she loved him and why she wanted him to go on their honeymoon night. He also expressed the possible danger of facing the strong Mughal army. Hadi Rani immediately replied that if she were to stop him that night, she would forever create a stain on Rajput valor and that people would never forgive them. She also said that only cowards were afraid of dangers and the brave face every danger valiantly and at ease. She persuaded and pressurized him to go. Rao Ratan Singh thus left with his forces towards the approaching Mughal army.

In this context, Lindsey Harlan in The *Goddesses' Henchmen: Gender in Indian Hero Worship* describes how Rajput women played an instrumental role in Rajput history and– "if a Rajput man can frighten lions, a Rajput woman can roar like a lioness"; it then identifies Rajput women as 'the secret of Rajput honor', also quoting the example of Hadi Rani as an "exemplar of Rajput feminine virtue and wifely duty".

Rao Ratan Singh, who started with his army, was so distracted by his wife's thoughts and her beauty that he stopped. He could not advance further. He sent one of his trusted lieutenants back to the palace with a message. He wanted to carry a memento from his wife as a token of love to the battlefield. The lieutenant arrived at the palace and delivered Rao Ratan Singh's message to Hadi Rani.

When the Hada Chauhan Rajputani, now a Chundawat queen, learned how distracted her husband was, she could not digest the fact that he wanted a memento at an odd hour–at a time when he should be galloping fast towards the approaching enemy. Something immediately clicked in her mind. She ordered her maidservant to bring a sword and salver. The maidservant obeyed.

Hadi Rani caught hold of the sword as the maidservant stood carrying the salver and the lieutenant waited. What happened next froze the hearts of the maidservant and the lieutenant. Uttering 'Jai Durge', at one powerful strike of the sword, Hadi Rani struck her head off! The maidservant screamed. The two realized what the memento was. The maidservant immediately put the bleeding head of Hadi Rani on the salver, covered it with a red cloth, and gave it to the lieutenant to deliver it to Rao Ratan Singh.

The lieutenant soon reached the spot where Rao Ratan Singh was waiting with his army. The Chundawat warrior's face brightened up as the salver covered with the red cloth came into view. He waited impatiently for the memento to be delivered to him. When he removed the cloth he was dumbfounded to see his queen's head. He realized his fault and regretted it. But he had to keep his queen's words. He had to fight the enemy bravely. With renewed vigor and with the lifeless Rani tied around his neck by her hair, Rao Ratan Singh marched towards the Mughal forces.

Lindsey Harlan in *Religion and Rajput Women* draws a symbolism of Hadi Rani's sacrifice citing the *jhumjhar* metaphor. To quote from this book: "When a jhumjhar's head survives its body, it may roll a great distance in order to achieve an auspicious destination, which is then marked by a shrine. Similarly, Hadi Rani's head travels about to attain its end, her husband's glory. This comparison also hinges on the male-female inversion, for Hari Rani's head does not animate the body from which it is severed but the body to which it is offered–the body of her husband. The symbolism of three types occurs: substitution, combination, and sacrifice."

To further quote from *Religion and Rajput Women* on the story of Hadi Rani: "Hari Rani had just been married to the Lord of Salumbar [one of the major estates of Mewar] when he was summoned by the Maharana to help repulse an attack by Aurangzeb. The husband was so enamored of his new bride that he had great difficulty pulling himself away from her to go and fight. Barely managing to leave her, he could muster no enthusiasm for the upcoming battle. When he reached the palace gates, he sent word back to Hari Rani that she should send him some souvenir to take to war with him so that he could feel she was by his side. Without hesitating, the devoted wife drew a sword and sliced off her head so that he could take that with him. When a maidservant delivered the head to him, he affixed it to his saddle and, inspired by his wife's example of devotion, rode off to do his duty as a soldier."

In the battle that followed, a devastated but nevertheless proud Rao Ratan Singh attacked the Mughal forces like a wounded fiery lion. He fought bravely, slaying fast the Mughal soldiers one after another. The Mughal forces retreated and fled. He thus achieved his goal, gaining victory for Mewar and facilitating Charumati's marriage with Maharana Raj Singh I. Now that his goal was met, he desired no longer to live, for he longed Hadi Rani's presence. He got to his knees and with his sword severed his neck from his body.

Had Hadi Rani not sacrifIced her head, Rao Ratan Singh would have continued to get distracted in battle which might have proved otherwise for the Mewari army. A bow to Hadi Rani for setting an example of sacrifice, valor, and duties of a wife!

41

How Naga Sadhus Defended Gokul from Abdali's Afghan Army in 1757

For centuries, Naga Sadhus, synonymous with 'valor and Dharma' defended Hindus and temples. This warrior saint community, numbering around 4,000, defended Gokul in 1757 from the robust Afghan forces of Ahmad Shah Abdali. They fought with trishuls (tridents) and daggers. More than 2,000 Naga Sadhus attained *Veergati* on the battlefield but they saved the temple of Gokul and defended the city. Abdali's forces couldn't advance into the city and retreated.

The antiquity of the existence of Naga Sadhus dates back thousands of years. Literary records and folklore attribute their founder to Dattatreya, a paradigmatic Sannyasi and the incarnation of the Trinity–Brahma, Vishnu, and Mahadev. Many monastic movements in Shaivism, Vaishnavism, and Shaktism were inspired by Dattatreya. The *Dashanami sampradaya* of monastic tradition was also inspired by Dattatreya. Adi Shankaracharya organized this *sampradaya* of monastic tradition into four mutts. He also organized a section of warrior sadhus to protect Sanatana Dharma. Later they came to be known as Naga Sadhus. They have no fear of death and their weapons have been the trishul, sword and stick. They also carry other weapons as well as musical instruments and conch shells. Their ash-covered bodies and matted locks differentiate them from other sadhus. To quote from Kanhaiyalal Maneklal Munshi's Foreword to Jadunath Sarkar's book *A History of Dasnami Naga Sanyasis:* "The Dashnamis are divided into two sections: The *shastradharis*, whoffectzee in sacred lore, and the *astradharis*, whoffectzee in arms. The sanyasis areffectzedd into four ranks–*Kutichak, Bahtidak, Hansa, and Paramahansa*–the last being the highest. The fighting wing is organised into akharas, and, in the past, played a historic role." Naga Sadhus are *astradharis*. Baba Rampuri in his book *Autobiography of a Sadhu: A Journey into Mystic India* has given a detailed account about Naga Sadhus and their akharas. An American born as William A. Gans, he claims to be the first westerner to become a Naga Sadhu.

Madhusudana Saraswati, a philosopher from the Advaita Vedanta tradition and a contemporary of Akbar, further reorganized a section of the Naga Sadhus in the 16th century to protect Hindus from the tyranny of the Mughals.

Ahmad Shah Abdali, also known as Ahmad Shah Durrani, was the founder of the Durrani Empire in Afghanistan. He ruled from 1747 and soon started expanding his empire through military conquests. He attacked India eight times from 1748 to 1767. He accompanied Nader Shah on a military expedition to India in 1739, he was then aged 17 years, during which he stayed in the Red Fort of Delhi for a few days. He was witness to the vast wealth of India then. After he ascended the throne of Afghanistan, he immediately started his conquests into the Indian territories. Abdali set out to attack the Mathura-Vrindavan-Gokul area in 1757 with a huge force.

Gokul is located at a distance of 15 kms to the south-east of Mathura, the birthplace of Shri Krishna. This region finds mention in the Ramayana and several ancient Indian texts. Shri Krishna played in Gokul during his childhood days, as described in the *Bhagavata Purana*. During the time of Abdali's invasion, the Mathura-Vrindavan-Gokul region, also known as Braj, was under Maharaja Suraj Mal, the Jat Raja of Bharatpur.

It was the Holi of 1757, dated 28th February. Pilgrims from across the country had assembled at Braj to celebrate Holi. When Suraj Mal learned about the approaching army of Abdali towards Braj, he sent his son Jawahar Singh with 5,000 men to offer resistance. The Afghan forces with over 40,000 soldiers were led by Jahan Khan. Both the armies met outside Chaumuha, eight miles from Mathura. A fierce battle ensued. Jawahar Singh and his men, comprising more of peasants, offered a brave fight. The battle continued for nine hours. The Abdali forces, superior in strength and weaponry, emerged victorious. About 3,000 Jat soldiers attained *Veergati*. According to *Tarikh-E-Alamgir Sani*, the number of casualties was 10,000 to 12,000 on both sides. Going by this account, casualties were more on the Afghan side–7,000 to 9,000 soldiers. This corroborates how the brave Hindus, for nine hours, fought ferociously to defend Braj. To quote about this battle from *Ahmad Shah Durrani: Father of Modern Afghanistan* by Ganda Singh: "Jahan Khan, guided by Najib-ud-Daulah, on the other hand, had commenced his slaughtering and scalp-gathering campaign with a greater vigour and on a much larger scale. All of a sudden, he swooped down upon the unsuspecting town of Mathura. Prince Jawahar Singh was there to defend it. Although taken by surprise, Jawahar Singh and his Jat 'peasantry were determined that it was only over their corpses that the ravager should enter the sacred capital of Braja'. Jawahar Singh issued out on the 28th of February with five thousand men to block the passage of the invader outside the village of Chaumuha, eight miles north of Mathura. But he was no match for the veteran Afghan general, and despite his stout

Jawahar Singh, prince of Bharatpur, in action against Abdali's forces in the battlefield in the outskirts of Mathura.

resistance for nine hours, he was pushed aside with a heavy loss of about three thousand lives. The Afghan victors pushed onto MathurI."

What followed was genocide of the Hindus, plunder, loot of wealth, destruction of temples, burning of the city, and captivity of women. It was 1st March 1757. To further quote from *Ahmad Shah Durrani: Father of Modern Afghanistan:* "It was mostly a city of priests and pilgrims, many of whom have come from outside for the Holi festIl... Jahan Khan had the fullest opportunity for a literal execution of his master's commands 'to slay and plunder'. His fury had been further inflamed by the resistance of the previous night and he was not in a mood to show mercy. He ordered an indiscriminate massacre of the people and the Holi was played afresh with the deep red blood of the Hindus. In addition to this carnage the city was set at fire and it burnt like a huge Ifire... Huge and heavy idols were broken to pieces under the blows of the ghazis' hatchets and were kicked about in lanes and streets like children's polo-balls."

Vrindavan faced the same fate. Jahan Khan committed genocide of the Hindus in Vrindavan, repeating exactly the same 'play of fire and sword' he followed in Mathura on 6th March 1757. To further quote Ganda Singh, who cites from Samin's Ioirs: "...'wherever you gazed you beheld only heaps of the slain; you could only pick your way with difficulty, owing to enormous number of bodies lying about and the amount oIlood spilt... At one place that we reached, we saw about two hundred dead children in a heap. Not one of the dead bodies had a head... The stench and fetor and effluvium in the air were such that it was painful to open your mouth or even draw a breath'."

Jadunath Sarkar in *A History of Dasnami Naga Sanyasis* writes, on the above incident on the genocide of Hindus by Abdali's Muslim forces at Mathura and Vrindavan, quoting Samin: "Ahmad Shah Abdali had issued that time a stern decree, ordering a general slaughter and burning of the whole country from Agra to Mathura. His faithful followers deluged the town of Mathura with blood. 'For seven days the water of the Jamuna (at this holy city) flowed of a blood red colour; The Sannyasis and the Bairagis were decapitated and their heads were defiled by being tied Ia cow's head'..."

Ahmad Shah Abdali was following Jahan Khan at a slow pace. By the time he was about to reach Mathura, Jahan Khan had already plundered the holy cities of Mathura and Vrindavan. The Afghan soldiers camped and waited for the Sultan to arrive. Abdali arrived near Mathura, crossed the Yamuna, and encamped at Mahaban on 15th March. While Mathura was at a distance of six miles, Gokul was two miles away from his camp. From there, Abdali detached a huge force for the plunder of Gokul.

During that time, around 4,000 Naga Sadhus camped in a small village outside Gokul. When they saw the advancing Muslim forces of Abdali, they immediately set to action. With their trishul*s* and daggers, they fell upon the Afghan soldiers in the outskirts of Gokul. In the fierce battle that followed, the Afghan soldiers froze witnessing the unmatched valor of the Naga Sadhus. About 4,000 Naga Sadhus fought against many thousands! Abdali's forces ultimately had to retreat after facing heavy casualties and when they saw defeat for them was certain. About 2,000 Naga Sadhus attained *Veergati* in that battle and hundreds wounded with casualties higher on the enemy side. But they saved Gokul from being plundered and looted. They defended the Hindus of Gokul, preventing another genocide. They saved the Gokul Dham temple. The Afghan forces could not even enter Gokul.

To quote Ganda Singh about the defense of Gokul by Naga Sadhus against Abdali's forces: "The latent martial spirit of the sturdy north Indian Nanga Sadhus of the Bairagi cult was roused in defence of their monstery and four thousand of these 'naked ash-besmeared warriors' issued out of the town to oppose the advance of the Afghans. A desperate struggle ensued. Two thousand of them fell dead on the scene of action along with as many of the Afghans."

To further quote Jadunath Sarkar, who cites from *Marathi Riyasat*, Panipat Prakaran, and *History of the Jats* by Qanungo: "The account of unopposed massacre and loot was relieved by the resistance of a body of 4,000 Naga monks. Of them, 2,000 laid down their lives but saved the shrine of the Deity at Gokul from defilement."

Had the Naga Sadhus not resisted, Gokul would have faced a similar fate as Mathura and Vrindavan.

42

Onake Obavva

A Guard's Wife who Fought against Hyder Ali's Forces

The freedom that India enjoys today is at the cost of the resistance offered by millions and sacrifice by lakhs of Dharmic warriors over a period of 1,400 years. It was not only kings and queens, but also soldiers and the common people who participated. Here is a story of the valor of Onake Obavva, the wife of a fort guard, who single-handedly killed hundreds of soldiers of Hyder Ali with an onake, a pestle, at the impregnable Chitradurga Fort of Karnataka. Untrained in the art of warfare, it was her bravery, her presence of mind, and her love for the motherland that robotically prompted her to act against the enemy. She is immortal in historical folklore and ballads.

Chitradurga is an ancient picturesque town with rock hills and huge towering boulders on the Vedavati river valley in Karnataka. Artifacts from the Stone Age and prehistoric times have been found here. This city finds mention in the Mahabharata and other ancient texts. It is believed to be the place where the Pandavas spent some time during their exile and where Bhima married Hidimbi. The city was also known as Hidimbapattana, Chinnamuladri, Perumalepura, Chitrakaldurga, and Mallarayanadurga. Various dynasties including

Mauryas, Satavahanas, Kadambas, Chalukyas, Rashtrakutas, Cholas, and Hoysalas ruled here. It was also part of the Vijayanagara Empire besides being a feudatory kingdom.

Chitradurga is home to the robust Chitradurga Fort that straddles several rock hills and a peak overlooking a flat valley. The fort was built over a period of three centuries from 10th to 13th by several dynasties, especially the Chalukyas, the Hoysalas, and the Vijayanagara kings, as evidenced by inscriptions found in and around the site. This fort has 19 open entrances, 38 smaller entry points, 35 secret entrances, and four entrances through hidden tunnels. Eighteen temples in the upper and one in the lower area adorn the fort site. These temples, built by different dynasties, are dedicated to Krishna, Hanuman, Nandi, and other deities. One temple is dedicated to Uchchangiamma, the tutelary deity of the Nayakas.

When Hyder Ali attacked the fort in 1779, Chitradurga was ruled by Ontisalaga Madakari Nayaka. Ontisalaga Madakari Nayaka's ancestors first ruled as feudatories under the Vijayanagara Empire, later they asserted their independence. Timmana Nayaka was the first chieftain of Chitradurga under this empire.

Not much information is available about Onake Obavva except her resistance to Hyder Ali's soldiers. She was a Chalavadi Holaya, one of the oldest communities to inhabit Karnataka and adjoining regions. Chalavadi Holayas were agriculturists as well as warriors. They were also disciples of Jagajyoti Basaveshwara, a Shaivite social reformer. Onake Obavva is considered to be from the scheduled caste. But going by the ancient varna system wherein by 'karma' i.e., work/ deeds, a person was classified, she was a Kshatriya. In ancient and medieval times, Kshatriyas were those who ruled and those who defended and protected the motherland from enemies. Onake Obavva defended her motherland fighting until death.

Onake Obavva was married to Kahale Mudda Hanuma, a guard of a watchtower at Chitradurga Fort. The watchtower was located near a crevice, which was one of the secret entrances to the fort through a hidden tunnel. Nearby that crevice was a pond where few residents of the fort area residing at that part fetched water for drinking.

Hyder Ali became the Sultan of Mysore in 1761. Prior to this, he was the commander of the army of Wodeyar Raja of Mysore. He attacked Chitradurga thrice, first in 1760, then in 1770, and the third in 1779. Ontisalaga Madakari Nayaka, who ascended the throne in 1754, repulsed Hyder Ali's attacks twice. And twice the Muslim ruler failed to enter the fort. In 1779, Hyder Ali and his troops laid siege to the Chitradurga Fort at the base, unable to enter. Madakari Nayaka had used the fort effectively for defense during the earlier two battles. So did he in the battle in 1779. Hyder Ali had been looking for an opportunity to enter the fort by any means. His men, at all four sides of the fort, stayed guard to see if anyone entered through a secret passage. After several days of siege, they saw a man entering the fort through a crevice in the rocks. Hyder Ali immediately set to action. He and his troops gathered near the crevice. There was room for entry of only one soldier at a time in the crevice, hence it was decided that the soldiers would enter the fort one by one.

Meanwhile, Kahale Mudda Hanuma, who was guarding the area near the opening of the crevice within the fort, went to have lunch at his home located nearby. Hanuma was more than confident that the enemies would never get to know about the secret tunnel through the rocks. Onake Obavva served him food. After she served the food, she noticed there was no drinking water left at her home. Carrying a pitcher and an onake, she set out towards the pond, located near the crevice. She used the onake, a long wooden club meant for pounding paddy grains, to support herself through the rocky tracks to the pond.

While she filled her pitcher with water from the pond, she heard a whispering sound emerging from inside the crevice. Onake Obavva was already aware of Hyder Ali's troops surrounding the fort at the base. She smelt something fishy. Immediately, she left the pitcher and holding her onake waited outside the crevice, hiding, all ready to strike. She saw an enemy soldier crawling out of the crevice. She hit him hard on the head to death. Then she pulled him out quietly and laid him on one side, out of view from the crevice. She killed one soldier after another and scores of the dead soldiers of Hyder Ali piled up with blood oozing from their heads. Onake did not stop. She continued until her husband Hanuma reached the spot. Hanuma saw over a hundred soldiers in a pool of blood. And he couldn't believe his eyes that Onake, a housewife engaged in household chores and never trained in fighting, could kill over a hundred of the enemy soldiers! A motivated Hanuma helped his wife in defending the fort. An exhausted Onake Obavva attained martyrdom after few hours. She was attacked by one of the enemy soldiers. Though it is not clearly mentioned how she was hit, it was probable that one of the enemy soldiers lying in the pool of blood regained consciousness and killed her.

Madakari Nayaka was defeated in that battle. But Onake Obavva single-handedly defended the fort for several hours and killed hundreds of the enemy soldiers before attaining *Veergati*.

The place in Chitradurga Fort, where Obavva killed Hyder Ali's soldiers, is named Obavvana Kindi (*kindi* meaning crevice) in her memory.

43

Prafulla Kumari Devi

Maharani of Bastar, who Challenged the British

The very utterance of Bastar ships one to the terrain of Naxal terrorists in Chhattisgarh. This region was once a flourishing kingdom in ancient and medieval India. For some time, the Bastar kingdom was ruled by Maharani Prafulla Kumari Devi from the Kakatiya dynasty by her parents and the Bhanja dynasty by marriage. She reigned from 1922 to 1936. During her rule, the British imposed their policies in her kingdom, which she didn't follow. This region has been rich in natural resources. The British were all geared up to hand over part of Bastar, rich in iron ore reserves, to the then Nizam of Hyderabad against a hefty sum. But this didn't materialize as the Maharani intervened and challenged it. She fell ill and required advanced treatment. She was taken to London at the advice of the British. There she was treacherously murdered in the name of her illness, as evidenced by a secret letter that later surfaced.

The Bastar region is an ancient city that finds mention in numerous ancient texts. In the Ramayana, the region is mentioned as Dandakaranya, meaning Dandak forest where Dandak Rakshash once lived and where Shri Ram, Sita, and Lakshman spent their initial years during their exile. It was part of the Kosala kingdom during the Mahabharata era. Several more dynasties ruled that region over several centuries. In the medieval era, that region was ruled by a Nagvanshi king. Annamaraja, the brother of Raja Prataparudra II of the Kakatiya dynasty defeated the Nagvanshi king and further re-established the kingdom with capital at Mudhota. Before he started his kingship, Annamaraja sought the blessings of his Kuldevi Danteshwari and built the Danteshwari temple at Dantewada at the confluence of the Sankani and Dankani rivers. Danteshwari temple is a Shaktipitha. It was at this place that the tooth of Sati fell thousands of years ago. Danteshwari was the presiding deity of the Kakatiyas. Maharani Prafulla Kumari Devi traced her ancestry from this lineage.

To quote from Wilfred Grigson's Maria *Gonds of Bastar:* "Bastar has in fact always been an almost unknown backwater of the river of Indian history. The late Chief, Maharani Prafulla Kumari Devi, at her accession in 1924 was the last legitimate survivor of one of the most ancient royal families of southern India, the Kakatiya, which reigned at Warangal from about A.D. 1150 to 1425, first possibly as feudatories of the Chalukya kings and then independently. In Bastar folk-song, Annam Deo, the first to reign in Bastar, is spoken of as 'Chalkibans Raja', which may be a corruption of 'Chalukya-bans' and indicate that the Kakatiya family was a cadet branch of the Chalukya. Pratap Rudra, the greatest and the last independent Kakatiya king of Warangal, lost his life and independence in battle with the Mohammedan invaders of the Deccan under Ahmad Shah Bahmani early in the fifteenth century and, according to Bastar tradition and folk-song, his brother Annam Deo fled across the Godavari into Bastar, which had been an outlying and loosely-held group of feudal dependencies of Warangal. For inscriptions show that before this, in the eleventh century, a Telugu line of Nagvansi kings ruled at Bastar IDantewara tahsil..."

According to the *Imperial Gazetteer of India*, Volume 7, dated 1908, the population of Bastar in 1901 was 306,501 persons in 2,525 inhabited villages. About two-thirds of the inhabitants comprised of Gonds and a considerable number of Halbas. Languages spoken were Halbi (a mixed dialect of Hindi, Oriya, and Marathi), Oriya, Telugu. Maria Gonds 'have a language peculiar to themselves'.

Maharani Prafulla Kumari Devi was born to Rani Kusumlata Devi and Raja Rudra Pratap Deo on 10th February 1910 at Bastar. After the death of Raja Rudra Pratap Deo in 1921, Maharani Prafulla Kumari Devi became the ruler as there was no male heir. Rudra's only son died at 10 months. Prafulla Kumari Devi ascended the throne of Bastar in 1922. She was then aged 12 years. She was married to Prafulla Chandra Bhanj Deo of Mayurbhanj of the Bhanj dynasty in 1927 at the age of 17. Prafulla Chandra was the nephew of the then Maharaja of Mayurbhanj.

Angma Dey Jhala writes in *'Courtly Indian Women in Late Imperial India'* published in *Journal of the RoI Asiatic Society*, "...rare phenomenon of a woman who ruled in her own name not just as a Regent for a male child or the hidden partner of a devoted husband. Jhala examines the Hindu Maharani Prafulla Kumari Devi of Bastar and the challenges that a queen regnant posed to her husband's sense of sex roles;" This statement by Jhala suggests it was not an easy task for Maharani Prafulla Kumari Devi to rule Bastar as a woman. Another local account suggests her husband supported her in whatever tasks she undertook for the welfare of her kingdom.

Maharani Prafulla Kumari Devi took up the cause of the local tribals and ensured that they were not exploited either by the British or other influential people of her kingdom. She worked for their welfare. The British annexed territories or allowed respective rulers of certain princely states to continue their rulership against payment of tribute. In 1863, the British made Bastar a part of the Jeypore state, allowing the rulers to rule against payment of tribute. But they also interfered in the internal affairs of the kingdom. Maharani Prafulla Kumari Devi emerged as a threat to the British as she interrupted their interferences.

Pramatha Nath Bose, a pioneering Indian geologist, and paleontologist visited the Bastar kingdom, especially in the hills of Bailadila, for research. Maharani Prafulla Kumari Devi facilitated his stay and other requirements. Once he completed his research, he visited the court of the Maharani and informed her about the rich iron ore deposits in the Bailadila hills. When the British came to know about the find, they entrusted more researchers and detected 14 spots of the world's best iron ore deposits estimated at 1,500 million tons. Hyderabad is connected to the borders of Bastar in the west.

The news about the existence of iron ore in Bastar invited the interest of the Nizam of Hyderabad. The British entered into a pact with the Nizam allowing the latter to take control of Bailadila hills against a hefty tribute. In this context, the then Viceroy of India, Linlithgow summoned Maharani Prafulla Kumari Devi. The meeting did take place but without success. Linlithgow could not convince her to cede the Bailadila hills to the Nizam. Several meetings took place but the Maharani remained adamant. In 1936, Maharani Prafulla Kumari Devi was 26 years old. It was then that the British started planning ways of eliminating her. As long as she remained the ruler of Bastar, she would never allow the Nizam or the British to take control of Bailadila hills.

The British then tried to convince her husband Prafulla Chandra Bhanj Deo for the same, even making a promise of giving him the Zamindari of a region including immense wealth, but in vain. In fact, he remained a loyal adviser to the queen and supported all her undertakings and decisions. This further irked the British. Because it was the British who facilitated the marriage for they thought of using Bhanj Deo as bait for their colonial interests. The Maharani had thrown away the wedding gifts she received from her in-laws because it was a forced marriage. Even Bhanj Deo initially, before marriage, remained a puppet of the British. But his perceptions changed after marriage. He fell in love with the Maharani and supported her in everything besides also advising her to not give in to the demands of the British.

During this time, Maharani Prafulla Kumari Devi fell ill. She was advised a surgical procedure on her appendix. When the British came to know about her illness, they proposed that she should go to London for the surgical procedure. The Maharani went to London. But there she died in the operation theatre of a nursing home on 26th February 1936. Was death a result of murder or her illness? It was murder, but this fact remained a secret until a covert letter exposed it. Rajiv Ranjan Prasad in his book *Dantakshetra* has published the secret letter. This letter was addressed to Michelle by an anonymous person. The letter mentioned Col. Meek giving some instructions to Michelle. It mentioned how the British were not able to give shape to their political aspirations in Bastar due to the intervention by Maharani Prafulla Kumari Devi, that the British could establish their suzerainty in Bastar only after her death, that she should not come back alive to India, that the British were completely dependent on Michelle for the task. That letter also mentioned rewarding Michelle with money and about a request to the lady for tearing the paper and setting it on fire after reading.

Maharani Prafulla Kumari Devi was succeeded by her son Pravir Chandra Bhanj Deo.

Had Prafulla Kumari Devi not challenged the British, Bailadila hills would have been ceded to the Nizam of Hyderabad. She ascended to the throne as a child and boldly ruled her kingdom until the young age of 26. Had she not been treacherously murdered by the British, the history of the Bastar region would have been different!

Naman to Prafulla Kumari Devi! Vande Mataram!!!

44

Rajachakravarty Pratapaditya of Jessore

Defeated Mughals in Several Battles

From a Baro Bhuyan, a soldier land-owner under the Mughals, he rose to be an independent ruler of a big kingdom comprising of southern and western Bengal including eastern Bihar. He led several battles against the Mughals to victory–Battle of Salka, Battle of Patna, Battle of Rajmahal, Battle of Kalindi, and Battle of Hijli. He also annexed Mughal territories into his kingdom. He had a robust naval force and an equally strong army divided into infantry, cavalry, artillery, archers, and elephant divisions. He was an ardent devotee of Goddess Kali. He was Rajachakravarty Pratapaditya Maharaj of Jessore.

Pratapaditya was born in 1561 at Jessore. His father Shridhara, also called Shrihari Vikramaditya, was an officer under Daud Khan of the Karrani dynasty of Bengal. After the fall of this dynasty at the hands of the Mughals, Shrihari along with the wealth of Karrani fled to the marshy lands of Jessore, located at the extreme south of Khulna, and established his kingdom there in 1574. Pratapaditya ascended the throne of Jessore in 1584 at the age of 23.

Initially, Pratapaditya ruled as a feudatory of the Mughals under Akbar. But he declared independence a few years later. He shifted his capital to Dhumghat at the confluence of the Jamuna and Ichhamati. During the expansion of his kingdom, he strengthened his army and naval base. He recruited even Afghans and Portuguese. His army comprised of infantry, cavalry, artillery, archers, and elephant divisions with each division under a head. An excellent war strategist, he also employed two war strategists–Sardar Shankar Chakraborty and Rudraditya Upadhyay, who were also the commanders-in-chief of his army. He always kept his naval force ready with war boats at the naval stations, as he anticipated attacks from the Arakanese and the Portuguese along the Bay of Bengal. He built shipyards and dockyards at Chandikhan, Dudhali, Jahajaghata, and Chakasri. The naval war vessels were kept equipped with artillery. Sixteenth-17th century traveler Abdul Latif and Dutch historian Jos Gommans have described in their accounts about the Jessore fleet consisting of hundreds of war boats, more than the Mughals in numerical strength. Pratapaditya involved in a number of welfare activities in his kingdom including the strengthening of infrastructure.

To quote from *Jessore* by Lewis Sydney Steward O'Malley: "For a time, says tradition, Pratapaditya prospered exceedingly. He adorned his kingdom with noble buildings, made roads, built temples, dug tanks and wells, and, in fact, did everything that a sovereign could do for the welfare of his subjects. The limits of his kingdom quickly extended, for he made war on his neighbours and came off victorious in every battle till all the surrounding country acknowledged his rule. Ultimately, he declared himself independent of the Emperor of Delhi, and so great was his power that he managed to defeat, one after another, the generals sent against him. These successes he owed to the favour of the goddess Jasohareswari (Kali), who, pleased with his zealous devotion to herself and his charity to all around him, had promised that she would aid him in every difficulty and never leave him unless he himself drove her away."

Jeshoreshwari, another name of Goddess Kali, was the patron deity of Jessore. According to historical folklore of the region, a general of Pratapaditya once saw a ray of light in a nearby forest. He went towards the source of the light where he found a Moorti of Goddess Kali. He immediately informed Maharaja Pratapaditya. The king brought the Moorti to his capital and built a temple. The Moorti was installed in the temple and worshipping began. According to legend, Jessore was the place where the palm of Shakti fell. Jeshoreshwari temple is thus considered a Shaktipitha. It was after he discovered the Moorti and constructed the temple that Pratapaditya started gaining victory after victory against the Mughals and expanded his kingdom. In the same book, *Jessore* describes how Pratapaditya later became arrogant and proud for the vast powers he held, he turned tyrannical towards the last years of his life. It was then that Goddess Kali withdrew Her favor for the king.

Pratapaditya won several battles against the Mughals–Battle of Salka, Battle of Patna, Battle of Rajmahal, Battle of Kalindi, and Battle of Hijli. Pratapaditya built around 19 forts besides also capturing forts that were under Mughal dominion. A few of these forts were in and around Jessore, a few around today's Kolkata, and one in Jaggaddala (now in Bangladesh).

Regarding Pratapaditya's defensive position while dealing against the Mughals, *Baharistan-i-Ghaibi* by 17th century historian Alauddin Isfahani says: "Pratapaditya raised a very strong fort like the fort of Salka at a place between the river Bhagirathi and the Kagarghata canal. Innumerable boats were kept ready for battle in the river, and Pratap himself was within the fort with big cannon, a huge army, elephants, and a large number of infantry equipped for the war." Pratapaditya, after fleeing from Jessore where the Mughals raided, raised along with his son Udayaditya the fort of Salka in no time with natural barriers on three sides rendering it almost impregnable. He was all ready for war in 1611. In the battle of Salka, the Mughals initially won but in the end, victory favored Pratapaditya. It was a major victory and soon after he sent a letter to the Mughals asking them to recognize him as the ruler of Bengal.

Mughals saw a threat in Pratapaditya's rise to power. The Mughal ruler sent Abram Khan, the Nawab of Patna to attack Pratapaditya and subdue Jessore. A uniqueness in war strategies followed by Pratapaditya was the building of structures against an approaching enemy. During the Battle of Salka, he built a fort in another location far from Jessore Fort and planned his attack from the newly constructed site. Before the battle was to commence, Pratapaditya built a two-sided structure near the Mautala citadel in Jessore. As the battle began, Pratapaditya's army fiercely attacked the Mughal forces from two directions along with the newly constructed two-sided structure. The two-way attack left the Mughals petrified. There were many casualties from Abram's side. Pratapaditya emerged victorious and Abram Khan was taken prisoner.

Rajmahal, now a sub-divisional town, located by the Ganga in Jharkhand, was under the Mughals. Sher Khan was then the nawab of the city. After defeating the Mughals in Patna, Pratapaditya marched towards Rajmahal with a huge force. A fierce battle ensued between the Jessore forces and Mughals on the banks of the Ganga in Rajmahal. The Mughals were defeated and Sher Khan fled from the battlefield. It was after this victory that Pratapaditya assumed the title of 'Rajachakravarty Pratapaditya'.

The Jessore king, in another naval battle at medinipur, against Nawab Taj Khan and Isha Khan of Hijli, emerged victorious. Isha Khan was killed in the battle.

In 1603, Pratapaditya confronted in a battle a huge force sent by Mughal ruler Jahangir. Among the enemy forces were 22 Umrah generals and Man Singh. The enemy forces camped at Basantpur. The battle took place near this area close to the banks of the Kalindi River. In the battle, Pratapaditya who gained a competitive advantage with his naval force and war boats killed 12 of those generals. The rest of the generals fled from the battlefield. Torrential rains further weakened the Mughal forces and Man Singh escaped from the battlefield with the help of Bhava Nand Majumdar, who worked in the court of Pratapaditya.

It was in the Battle of Kagarghat in 1612 that Pratapaditya was defeated by the Mughals. The defeat was a result of treachery by Bhava Nand Majumdar. He helped the Mughals defeat his own king. Traitors, over time, had done greater damage to the motherland than enemies. To quote from *Hindu Castes and Sects* by Jogendra Nath Bhattacharya: "The great Pratapaditya, whose father had been the prime minister of the last Patan King of Bengal, and who at the time of the conquest of the province by the Moguls carved out an independent kingdom in its seaboard, was a Bangaja. For a time, Pratapaditya defied the great Akbar, and the conquest of his kingdom was ultimately effected by Raja Man Sing, chiefly through the treachery of Bhava Nand Majumdar, who had been in the service of Pratapaditya as a pet Brahman boy, and who subsequently became the founder of the Nadiya Raj family through the favour of the imperial general whom he had helped."

Many freedom fighters from Bengal later drew inspiration from Pratapaditya.

45

Kapilendra Deva

Defeated Sultans of Bengal, Jaunpur, Malwa, Bahmani Kingdom

Kapilendra Deva! He was the founder of the Routray dynasty, more popular as the Suryavamsha Gajapati Empire. He rose to power from a humble position, carving out an extensive empire with boundaries stretching beyond what the earlier kings ruled. He won several battles against Islamic invaders. He defeated Sultans of Bengal, Jaunpur, Malwa, and Gulbarga. He helped the Velamas of Andhra Pradesh regain their territories from Humayun Shah of the Bahmani Sultanate. He defeated Humayun Shah in Devarakonda and after that victory, Velamas became his vassal rulers. Kapilendra Deva had a robust army, including an advanced elephant battalion. He patronized art and literature. Sanskrit and Odia literature flourished under his reign. He built many temples. He was one of the greatest rulers of the Suryavamsha Gajapati Empire.

Orissa, also called Odra, was known as Kalinga and Utkal in ancient times. This kingdom finds mention in several ancient texts including the Mahabharata, *Vayu Purana, Mahagovinda Suttanta*, and more. There are archaeological evidences, especially Acheulian tools dating to the Lower Paleolithic era, suggesting pre-historic human settlement in this region. Asurgarh Fort excavations led to the discovery of an advanced civilization dating back 2,500 to 3,500 years. Various dynasties including Mauryas, Mahameghavahanas, Guptas, Pauravas, Somavamsis, Bhauma, Eastern Ganga, and Gajapatis ruled Odisha.

Kapilendra Deva was born to Bellama and Jageswara Routa. The Gopinathpur inscription of 1447 CE describes his birth thus: "By the order of the Lord of Nilagiri (blue hill) (who is) the lord of the three worlds (Jagannatha), there was born in the Odradesa a king named Kapilendra, the ornament of the solar race." Kapilendra Deva initially served in the Eastern Ganga army of Bhanu Deva IV, who ruled from 1424 to 1434. Bhanu Deva IV honored him with the title of Bhramaravara before he sent him to deal with Hushang Shah Gori, the Sultan of Malwa. Bhramaravara was a title conferred to warriors from the royal family, which suggests Kapilendra Deva was born in a royal family. Kapilendra Deva was also conferred the titles of Rauta, meaning a horseman, and Mahapatra, meaning an officer in the Ganga army. Bhanu Deva IV choosing Kapilendra Deva for negotiations with Hushang Shah Gori also suggests his rising to prominence in the Ganga army, especially to a higher post. Kapilendra Deva usurped the throne of Orissa when Bhanu Deva IV was engaged in a battle in the south in 1434. Though initially, feudatories of the Ganga dynasty including few officers of the earlier king refused to acknowledge his kingship, he ultimately handled the rebellions successfully.

The *Madala Panji*, a chronicle of the Jagannath Temple of Puri, starting from the 12th century, describes historical records of the kings of Orissa. This chronicle depicts the coronation of Kapilendra Deva as Gajapati of the kingdom succeeding Bhanu Deva IV. It mentions the coronation date as *2 kākara śukḷa 4 aṅka 2*, corresponding to 29th June 1435 of the Gregorian calendar.

Gajapati Kapilendra Deva worshipping Prabhu Jagannath at the Puri shrine.

According to accounts in *Oriya Mahabharata* by Sarala Das, a poet and a contemporary of Kapilendra Deva, the latter is described as the servant of the Lord Jagannath. Since the time of eastern Ganga king Ananga Bhima Deva III, who ruled from 1211 to 1238 CE, the kings of Orissa had regarded *Bhagwan* (God) Jagannath as the real king and themselves to be His servants. Ananga Bhima Deva III formally dedicated his kingdom to Jagannath and declared himself to be His deputy and first servant. Since then all subsequent kings continued that tradition. In the opening part of Sarala's *Mahabharata*, Kapilendra Deva is addressed as Maharaja Kapilesvara and represented as the first servant of Jagannath.

Kapilendra Deva inherited the military tradition of the Eastern Gangas. He furthered strengthened his military base for expanding his kingdom through conquests. He always kept a standing army ready to counter any possible war. He had a huge elephant force–200,000 war elephants, which was a competitive advantage when compared with other kingdoms. Sarala Das in his book *Oriya Mahabharata* has given a detailed description of the military divisions of Kapilendra Deva's army including weaponry and musical instruments used in warfare. The Gajapati military was divided into six divisions, viz., Hantakaru Dala, Aguani Thata, Pradhana Vala, Pachhiani Thata, Angavala, and Paridhana. Pradhana Vala was the main division and the Angavala comprised of specially deployed bodyguards. The Hantakaru Dala remained in the forefront of the marching army and the Aguani Thata marched ahead of the main army. Pachhiani Thata took the rear guard position in battles. Kapilendra Deva also had a special division for taking charge of conquered forts and areas. Paridhana comprised of this contingent of the army. Sarala Das has also described in his book Kapilendra Deva's breaking enemy's fort gates and walls using iron instruments, horses, and elephants.

During the time of Kapilendra Deva, Muslim rulers were powerful in several regions. He subjugated them all in battles and raised the Hindu flag high. Hindu saints persecuted in Muslim-dominated kingdoms found a safe haven in Orissa. To quote from *Sarala Dasa* by Krishna Chandra Panigrahi: "There can be hardly any doubt that Kapilendra was a great conqueror, even if we reject in the absence of any conclusive evidence, the statement of the Veligalam copper plates to the effect that Kapilendra successfully invaded Malwa and Delhi or that he proceeded as far as Hampe. The empire which he founded formed a bulwark against the Muslim kingdoms in northern India and the Deccan plateau. Orissa became the standard-bearer of Hindu culture, and scholars like Vasudeva Sarvabhauma and religious teachers like Chaitanya came to live there."

The Sultans of Jaunpur, Bengal, Malwa, and the Deccan had their eyes on the Gajapati kingdom. As soon as Kapilendra Deva ascended the throne of Orissa, the Jaunpur Sultanate and the Bengal Sultanate forces attacked one after another. The king entrusted one of his most trusted and bravest generals Gopinath Mahapatra for the task. The Gajapati forces emerged victorious in both battles. Later, Kapilendra Deva encountered the Sultan of Bengal once again. In the first battle against Bengal, Shamsuddin Ahmad Shah of the Ganesha dynasty was the Sultan, who ruled for three years till 1436, and in the second battle, Nasiruddin Mahmud Shah of the Ilyas Shahi dynasty was the Sultan.

Neighboring Muslim rulers feared Kapilendra, learning about the strength of his army and war elephants. By then, the Gajapati king had already subdued a few Sultans. Few Muslim chiefs, who raided Hindu kingdoms, taking captive innocent Hindus to sell them as slaves in Muslim kingdoms, dreaded Kapilendra and stopped their atrocities. To quote from *History of Orissa* by R.D. Banerji: "The *Burhan-i-Maa'sir* states that a chief named Sanjar Khan was engaged in the delightful pastime of raiding Hindu kingdoms and capturing noncombatants in order to sell them as slaves in Musalman kingdoms. Hearing this, the Bahmani Sultan Alauddin Ahmad Shah is stated to have said that it was dangerous to meddle with a man who possessed more than two hundred thousand war elephants, while he himself did not possess even two hundred. This is just the beginning of Kapilendra's activities outside Orissa proper when he started to increase the original limits of the kingdom of the Gangas to found an empire."

According to the Gopinathpur inscription, the Bengal Sultanate forces advanced towards Orissa. In the fierce battle that followed, the Gajapati army won. But Kapilendra did not stop. He along with his forces intruded into the territories of Gauda (Bengal) and annexed the region to the west of the river Ganga after defeating them. The Gajapati king also captured the Gar Mandaran Fort from Sultan Nasiruddin Mahmud Shah. Gopinath Mahapatra was again the general of the Oriya army. An inscription in the Jagannath temple of Puri dated 1450 CE describes the battle and mentions the Sultan as Malika Parisa, who was Nasiruddin Mahmud Shah. After that victory, Kapilendra Deva assumed the title of Gaudeswara.

In 1457, Kapilendra Deva attacked Mahmud Khalji, the Sultan of Malwa, and stamped his victory. He captured the fort of Mahur. The Veligalani plates and Chiruvrolu inscriptions describe the Gajapati expedition in Malwa. He also attacked the Bahmani Sultan of Gulbarga and captured the fort of Bidar.

In 1456 CE, Bahmani Sultan Humayun Shah sent a huge force under general Sikander Khan and raided the territories of the Velama chiefs of Andhra Pradesh (present Telangana). Bahmani Sultanate forces occupied Devarakonda, presently in the Nalgonda district. Finding no other way, the Velama chiefs sought the help of Kapilendra Deva. The Gajapati king marched towards Devarakonda with a huge force. A battle between Humayun Shah's forces and Kapilendra Deva's forces took place in Devarakonda. In that battle, Humayun Shah was severely defeated, there were many casualties from his side. The surviving army of Shah fled from the battlefield and the Gajapati forces pursued them for around 80 miles! After that failed expedition, the Bahmani Sultan never dared to attack Telangana or Orissa. The Velama chiefs recognized Kapilendra Deva's suzerainty and became vassal rulers of Telangana under the Gajapati Empire. The battle finds description in Muslim records and also in Sarala's *Oriya Mahabharata.*

To quote from *History of Orissa* by R.D. Banerji about Kapilendra's further conquests of the Sultanate territories: "In 1464-65, Kapilendra had succeeded in conquering the whole of the eastern coast of the Bay of Bengal as far as the South Arcot district. Except Kharavela no other king of Kalinga or Orissa had succeeded in ruling over such a wide stretch of the eastern coastland."

Kapilendra Deva was a Vaishnavite and a great patron of Vedic culture. He expanded the Jagannath temple and offered many donations of gold. His donation of gold ornaments to the deities finds description in inscriptions at the Jagannath temple on the left side of the Jaya Vijaya doorway. A scholar in Sanskrit, he wrote a play titled *Parshuram Bijaya* in this ancient language. He also patronized the Odissi dance and drama. Art and literature flourished under him. The Oriya language and literature including Sanskrit saw a solid base under his reign. Sarala Das, his contemporary, who also served in his army as described by himself in his accounts, laid the foundation of Oriya literature through his several works including Mahabharata, *Vilanka Ramayana*, and *Chandi Parana*. Kapilendra Deva built many temples. He looked after the welfare of his subjects. Orissa flourished during his reign.

Kapilendra Deva ruled until 1467 CE.

46

Role of Bishnupriya Manipuris in Early Phase of Freedom Struggle

Now an ethnic and linguistic minority and once a ruling class of Manipur, the Bishnupriya Manipuri community faced mass exodus from their home state during the latter part of the 18th century due to Burmese invasions and internal conflicts. They settled in parts of Assam, Tripura, and Bangladesh. They were also called 'Khumals' and 'Khalachais' or 'Kalisa'. Manipuris are divided into two sub-groups called the Bishnupriya and the Meitei. To quote from the book *The Background of Assamese Culture* by Raj Mohan Nath: "…the Khalachais were the first cultured race in possession of the Manipur Valley, and they were connected more with the neighbouring kingdom of Kamrupa than with other countries… It is also very likely that in very early rimes they were influenced by the Vishnu cult–either from Kamarupa or other parts of India and they named their capital town as Vishnupur." The term 'Bishnupriya' traces its roots to Vishnu, meaning 'devotees of Vishnu' and from their capital Bishnupur in Manipur. Bishnupriya Manipuris have been termed 'Mayangs' by G.A. Grierson, a linguist under the British Government in India. To quote from *Linguistic Survey of India*, Vol. V by G.A. Grierson: "Except for their language the Mayangs are indistinguishable from the general Manipuri population. All of them can speak Meithei. They are also known as Bishunpuriya Manipuris, or as Kalisa Manipuris..." Bishnupriya Manipuris played an instrumental role in India's struggle for freedom.

Bishnupriya Manipuris are the descendants of Pandava prince Arjuna and Manipuri princess Chitrangada. It was during his exile that Arjuna visited the north-east where he married Manipuri princess Chitrangada and Naga princess Uloopi. Apokpa is the *Kuldevta*, the ancestral tutelary deity, of the Bishnupriya Manipuris. He is the sixth generation from Babruvahana, the son of Arjuna and Chitrangada. This genealogy finds description in the *Khumal Purana*. There is temple for every 12-20 Bishnupriya Manipuri families in the village/ town. All religious and cultural festivities, right from Durga Puja, Jaggannath Puja to Shivratri, Janmasthami, etc., are celebrated with great zest in these temples with active participation from each and every member (of all ages) of the local community. One ritual worth mentioning here is *Kapokor Pali*. *Kapok* means 'puffed rice' and *pali* means 'festivity'. Puffed rice mixed in light jaggery is offered to Bhagwan Krishna at the local temple starting from *Lakshmi Poornima (Sharad Poornima)* for one month till the next Poornima. All residents of the village gather in the village temple to listen to the *Mahabharata* and the Bhagavad Gita. One who is well versed in the scriptures reads out verses from the *Gita* or *Mahabharata* and explains the same in the Bishnupriya Manipuri language. And this continues during the whole month every dusk for several hours. Before the reading of the sacred book commences, devotees sing *bhajans* and play drums invoking the deities. In the Bishnupriya Manipuri community, Rathyatra is called *Kaang*. It is celebrated for nine days in every home. On the first day and last day, the Rath of Jagannath (one of triads–Jagannath,

Balabhadra and Subhadra) is drawn by devotees as a ritual in the streets, the first being called *Kaang* and the last (9th day) *Fira Kaang*. On all nine days, Shri Jagannath is worshipped to the accompaniment of *bhajans*, especially on the Daashavatar of Bhagwan Vishnu, playing of dhol and other instruments after dusk at the local temple. All devotees encompassing the young and the old including children assemble in the temple and participate in the celebration with zest. This is followed by consumption of fruit *prasad* and *khichdi prasad*. A must-offer fruit for Shri Jagannath is the ripened jackfruit. Bishnupriya Manipuris have great reverence for their ancestors. Every mid-April, they offer *Laamor Baat*, an offering of food to the ancestors and departed souls, seeking their blessings. A variety of vegetarian delicacies are prepared, which are offered on a banana leaf in an open field, near a water body, or under a tree. They also offer homage to their ancestors in the morning of *Mahalaya* (the first day of Durga Puja that falls in October-November). It is done either at home in an open place where Ganga *jal* is offered with flowers to the accompaniment of chanting of mantras, lighting of *diyas*, and burning of incense. The *gotra* of the person is mentioned by the chanter (generally a *pujari*, a temple priest) and gradually the departed souls, dating back to generations, are invoked and their blessings sought. Raw rice, pulses, spices, vegetables, etc., which is termed *sidda* are offered in the local temple in the name of the ancestors. These are used in the preparation/ cooking of *bhog*, which are then offered to the deities of the temple. The *bhog* and the delicacies prepared are consumed as *prasad*. Bishnupriya Manipuris are one of the few communities where almost 99 per cent are still Hindus. Presently, the Bishnupriya Manipuris are facing an ethnic identity crisis.

The role of Bishnupriya Manipuris in the 1857 War of Independence finds description in letters by Captain M.G. Allen dated 4th Dec

1857, commander of Arakan Battalion dated 19th May 1857, superintendent of Sylhet dated 29th November 1857 and by collectors of Sylhet dated 22nd October and 24th November respectively–all addressed to their respective British authorities.

Ever since the British looted Indian treasury, freedom fighters across the country had tried to reclaim the same. For example, in 1824 when the British were transporting treasury from Jawalapur to Saharanpur, escorted by 200 British soldiers, freedom fighter Kalyan Singh Gurjar along with his men attacked them. They reclaimed the treasury and killed a number of British forces. There have been several such incidents reported, hence, the British were more than cautious in this regard. Manipuri sepoys stationed in Sylhet demanded the British officials to deliver half their treasury. Mr. Larkin, then collector of Sylhet and G.N. Dod, a contemporary writer, refused to give in to the demands. They got the Sylhet treasury shifted to Fort William in Calcutta. Meanwhile, the Sepoy Mutiny began on 10th May 1857 in Meerut. Indian sepoys stationed across several parts of the country started revolting. Nutan Singha, a sepoy left his post as a soldier, went to Cachar (Assam) and started motivating the Bishnupriya Manipuris to rise in revolt against the British. One of his associates was Pulor Singha. They maintained a close connection with the 33 BNI Company of Chittagong sepoys who revolted. They planned to march towards Manipur and attack British posts. The British came to know about the joint planned attack and learnt that many of them had assembled at Pratapgarh (now in Karimganj district of Assam). They arrested Pulor Singha at Sylhet. British forces marched towards Pratapgarh and a fierce fight ensued. It was the mid of December 1857. The commander of the British forces was killed in the encounter. The local Bishnupriya Manipuris of Pratapgarh attacked the British post and another fight ensued. This was followed by the arrest of around 50 Bishnupriya Manipuri freedom fighters including Gillou Singha, Paisananda Singha, Tulsidas Singha, Shyam Singha, Kailash Chandra Singha, Bhagabati Mishra, Tabina Singha to name a few. While few of them were banished, few were executed, and few imprisoned.

British forces led by Major Byang counter marched from Pratapgarh to Latu (now in Karimganj district of Assam) on the banks of the river Kushiara. The sepoys and freedom fighters started firing at the British soldiers from a stretch on Malegar hillock. An aggressive skirmish followed. It was the morning of 18th December 1857. Around 30 freedom fighters attained martyrdom in the Battle of Latu.

The British further checked the advances of the freedom fighters in Cachar. While 37 freedom fighters were killed in action, 39 were executed and two died of wounds. The total number of martyred soldiers was 110.

Many Zamindars from across India collected heavy taxes from the farmers on behalf of the British. The farmers of Bhanubil area (now part of Bangladesh) revolted against the tax collection from 1901. They were led by freedom fighter Panchanan Sarma, also called Panchanan Thakur. Amzad Ali Khan was then the Zamindar of Bhanubil. The Bishnupriya Manipuris of Tetoi Gaon, Ghuramara, and other villages in Bhanubil refused to pay taxes. 'Free tax, free land' was their firm slogan. Panchanan Sarma's associates were Raman Singha, Chauba Singha, Gobardhan Singha, Rupchand Singha, to name a few. Several freedom fighters were arrested by the British. Panchanan Sarma was imprisoned at Sylhet Jail and tortured for two years. Arrested amongst others were Rupchand Singha, Purnachan Sinha, Krishna Mani Sharma, Bijoy Sinha, Thongbabu Sinha, Kunjalata Sinha, Dhala Sinha, and Mohan Sinha. While Baikunthanath Sharma was imprisoned for five years, Khamtal Sinha, Raja Sinha, and Babu Chand Sinha faced six months imprisonment each. Houses of Bishnupriya Manipuris, who revolted, were trampled upon and broken using elephants. Many families were forced to leave their homes. Many farmers received notices wherein they were not allowed to sell their lands due to non-payment of land tax. Here is an example of one such notice sent by the British to farmer Dhala Sinha, quoted from the book *Bishnupriya Manipuris in Freedom and other Movements* by Braja Gopal Sinha:

"To

Dhala Sinha, Accused

Since case No, 80, Dtd 20.12.1930 in favour of appealant Md. Hyder Ali Khan, case No-47 V9. As you are unable to clear land Tax, you are not entitled to sale the Deed or Decree of immovable property. It is prohibited until further order."

The Bhanubil peasant agitation continued until 1937 after the Government of India Act was passed in 1935, which was implemented two years later. The imprisoned freedom fighters were released.

Participation of Bishnupriya Manipuris in freedom struggle continued until India gained independence.

47

Chhatrasal

Defeated Mughals in Many Battles; Reclaimed Bundelkhand

Maharaja Chhatrasal was the Bundela Raja of the Bundelkhand region and a contemporary of Chhatrapati Shivaji Maharaj. He led the first attack to victory with an army of five horsemen and 25 swordsmen in 1671 at the age of 22. Within a period of 10 years, he won many battles against the Mughals defeating many renowned Mughal generals and conquered the Mughal territories of Chitrakoot, Chhatarpur, Panna, Kalpi, Sagar, Garhakota, Shahgarh, Damoh, and more regions. Chhatrasal was immensely inspired by the feats of Chhatrapati Shivaji. He traveled to Maharashtra to meet Shivaji and sought his guidance. At the age of 79, he lost a battle against Nawab of Farrukhabad of UP, but with the help of Marathas, he defeated him and regained his territories. Bundelkhand prospered under his reign.

Bundelkhand, earlier known as Jejabhukti or Jejakabhukti, was a large kingdom with several principalities under several chiefs. Today, parts of this region are in Uttar Pradesh and Madhya Pradesh. There were several Bundela dynasties, who trace their ancestry to Suryavansha, i.e., the solar dynasty. According to an account by Kavi Gorelal, who wrote a biography of Chhatrasal in verse form, as described by Ravindra K. Jain in his book *Between History and Legend: Status and Power in Bundelkhand*, the first ancestor of the Bundelas was Brahma. One of their ancestors Kiratdeva was the seventh generation descendant of Vihagaraja, the son of Brahma. Kashi king Virabhadra traced his ancestry to Kiratdeva. Jagdas was one of the sons of Virabhadra. Denied a kingdom, he came to the shrine of Goddess Vindhyavasini at Vindhyachal, a northern offshoot of the Vindhya ranges, and worshipped Her. The Goddess, pleased with his *tapasya* (penance), blessed him that his son would be king. The son born to Jagdas was Bundela. Since then, Vindhyavasini was the Kuldevi, the family deity of the Bundelas.

Chhatrasal was born on 4th May 1649 to Rani Lal Kunwar and Raja Champat Rai at Kachar Kachnai in Tikamgarh in the Bundelkhand region of Madhya Pradesh. Champat Rai was the Bundela chief of Mahoba and a vassal ruler under the Raja of Orchha when Chhatrasal was born. Raja Rudra Pratap Singh, a Bundela chief of Orchha, was an ancestor of Chhatrasal.

Bundela kings bravely resisted Islamic invaders for several centuries. Mughal rulers Babur and Humayun failed to annex their kingdoms or turn them into vassal rulers. After the fall of Kalinjar, a Bundela principality, at the hands of Sher Shah Suri, strongholds of Bundelkhand in later years fell into the hands of Akbar. Since the time of Akbar, those strongholds became feudatories or vassal rulers under the Mughals and incorporated under the Mughal *subah* (province) of Allahabad. During the reign of Shah Jahan, the grandson of Akbar, Jujhar Singh, Bundela Raja of Orchha asserted his independence in 1626. That invited the wrath of the Mughals. Jujhar Singh successfully resisted their attacks. He further attacked another territory of the Mughals. Shah Jahan sent his son Aurangzeb along with a huge force to subjugate Orchha in 1635. Jujhar Singh lost the battle, he was driven out of his kingdom. What followed was the loot of wealth by the Mughals, destruction of temples and heritage sites, the enslavement of the royal women in the homes of Mughal nobles, and more atrocities. The Mughals forcibly converted the two sons of Jujhar Singh to Islam. The third refused to convert for which he was executed. Aurangzeb turned the royal palace of Orchha into a mosque. To quote from *Advanced Study in the History of Modern India 1707-1813* by Jaswant Lal Mehta: "Jujhar Singh's family and treasure of the estimated value of fifty lakhs of rupees, fell into the hands of the Mughals. Aurangzeb converted two of his sons to Islam by force, while the third one, who refused to obey him, was executed. The ladies of Jujhar Singh's family were enslaved and made to serve as menials in the houses of the Mughal nobles. The splendid royal temple of Orchha was destroyed and converted into a mosque. This was the first display of religious intolerance by Aurangzeb in his early youth. Unfortunately, his policy was endorsed by Shah Jahan to the great joy of the fanatical element, which had remained subdued since the days of Akbar the Great."

Raja Champat Rai of Mahoba, a vassal of the Orchha kingdom, refused to accept the suzerainty of the Mughals after the defeat of his Maharaja Jujhar Singh. Meanwhile, the Mughals brought more principalities of Bundelkhand under their realm. Raja Champat Rai successfully resisted the Mughals and maintained his independence for 26 years.

Chhatrasal grew up seeing his father bravely fight the Mughals. He learned the art of warfare from a very young age and soon became an expert in the use of weapons and fighting on the battlefield. He had a 'strong intellect and sturdy temperament'. No warrior in his kingdom could match him in the use of the 'match-lock, spear-sword, dagger, stiletto, battle-axe, bow and arrow, and other war like weapons'.

In 1661, when the Mughals could not subjugate Mahoba, they got Raja Champat Rai treacherously murdered. Chhatrasal was then aged 12 years. His brother Angad Rai, was younger than him. All the while, his father was his mentor and Guru. He was yet to learn the art of using weapons. Raja Champat Rai was a friend of Raja Jai Singh, the governor of the Deccan. Chhatrasal saw in Raja Jai Singh a fatherly figure. The young Chhatrasal joined the army of Raja Jai Singh to enhance his skills in the use of arms. Chhatrasal also became an expert in guerrilla warfare tactics.

Since his young age, Chhatrasal drew inspiration from Shivaji Maharaj, who by then had defeated the Sultanates of the Deccan and the Mughals, re-established Hindu supremacy in several regions, and defended Hindus and temples. Determined to seek guidance from Shivaji, Chhatrasal traveled all the way to Maharashtra to meet him. Chhatrasal expressed interest in joining Shivaji's army. An elated Shivaji, seeing in the young warrior's capacity to subdue the enemies, motivated him to liberate his ancestral lands. Shivaji said thus to Chhatrasal, as quoted from *Outline of the History of Charkhari State* by Mata Din Trivedi: "Illustrious Chief! Conquer and subdue your foes! Resume and rule your native land! Destroy the Emperor's army! Slay the Turks, and the Moghals, and trust not that deceitful race. And whenever they evince an intention of attacking you, I will distract their attention and subvert their plans by active cooperation. When they opposed us, Shree Maharanee Bhawani came to our aid: confiding in her favour and protection, I fear no Muslim power. Numerous were the nobles of that deceitful race by whom I was assailed, on whom I tried the temper of my blade and whom I slew. Return then to your native land, levy an army, expel the invaders, grasp the sword and Kanhaiyajee will protect you in the day of battle: for does not Chhatri faith consist in protecting the cow and the Brahmans, in guarding the *Vedas*, in showing skill and valour in battle? And if you lose your life, will you not through the solar orb enter the mansions of bliss, enjoying plenitude of happiness and repose? If victorious, you will repossess your country I immortalize your name..." With renewed energy and inspiration, Chhatrasal came back to Mahoba and was all geared up to attack the Mughals.

During that time, Fidai Khan Koka, also known as Muzaffar Hussain, master of ordnance at the court of Aurangzeb, released an imperial mandate for Orchha, following the advice of the Mughal ruler. According to the mandate, Hindu rituals and customs such as offering worship to the deity enshrined in Moortis, blowing of *shanka* (conch shells), ringing of bells, applying *tilak* on the forehead, and offerings to the ancestors were ordered to be suppressed. The mandate ordered the destruction of temples and the building of mosques in the temple premises. Further instructions were given that if the Hindus repaired the temples, the upper structures be demolished and minarets erected in their place. It also ordered the appointment of mullahs for offering prayers in loud voices and the appointment of qazis for the administration of justice. When Chhatrasal heard about the mandate, he attacked the Mughal territory and emerged victorious with an army of five horsemen and 25 swordsmen. He was then aged only 22 years in 1671! Chhatrasal was then coronated the Maharaja of Bundelkhand.

Chhatrasal maintained an army of around 20,000 soldiers. Within a period of 10 years, the Bundela king won many battles against the Mughals defeating many renowned Mughal generals including Rohilla Khan, Sadruddin, Mohammad Hashim Khan, Sheikh Anwar, Kaliq, Munawwar Khan, Sayyid Latif, Tahauwar Khan, Bahlol Khan, Abdus Ahmed, and more. He conquered the Mughal territories of Chitrakoot, Chhatarpur, Panna, Kalpi, Sagar, Garhakota, Shahgarh, Damoh, and more regions. In all of those battles, the Mughal soldiers always outnumbered his army. He re-established Hindu supremacy in the regions that belonged to his ancestors and which were taken by the Mughals.

Chhatrasal exploited his guerrilla warfare skills to defeat the enemies. For instance, Mughal general Mohammad Hashim Khan attacked the Bundela warrior with a large army. As per his guerrilla strategies, witnessing the huge force, Chhatrasal feigned retreat. Suddenly, divided into groups, Chhattrasal's forces attacked the enemies and inflicted upon them a crushing defeat. In another instance, Aurangzeb sent Tahauwar Khan with 30,000 men against Chhatrasal. A series of battles took place between the Mughal and Bundela forces. Every time, the Mughals lost. At last, the surviving Mughal soldiers fled. Chhatrasal then 'took Kalinjar and stormed Kalpi, extending his dominion including Kalpi in the north to Saugor in the south, and from Kalinjar on the east to Bhelsa on the west'. Chhatrasal was never defeated. He remained the undisputed ruler for 57 years.

At the age of 79, Maharaja Chhatrasal lost a battle against Muhammad Khan Bangash, the Nawab of Farrukhabad of UP. The Raja sought help from the Marathas in 1728. For some time, he did not receive any help as the Marathas were busy in battles in defending the Maratha region. Baji Rao was then the Peshwa. In 1729, Chhatrasal wrote a letter to Peshwa Baji Rao, again seeking help. Baji Rao immediately responded, personally leading the Maratha army towards Bundelkhand. The Peshwa not only helped Chhatrasal defeat Bangash but also helped him regain more territories from the Mughals. Chhatrasal declared Peshwa Baji Rao as his 'adopted son' and gave him few parts of his kingdom as gifts in return for his military support though the latter asked for nothing.

To quote from *Advanced Study in the History of Modern India 1707-1813:* "In his 'epic struggle' against the Mughals, Chhatrasal was 'greatly influenced' by the examples of Chhatrapati Shivaji, Balaji Vishwanath, and Baji Rao I. There is no denying the fact that 'the revolt which he engineered in Bundelkhand, and kept going for over forty years, greatly facilitated the rapid disintegration of the Mughal empire'?"

Maharaja Chhatrasal was not only a great soldier but also an able administrator. He was a patron of literature and the arts. He had numerous poets in his court. Chhatrasal became a disciple of Mahamati Prannathji of the Pranami Sampradaya, a Krishnaite community. The king met his Guru at Panna in 1683 on the way to a battle against the Mughals. Prannathji gave him his own sword and blessed him to be always victorious and remain a great emperor. Later, Chhatrasal often took the advice of his Guru on political, social, and economic matters.

Maharaja Chhatrasal ruled until 20th December 1731. He breathed his last at the age of 82. Before his death, he divided his kingdom amongst his three sons Harde Sah, Jagat Rai, Bharti Chand, and his adopted son Baji Rao.

Naman to the brave warrior! Jai Hind!!!

48

Bhoja Paramara

Resisted Attacks of Ghaznavid Forces in 11th Century

Raja Bhoja was one of the greatest and most illustrious kings of India from the Paramara (also called Parmar) dynasty of Malwa in the 11th century. He provided military support to Anandapala, the Hindu Shahi ruler of Lahore in the battle against Mahmud of Ghazni. He resisted the attacks of a few armies of Mahmud of Ghazni at the borders. Mahmud of Ghazni, during one of his Indian expeditions, hastily retreated from Gujarat and did not advance into the Indian territories further. It was because Raja Bhoja marched with a huge army to attack Mahmud and the latter fled through another route. Muslim invaders, during his rule, were kept at bay. Bhoja assumed many titles–Parama-Bhattaraka, Maharajadhiraja, Parameshvara, and Bhoja Deva, all evidenced by inscriptions; Bhojasvamindeva and Tribhuvan Narayanadeva inscribed in the Samadhishvara Temple at Chittor Fort; and Triloka Narayana mentioned in the book *Ganaratna Mahodadhi*. He was a patron of art, culture, and literature. A scholar and a poet, he authored 84 books in Sanskrit on topics ranging from astrology, hygiene, lexicography, horses, Dharma, Shaivism to astronomy, statecraft, Sanskrit grammar for poetic and rhetorical compositions, meditations, chemistry, and the list goes on. He constructed hundreds of temples including 104 temples in Dhara, his capital. The establishment of Bhoj Shala, a center for Sanskrit studies in Dhar, is attributed to him. He laid the foundation of Bhopal. Sheldon Pollock describes Raja Bhoja as 'the most celebrated poet-king and philosopher-king of his time, and perhaps of any Indian time'.

Bhoja Paramara was born to Rani Savitri and Raja Sindhuraja. There are no exact records on his birth date, but going by several related literary sources examined by Mahesh Singh in his book *Bhoja Paramara and His Times*, Bhoja may have been born sometime between 982 and 989 CE. Bhoja was highly educated since his childhood. According to the same source, the author quoting P.T. Srinivasa Iyengar's *Ija Raja* describes thus: "...like a ksatriya prince Bhoja underwent an extensive course of studies. He mastered Sastras on King's craft, achieved skill in the use of thirty-six weapons of warfare, and mastered the sixty-four arts. He became an accomplished poet and scholar who could hold his own in learned debates against the greatest scholars of his time." Bhoja was tutored under the guidance of learned scholars. He was well versed in all the branches of learning and was a scholar of Sanskrit.

Bhoja was the ninth ruler of the Paramara dynasty, ascending the throne of Malwa in 1010 CE. The Udaipur prasasti describes in detail the earlier Paramara kings with the first king being Krishnarajadeva, also known as Upendraraja. Prasastis, meaning 'in praise for', are special inscriptions in the form of poetry or ornate prose, usually composed by court poets. Land grants of Vakpati and Bhoja including Nagpur *prasasti* and the Sanskrit epic poem *Navasahasahkacarita* by Padmagupta (the court poet of Raja Sindhuraja, also known as Navasahasanka) contain some information about the genealogy of rulers of this dynasty. Paramaras trace their ancestry as Agnivanshis while few historians describe them to be descendants or vassal rulers of Rashtrakutas. Garuda, the *vahana* of Vishnu, figured on the flags of the Paramaras.

Malwa finds mention in several ancient Indian texts. Early Stone Age and lower Paleolithic artifacts have been found here. This kingdom is believed to have been founded by Muchukunda of the Ishvaku dynasty many thousands of years ago. Muchukunda protected the Devas from the onslaught by Asuras till the time Kartikeya undertook the role of commander of Devas. This region was earlier known as Mahishmati and Avanti. It was one of the 16 *mahajanapadas,* meaning kingdoms, during ancient times. Malwa draws its name from an ancient Indian tribe of Malavas of the Avanti kingdom. After the Ishvakus and before the Paramaras, various dynasties including Nandas, Mauryas, Kushanas, Shakas, Satavahanas, Guptas, Gurjar Pratiharas, and Rashtrakutas ruled this region.

The Paramara dynasty rose to an imperial rank during the time of Bhoja. Soon after his ascension to the throne, he started expanding his empire. His kingdom soon extended from Vidisha in the east to river Sabarmati in the west, from Chittor in the north to upper Konkan in the south.

During Bhoja's times, Mahmud of Ghazni plundered the north-western parts of the country, destroying temples, looting wealth, committing genocide of Hindus, and taking women as captives. Bhoja stopped his other expeditions and focused on securing the boundaries of his territories from Sultan Mahmud. He arrayed all his forces on the northern boundary of his kingdom, all ready to offer strong resistance against possible Muslim attacks.

Bhoja also provided military aid to Raja Anandapala, the Hindu Shahi ruler of Lahore, to resist Mahmud. Anandapala was also helped by other Hindu rulers from northern India, evidenced by Persian historian Firishta's account. The Hindu army against Mahmud's forces was almost winning when Anandapala's elephant turned berserk when pierced by an arrow and it fled from the battlefield. Anandapala was the commander and the king. His action, especially his elephant's action, confused the Hindu soldiers. Misunderstanding him to be fleeing from the battlefield, they retreated too, resulting in the Muslim forces pursuing and slaughtering many of them. Anandapala's kingdom was plundered and the Hindu Shahi prince Trilochanpala fled towards the north of India. According to *Bhoja Paramara and His Times,* Trilochanpala sought refuge in Bhoja's kingdom. To quote from this book: "It is possible that Trilochanapala, after his father's defeat, may have fled to the Malwa kingdom where Bhoja is said to have given him refuge. It may be said that the defeat of Anandapala was the defeat of the Hindus directly or indirectly. Giving shelter to the son of Anandapala amounted to Bhoja's direct challenge to the might of Mahmud."

According to the Udaipur prasasti, Bhoja emerged victorious against the Turuskas, generally meaning Muslim invaders. During his time, it was Sultan Mahmud of Ghazni, who was the Muslim invader, who attacked India. Verse 19 of this inscription records Bhoja's victory, though there is no detailed description of the battle. According to various historians, Raja Bhoja did resist attacks of the forces of Mahmud at the borders and checked them from entering into his kingdom but did not involve in the battle against the Mahmud directly. German Indologist Lorenz Franz Kielhorn, citing from Orissa annals, identifies Bhoja's repulsing of the invasion of Mahmud from Sindh. Mahesh Singh, further citing from the *Bhavishya Purana*, mentions in his book Bhoja's victory over the Arabs; he also describes the varying opinions of historians on this.

Sultan Mahmud of Ghazni attacked Somnath in the middle of January 1025 CE. The local ruler offered resistance but in vain. After

Raja Bhoja Paramara at a literary durbar, engaging with scholars at the temple of Saraswati at Sanskrit University of Dhara.

the expedition, Mahmud did not further advance towards the other kingdoms and left for his capital. Furthermore, he took another route, an inhospitable but safer one, to return to his kingdom. Historians including Muslim chroniclers have described the reason for this retreat. To quote from *Bhoja Paramara and His Times:* "After the fall of Somnath in the middle of January 1025, Mahmud did not stay for long in India. What was the reason for Mahmud's hasty retreat only a month and a half after the Somnath conquest? What caused Mahmud to leave so rich a country and to rush back through inhospitable Kachchha? In this connection, we may cite the statements of the later Muslim Chroniclers."

Kitab-Zain-ul-Akbar by 11th century Persian historian Gardizi has one of the earliest records about Mahmud of Ghazni. This book has the answer to Mamhud's hasty retreat from India. To quote from the same aforementioned reference: "… from that place Mahmud turned back, the reason being that Paramdeo, who was the king of the Hindus, was on the way, and Amir Mahmud feared lest this great victory might be spoiled. He did not come back by the direct way but took a guide and marching by the way of Mansura and the bank of the Sihun, went towards Multan." Paramdeo referred to by Gardizi in *Kitab-Zain-ul-Akbar* is the Paramara king Bhoja. This record suggests that Raja Bhoja advanced with a huge army towards Gujarat to attack Mahmud and when the Sultan heard about it, fearing defeat, he retreated to Multan through another road, as he feared Bhoja might check him on the way in the earlier route. Twelvth-13th century Arab historian Ali ibn al-Athir also gives the same reason in his accounts. *Tabaqat-i-Akbari* by 16th century historian Nizamuddin Ahmad, a contemporary of Akbar, further describes the same reason. This book describes how "Paramadeo stood ready with his formidable army to deal with Mahmud on his return' route. When Mahmud learned about this route, he changed his way and reached Multan via Sindh to avoid a battle. Nizamuddin refers to Bhoja as Paramadeo. Thus, it was owing to the terror of Bhoja that 'Mahmud beat a hasty retreat".

Raja Bhoja kept Muslim invaders at bay during his rule. He played an instrumental role in checking their advance into the Indian territories. Mahesh Singh writes thus: "From this, it appears that by A.D. 1025 Bhoja was an unchallenged master of a vast empire. Alberuni also writes that Bhoja was the ruler of Malwa. Bhoja had a regular standing army. He is said to have despatched troops to the Raja of Delhi for his war against Turks. Although on account of the retreat of Mahmud of Ghazni, Bhoja had no opportunity to cross swords with him, there is no doubt that he was sufficiently powerful to force the ruler of Ghazni to retreat. His contribution to the defence of north India from the onslaughts of Turks is unmatched and deserves notice."

Malwa flourished during the reign of Raja Bhoja. The Paramara king donated his wealth to those who sought it. To quote from *Bhoja Raja* by Iyengar: "Bhoja would go daily to the 'pavilion of distribution' and bestow gold on petitioners waiting at his gate and summoned one after another by his attendants." The king often moved around his kingdom along with a few of his subjects to familiarize himself with the state of affairs. He facilitated his courtiers to speak their minds freely without fear of royal displeasure. Raja Bhoja greatly patronized art and literature. He established a Sanskrit University at Dhara called the temple of Saraswati where scholars from across the country gathered, engaged in discourses, and imparted knowledge. He interacted with scholars regularly and held literary *darbars* (discussions). Bhoja wrote around 84 books in Sanskrit.

Muslim monuments exist at the site where the temple of Saraswati once flourished. Islamic invaders built mosques and tombs at hundreds of Hindu temple sites. To quote from Iyengar's *Raja Bhoja:* "There are two Sanskrit grammatical inscriptions in the Nagari characters, on two stone pillars in the mosque near the tomb of Moulana Kamaluddin at Dhar. The mosque is still popularly called Bhoja Raja Ki Nisai or Raja Bhoja's College. This corroborates the fact that the mosque was built on the site of Raja Bhoja's College, held in a spacious and splendid temple of Sarasvati, the Goddess of Learning and Arts, discovered in the same mosque in 1902. There is ample evidence to show that the mosque was built not only with the materials of the temple but on the very site of it. The existence of numerous mutilated large Nagari inscriptions on the pavement and of a part of the plinth of the original temple with a *Go-Mukha*on the north-east corner proves the fact beyond doubt. Moreover, the image itself of Sarasvati (Goddess of Learning) recording its installation in the temple by Raja Bhoja himself in Samvat 1091 (A. D. 1035) exists in the British museum."

Temples dedicated to Vishnu, Shiva, and Surya in particular and other deities, in general, were built under the patronage of Raja Bhoja. The Paramara king built 104 temples in his capital Dhara alone and more temples across his kingdom. Most of those temples were later vandalized and destroyed by Islamic invaders over a period of several centuries. Bhoja also granted land to Brahmanas who came from other kingdoms and settled in Malwa. A copperplate grant of 1022 CE of Bhoja describes a land grant–the village of Viranaka by the Paramara king to Dhanapati Bhatta who migrated to Malwa from another kingdom.

To quote from *Bhoja Raja:* "Bhoja left such deep imprints on the sands of time that he became the one great Indian Emperor remembered by prince and peasant alike even up to day."

49

Birsa Munda

Spearheaded Revolt against British in Tribal Regions; Martyred at 24

During a short period of a few years, Birsa Munda spearheaded the Indian freedom struggle movement in the tribal regions of the then Bengal Presidency (that spread to today's regions of Bengal, Bihar, Odisha, Madhya Pradesh, and Jharkhand). He led an armed struggle against the British, attacking British posts and involving them in guerrilla fights. He played an instrumental role in preventing Christian missionary activities in his region. He converted during childhood while studying in a German mission school, but reconverted to the Sanatana faith and motivated many other tribals for *ghar wapsi* (return home or return to roots). He revived the traditional tribal culture and advised his followers to pursue the original traditional religious system. Missionaries raised their voice against him. He was also known as Birsa Bhagwan. Birsa Munda attained martyrdom at the age of 24.

Birsa Munda was born to Karmi Munda and Sugana Munda on 15th November 1875 at Ulihatu village in Lohardaga, then under the Bengal presidency and presently Jharkhand. He belonged to the Munda community, today comprising one of India's largest scheduled tribes. This community speaks Mundari with 30 out of 514 scheduled tribes speaking this language. Munda is a Sanskrit term, meaning 'headman'.

Birsa's father Sugana Munda was a farm laborer. The family was very poor when Birsa was born. Soon after his birth, the family migrated to Chalkhed owing to a dispute with the farmland owner. Birsa was highly talented since his childhood. As he grew up, he helped his parents in additional chores like taking the goats and sheep for grazing. He was an expert in playing the flute. Some thousands of years ago, Krishna played the flute while doing his pastime job as a cowherd–people, young and old, men and women, animals and birds gathered around Him to listen to His enchanting *bansuri* notes. Likewise, when people listened to Birsa's flute notes, they gathered around him and submerged themselves in the sea of ecstasy. To quote about Birsa's childhood from the book *Birsa Munda* by Neeraj: "Like the other Munda children, he would also play with soil and sand. As he grew up, his body began to build strong and well-shaped. When Birsa grew older, he began to take the herds of sheep and goats to the jungle for grazing, like his friends did. In the jungle, Birsa would play flute. Soon he became so proficient in playing flute that people would come to gather around him to listen to the sweet, melodious tune of his flute."

Due to poverty, Birsa was sent to his maternal uncle's house at Ayumavatu village where after two years he was enrolled in a school run by Jaipal Naag. Noticing Birsa's talent, Naag suggested that he get enrolled at the German Mission School. But the German school took only Christians. Birsa and his family members were converted to Christianity at Chaibasa and Birsa Munda was christened as Birsa David in 1886. He was then 11 years old. Little did Birsa know what conversion to another religion meant! He studied in this school for four years. Once, the father of the missionary school was narrating to the students about the Kingdom of Heaven. Birsa, who had been witness to poverty, exploitation of the tribals by both the landlords and the British, asked the father where the 'Kingdom of Heaven' was located. He gave a reason that all he could see around him was no Heaven but exploitation of the poor by the rich and the foreigners. The father was left speechless at the wisdom of the young Birsa, then a teenager.

During that time, freedom struggle activities were gaining ground and the racket of conversion of the tribal Hindus to Christianity being gradually exposed. Sugana Munda, a participant of the Sardari movement, came to Chaibasa and withdrew his son Birsa from the German Mission School in 1890. Birsa studied in that school for four years. Sugana Munda reconverted to his original Sanatana faith along with his family and started following the age-old tribal traditional religious practices. Birsa David again became Birsa Munda at the age of 15. He remained a Christian for only four years. Birsa migrated to Banagan village.

Farmers across India had been living a comfortable life and earned revenue from their crop yields. The British started looting them in the name of taxes that soon resulted in the farmers' impoverishment. Besides, the British also appropriated the land rights of many. It was the same condition in the tribal regions where the Munda community that Birsa Munda belonged to lived. Soon many tribal farmers not only became poor but also lost their land rights. Besides, many farmers, who once had their own farmlands, became farm laborers as a result of British oppression. The British imposed taxes even for the grazing of animals in forests. The young Birsa Munda had been witness to the British oppression as he migrated from one place to another. He was witness to how the British exploited the tribals and how many zamindars (landlords), subservient to the British, further exploited them. During Birsa's time, the tribal agrarian system was almost transformed into a feudal system by the British, and his community people exploited to the zenith.

The Sardari movement had gained momentum by then in the Chhotanagpur region. Birsa's father actively participated in the revolt against the British and the zamindars loyal to the British. Sardar here meant a 'leader' and the movement was directed towards restoring Adivasi land rights–there were several leaders. To quote from JSTOR journal article *'The Sardari Larai of the Mundas of Chhotanagpur'* by Piyush Kamal Sinha about this movement: "The basic philosophy of the Sardar movement was that the adivasis were the first people to clear the lands of Chhotanagpur and as such, they had an inalienable right to free access to Chhotanagpur's land. However, with the emergence of the Raja and later, Maharaja of Chhotanagpur, the adivasis were expected to make voluntary payment of 'subscriptions' to the central authority. The adivasis rejected this principle since it was alien to their society." Birsa Munda was still studying in the German missionary school when in 1889, the Mundas and another tribe called Oraons seized land from the zamindars. To further quote from the above reference by Piyush Kamal Sinha: "Groups of Mundas and Oraons seized land and resisted the efforts of landlords and the police to remove them, sometimes passive but at other times the adivasis assaulted the police or landlords' agents. Sometimes the protestors proceeded to distribute the land among themselves. In 1889, some adivasis even seized the crops of those who were not joining in the movement. Another form of direct action was their refusal to pay unfair rent increases." It was after this that Sugana Munda removed his son Birsa from the missionary school and reconverted to the original faith. Birsa Munda, seeing his family's participation in the Sardari movement, was greatly inspired. He joined this movement in the Porhat area.

Birsa Munda decided to actively participate for the cause of the tribals. He led a series of revolts against the British. Many tribals joined him. He became their leader. Birsa Munda, an expert in archery and other guerrilla warfare techniques, not only trained himself further but also his group of hundreds and thousands of freedom fighters. He formed a guerrilla army. He motivated hundreds of farmers to revolt against the British policies and fight for their land rights. Under his leadership, many farmers stopped paying taxes to the British.

Meanwhile, Birsa Munda realized that the upliftment of his community could happen only through a collective effort. He was against the activities of the missionaries converting the tribals to Christianity. He was aged only 20 when he led a movement against the church and the missionaries. To reconvert his community members and bring them back into the ancient religious fold followed by the community for centuries, he started propagating a religion that had two main aspects–worshipping of *Singbonga*, meaning 'Sun God' as the Almighty, and giving up of 'Haria', an intoxicating drink made of rice. Birsa had grown up seeing how the 'Haria' drink negatively affected the tribal communities. Birsa also started healing people. Soon the young Munda man, aged less than 20, emerged as a leader and an incarnation of God. The Mundas and other tribes saw in him 'a savior'. He came to be known as 'Dharti Aba' and 'Bhagwan'. Many tribals, who converted to Christianity, reconverted and started following the religion being propagated by Birsa. The Christian missionaries rampant in the region saw in him a threat. He became an enemy of both the British and the missionaries. He was imprisoned. But after his release from jail, he emerged as a greater leader.

Birsa Munda prevented cow-slaughter in his region and raised his voice against it. He raised a voice against the conversion of tribals by the Christian missionaries and saved many from falling into the conversion trap. He said that Munda Raj had begun and that the rule of Queen Victoria was over.

To quote from *This is Our Homeland:* "The Kherwar uprising and the Birsa Munda movement were the most important of the late-18th century struggles against British rule and their local agents. The long struggle led by Birsa Munda was directed at British policies that allowed the zamindars (landowners) and money-lenders Iharshly exploit the adivasiffecte collective aspiration of adivasi communities to protect their resources and cultural practices was strongly reflected in the Santhal Hul and became the inspiration of Ulgulan–the famous Munda rebellion in Jharkhand under the leadership of Birsa Munda."

The British fired to death hundreds of tribal freedom fighters besides also imprisoning many. But they were unable to catch Birsa Munda. The British announced a reward for those who would provide information about his whereabouts but in vain. For two years, Birsa Munda remained in hiding then but during that period he spearheaded his groups to continue their guerrilla attacks on the British. During his hiding, he also visited the Jagannath shrine of Puri.

The British ultimately caught Birsa Munda from Jamkopai forest in Chakradharpur in March 1900 and sent him for trial. He breathed his last in Ranchi jail during the trial after three months on 9th June 1900 at the age of 24.

At a young age, Birsa Munda left an indelible imprint in the minds of the tribals, inspiring later freedom fighters and battlers against Christian missionaries. Vande Mataram!

50

Rash Behari Bose

Founded INA in Foreign Lands for the Freedom of India

He was involved in the attempt to assassinate Lord Hardinge, then British Viceroy of India, in December 1912. He took a lead role in the Ghadar Rebellion that involved Indians settled abroad to rise in armed conflict against the British. In 1915, he fled to Japan in the name of Priyanath Tagore where for three years he stayed in oblivion, changing identities and residences to avoid arrest by the British. On 1st September 1942, he formed the Indian National Army (INA) as the military wing of his organization called the Indian Independence League for the freedom of India. He ideated it in March end of 1942 in Tokyo with the support of the Indian prisoners of war in Japan. He handed over his leadership of INA to Netaji Subhash Chandra Bose, who further reorganized and expanded it. INA led several battles against the British and ultimately forced the British to leave India. He was Rash Behari Bose.

Rash Behari Bose, also known as Rasu, was born to Bhubaneswari Debi and Benode Behari Bose on 25th May 1886 at Subaldaha village of Purba Bardhaman in Bengal. He studied in the local village *pathsala* (school) and then completed his college education at Dupleix College and Morton School. He was guided by his grandfather Kalicharan Bose during his school days. In his village, he learned the art of fighting with sticks. Right from his childhood, Rash Behari Bose heard a lot about freedom fighters and oppression by the British. His school teacher Bakkeswar and Charu Chandra Roy, the principal of Dupleix College, further motivated him to fight for the freedom of the motherland. He completed his higher education in France and Germany, earning degrees in Medical Sciences and Engineering.

During the last decades of the 19th century, after the Revolt of 1857, several organizations were formed in Bengal and the members resorted to armed conflict against the British for the independence of India. By the beginning of the 20th century, Bengal saw the mushrooming of three secret organizations, committed to overthrowing the British. These were the Anushilan Samiti, Yugantar, and Bengal Volunteers.

Anushilan Samiti connected local youth groups and *akharas* (gyms). Rash Behari Bose became a member of Anushilan Samiti. Amongst the leaders of the secret group were Aurobindo Ghosh and his brother Barin Ghosh. Since 1906, Barin and his group members had been experimenting with the production of explosives, and their cause was further supported by Ullaskar Dutt, a self-taught chemist and an expert in bomb-making. Their secret base was the Muraripukur garden house owned by Barin Ghosh in the Manicktolla suburbs of Calcutta. Thereafter, with the bombs they created, Anushilan Samiti targeted to kill Andrew Henderson Leith Fraser, the Lieutenant Governor of Bengal. They made several attempts, and though they were successful in the 4th attempt in December 1907, Fraser escaped unhurt. Security operations tightened in Bengal thereafter. In January

1908, during the testing of a more powerful bomb, an accidental explosion led to the death of freedom fighter Prafulla Kumar Chakraborty. That further alerted the British. In March 1908, Anushilan Samiti members targeted to assassinate Douglas Kingsford, the Chief Magistrate of the Presidency Court of Alipore; he was notorious for torturing freedom fighters and inflicting them with rigorous punishment. The next attempt was made by Prafulla Chaki and Khudiram Bose, both members of Anushilan Samiti, but instead of Douglas, his wife and daughter succumbed to the bomb injuries. Meanwhile, an insider of the Samiti, especially an infiltrator, gave some info about the course of events to the British. This led to the arrest of several leaders and members of Anushilan Samiti. They were tried in court, which came to be known as the Alipore bomb case trials. It was a series of trials against Anushilan Samiti members at Alipore for 'waging war against the Government'. The trials continued until 1909. The British looked for all the suspects including Rash Behari Bose. To avoid arrest, Rash Behari Bose shifted base in 1908 from Bengal to Dehradun, where he worked as a head clerk at the Forest Research Institute.

From Dehradun, Rash Behari Bose stayed secretly connected with his fellow freedom fighters in Bengal. He also connected with more freedom fighters in present Uttar Pradesh and Punjab. In 1912, he masterminded the assassination of Charles Hardinge, the Viceroy and Governor-General of British India, in Delhi. While Hardinge was in a ceremonial procession transferring the capital from Calcutta to New Delhi, freedom fighter Basanta Kumar Biswas, disguised as a woman, attacked him with a bomb near Red Fort. Rash Behari Bose was in Delhi during the attack. He immediately took a train and returned to Dehradun and joined office the next day and feigned condemning the attack. Thus he avoided arrest. Basanta Kumar Biswas was arrested and tortured by the British; he did not provide any information about Bose and other fellow freedom fighters. He was hanged on 11th May 1915 at Ambala Central Jail in Punjab. He was then aged 20 years.

In 1913, Rash Behari Bose played an instrumental role in organizing the Ghadar forces in India for war against the British. It was on 12th April 1913 that the Indian workers in the Pacific Coast, including Canada and the USA, that majorly comprised of Sikhs formed a group called the Ghadar Party. Sohan Singh Bhakna was the key founder. Another founding member was Har Dayal. The objective behind its establishment was to secure India's independence from British rule. Its headquarters was in San Francisco. Ghadar Party soon gained support from Indian expatriates from foreign lands worldwide. After World War I, Ghadar Party came to India to start the rebellion against the British on Indian soil where Rash Behari Bose took a leadership role. They started organizing uprisings in Punjab in 1915, challenging the supremacy of the British. More freedom fighters from across the country joined the Ghadar Party to give shape to the movement in a big way. Meanwhile, World War I had started and Rash Behari Bose including other Ghadar leaders entrusted hundreds of Ghadar members to infiltrate into the army to further enhance their plans. On 25th January 1915, at a meeting in Amritsar by Ghadar, members which also included Rash Behari Bose and Kartar Singh Sarabha, 21st February 1915 was chosen for attacking the British with arms. It was because of a traitor within the Ghadar Party that the British came to know beforehand about the war plans. Accordingly, the British arrested many freedom fighters and foiled their attempt. To avoid arrest, Rash Behari Bose, then aged 29, fled to Japan in the name of Priyanath Tagore where, for three years, he stayed in oblivion, changing identities and residences, as there were British spies everywhere. Various Pan-Asian groups, that promoted the political and economic unity and cooperation of Asian peoples, gave him shelter. Besides, the British, who were suspicious of Bose's presence in Japan, kept pressing the Japanese Government for his extradition.

Rash Behari Bose also found refuge at Shinjuku City in Tokyo at the house of noted Pan-Asian supporter Aizo Soma, the son of a Samurai and Kokko Soma, who were owners of Nakamuraya bakery in the same city. He met Toshiko Soma, their daughter. People around looked at him with suspicion for staying with the Soma family. Moreover, British spies were only looking for Bose to assassinate him. It was then that Toyama Mitsuru, a Japanese ultranationalist and a strong advocate of Pan-Asianism, proposed the marriage of Rash Behari Bose with Toshiko Soma. Toyama Mitsuru was the founder of Black Ocean Society, a secret ultranationalist group, and Black Dragon Society, a prominent paramilitary ultranationalist group, both based in Japan. To quote from *The Two Great Indians in Japan* by J.G. Ohsawa about how Toyama helped Bose: "The British Embassy mobilized a private detective group and offered a prize for Bose's capture. But Mr. Toyama always managed to outwit the people of the BritiIEmbassy and the detective group... Bose might have been assassinated any moment. Soma thought one must be always with him as the pursuit of the British Embassy became pressing day by day. Mr. Toyama could not solve this problem. He called Mr. Soma one day and asked him to give his daughter Tosiko, then 20 yearI old, in marriage to the poor young Indian–who was always under threat of brutal attack."

Initially, the Soma family was apprehensive about the marriage but later they agreed. Toshiko Soma took three weeks to take a decision and ultimately gave her consent. Rash Behari Bose married Toshiko Soma in July 1918. He became a Japanese citizen in 1923. He started working as a journalist and writer. He also introduced the Indian style of curry in Japan. Rash Behari Bose taught his wife Toshiko Soma how to wear a saree and taught her the Bengali language. They were blessed with a son Masahide Bose and a daughter Tetsuko. Toshiko's health started declining and she breathed her last on 4th March 1925 at the age of 28. After her death, Bose never remarried.

Meanwhile, Rash Behari Bose teamed up with Aiyappan Pillai Madhavan Nair, an Indian engineer who quit his job to join India's freedom struggle. Together they persuaded Japanese authorities to stand for the cause of India and officially provide support for India's independence. Bose established the Indian Independence League that traces its early formation in the 1920s by Indian nationalists including Bose. The key purpose of the organization was to work towards the removal of British colonial rule from India. For gaining support, he convened two conferences, the first from 28th to 30th March 1942 in Tokyo and the second on 22nd June 1942 in Bangkok. In the second conference, Rash Behari Bose proposed the name of Subhash Chandra Bose as the leader of the organization and persuaded Japanese authorities to recognize him and support him. On 1st September in 1942, Rash Behari Bose formed the Indian National Army (INA) as the military wing of the Indian Independence League. He ideated it in March end of 1942 in Tokyo with the support of the Indian prisoners of war in Japan. Anand Mohan Sahay and military officer Mohan Singh were the key people who helped him form it. Netaji Bose kept up Rash Behari Bose's words. He joined as the president and further expanded the INA as Azad Hind Fauz. Netaji Bose established the Azad Hind Govt on 21st October 1943 in Singapore, which was recognized by 11 countries.

To quote from *The Indian National Army: Second Front of the Indian Independence Movement* by K.K. Ghosh: "The prominent Indian who took initiative in organizing the Indians in East Asia for India's independence after the outbreak olhe Pacific War was Rash

Behari Bose... In his political ideas, he was a Iiever in the complete freedom of India... Rash Behari Bose, like other revolutionaries, believed in violent methods in the achievement of India's freedom. In India, he 'devoted his efforts to fomenting revolt amongle Indian troops which served the British'... During his stay in Japan, Rash Behari Bose's efforts 'consisted… of acquainting the people of Japan with the Indian problems'. He also strongly believed in mobilizing Japanese help for India's freedom in case of a war between Japan and BrIin–an event which appeared to him inevitable... Rash Behari Bose contacted the Japanese high military authorities to secure their help for organizing a movement in East Asia for India's freedom. He tried to impress it on them that without the elimination of the British power from India, Japan's Co-Prosperity Sphere could not be free from danger. His efforts seemed to have succeeded in persuading the Japanese Government about the desirability of adopting a non-hostile attitude towards the Indian communities in the occupied countries and helping their nationalist activities. The sympathetic attitude of the Japanese Government was evident."

After the alliance with Japan, the Azad Hind Fauz won several battles in Burma and the north-east. The Azad Hind Fauz hoisted the National Flag in the Andamans and Manipur. After Japan surrendered on 15th August 1945, Azad Hind Fauz's support of Japan ended. By then 26,000 Azad Hind Fauz soldiers died in action for the freedom of India. Japan saw no other option than to surrender, as the nuclear bombing of Nagasaki and Hiroshima by the US on 6th and 9th August had already paralyzed the island country, and not surrendering would have led to further bombings, which could have had a devastating effect. With Japan's withdrawal, its support to the Azad Hind Fauz ended. Many INA soldiers were taken as prisoners of war.

Later after the British tried INA soldiers in Red Fort (famous as INA trials), Indian soldiers in the Army, and Navy revolted in large numbers, which ultimately forced the British to leave India. There are several documentary evidence that prove INA trials that triggered another 1857 type revolt that led to India's freedom. Clement Attlee, who was the British Prime Minister from 1945 to 1951, had said Gandhi's role in the Indian freedom struggle was minimal.

Had Rash Behari Bose not given shape to the INA, India might not have achieved independence in 1947!

Rash Behari Bose breathed his last on 21st January 1945 at the age of 58.

Naman to the brave warrior! Vande Mataram!!!

51

U. Kiang Nangbah

Organized Military-Style Attacks on the British in 1861-62

Almost the whole of India, except Meghalaya, must have never heard about U. Kiang Nangbah. Like thousands and lakhs of freedom fighters, his name is in oblivion in national history textbooks. U. Kiang Nangbah, a Khasi, led the third Jaintia Rebellion against the British. With an army of 200 men, he laid siege to the British military post at Jowai in Meghalaya, storming the post. He mobilized a huge force, comprising of village men numbering over 50,000, and made preparations for war against the British. He organized military-style attacks on the British. For nearly a year, Nangbah and other Khasi leaders created havoc on the British, defeating them at several places. The Khasis stopped paying taxes. The British deputed a larger force in the Jaintia Hills. Nangbah was taken prisoner through treachery with the help of two traitors on 27th December 1862. He was publicly hanged by the British, three days later, at Jowai on 30th December 1862.

U. Kiang Nangbah was born to Ka Rimai Nangbah at Tpep Pale in Jowai in the West Jaintia Hills of Meghalaya. He belonged to the Pnar Khasi, also known as the Jaintia community, a sub-tribe of the

Khasis, an indigenous ethnic group from Meghalaya and other parts of the north-east. Pnar Khasis majorly inhabit the Jaintia Hills. The Khasis have been granted the status of Scheduled Tribe under the Constitution of India. This community follows the matrilineal system of descent and inheritance. They are believed to be the largest surviving matrilineal culture in the world at present according to a report by T. Laird published by ICIMOD (International Centre for Integrated Mountain Development). Women play a dominant role in the Khasi society with the youngest daughter in a family inheriting all ancestral property. The birth of a girl is always celebrated. The Khasis find mention in several ancient texts. Raja Lalityaditya Muktapida of Kashmir during his military expedition to the north-east around the eighth century CE, came across a *Stri-Rajya*, meaning the kingdom of females, also known as Pramilar Desh ruled by a woman. This *Stri-Rajya* mentioned in ancient historical records is the stretch inhabited by the Khasi tribe.

Not much information is available about when U. Kiang Nangbah was born and about his childhood. The Jaintia Hills was annexed by the British in 1835. U. Kiang Nangbah was then a child. He was a farmer when he joined the freedom struggle movement. He was an expert piper and with the tunes of his pipe, he motivated the youth of Jaintia Hills to fight for the freedom of the motherland. U. Kiang Nangbah was of 'ordinary feature and of average physique'.

The British established their supremacy in parts of the north-east after the Treaty of Yandaboo was signed in 1826 with Burma. It was a peace treaty that led to the end of the First Anglo-Burmese War. The war that continued for two years led to the death of 15,000 European and Indian soldiers. As per the treaty, the British would occupy Assam, Manipur, Rakhine (Arakan), and the Taninthayi (Tenasserim) coast south of the Salween River besides supremacy in Cachar and the

Jaintia Hills. After the treaty was signed, the British planted tea gardens in most of these places and stationed British planters and forces. The road leading from the Brahmaputra valley to Cachar and other regions of the Barak valley was hilly, treacherous, and daunting. There were no direct roads that connected the two valleys. Before the treaty of Yandaboo was signed, the British had already established their supremacy in the Barak valley. After the treaty was signed, the British found it difficult and time-consuming to maintain a communication link between the two valleys. The British wanted to establish a strategic road to link the two valleys, from Guwahati to Sylhet. That would mean it should be constructed via the Khasi hills for the road to be short and less time-consuming. Passage through the Khasi hills would save the British several weeks of time. The British gave a proposal to U. Tirot Sing, the Raja of Nongkhlaw, a principality in the Khasi Hills. Sing accepted the proposal, as good roads would also benefit the local tribe. But when the British stationed forces along with the laborers, he smelt something fishy. It was then that Tirot Sing declared war against the British. The war continued from 1829 to 1833 until a traitor helped the British arrest Sing. At Dhaka Jail, Sing breathed his last in 1835. U. Kiang Nangbah was a child when Sing attained martyrdom. The Jaintias opposed the building of roads by the British. Besides, the British imposed taxes on the population. Wherever there was opposition, the colonial power responded by burning the respective villages, destroying crops, and arresting the freedom fighters. U. Kiang Nangbah grew up witnessing this oppression by the British.

The young Pnar Khasi freedom fighter visited from place to place across Jaintia Hills and spread awareness about the cruel policies of the British, and how foreign occupation had curtailed their freedom. He motivated people of all age groups wherever he went. By 1860, Nangbah organized a secret force to revolt against the British. As he believed in armed conflict against the British, his brother called him a fanatic.

After the annexation of Jaintia Hills, the power of the then Raja ceased and the British entrusted the existing traditional chiefs, i.e., heads of local units, called Dalois, to assist in the administration and other internal affairs of the Hills. There were seven Dalois in the post-medieval period. Later, the number increased to 12 and then 20 along with two Sirdars. Meanwhile, after two Jaintia Rebellions, the British confiscated homemade weapons of the Pnar Khasis. British forces remained alert against any possible uprising. The British curbing the age-old power of the Daloi to three years instead of a lifetime created resentment among the people. Furthermore, before 1860, John Bird Shadwell, British Assistant Commissioner of the Khasi and Jaintia Hills convoked a meeting of the Dalois and laid instructions for collecting taxes and enumeration of a census. But the meeting turned ineffective as the Dalois, though representatives of the British, were against the collection of taxes from the local population. But to continue holding their posts, the Dalois had to follow the orders of the British.

U. Manick was the Daloi of Jowai during this time. He held a *durbar* (meeting) where delegates from all over the Jaintia Hills attended. They discussed the taxation schemes enforced by the British and on census enumeration. U. Kiang Nangbah denounced the policy of the British and declared that the people of Jaintia Hills would not pay any tax to the foreign power. He further openly declared about organizing an armed rebellion to drive the British away from the motherland.

According to the Pnar Khasi tradition, going to war was ascertained through some divine happenings including examining omens. For gaining the support of the Khasis for war against the British, U. Kiang

Nangbah tried to prove that he was an enlightened son of Heaven. To quote from *The History and Culture of the Khasi People* by Hamlet Bareh: "A tradition narrates that he claimed himself an enlightened son of the heaven and a prophet of the new age. The Khasis of old never went to war without having clearly ascertained whether the battle was worth fitting through a system of divination. Durbars were held at Madan Sintu Ksiar in Jowai's suburbs where omens were examined by people with results which supported his claims. The same tradition tells that he hailed from Jowai and came off the respectable priestly house whose paternal ancestry was from Nongbah. U. Kiang Nongbah was a sweet piper and with the tunes of his pipe, he incited and roused the hearts of patriots."

During a dancing festival, a sacred practice of the Khasis, which involved the use of weapons, especially shields and swords, the British police interfered. Hundreds of Khasis had gathered to witness the dance and to be part of the festival on 28th December 1861. U. Salomon, the Khasi officer in-charge of the British police post at Jowai, met the special performers, who were 10 in number, and asked them to surrender their weapons. Upon refusal, the police not only confiscated their weapons but also opened fire to disperse the crowd. They also destroyed the weapons in front of the Khasis. Many fled and a few of them took shelter at the residence of U. Kiang Nangbah.

Soon, U. Kiang Nangbah made preparations for the revolt. Durbars were held at several places to discuss the plans and proceedings of the revolt. With a group of 200 men, U. Kiang Nangbah and other brave Kiangs laid siege to the military post at Jowai and stormed it. He sent word to the other leaders to start preparations for war against the British. To avoid food shortages during and after the war, Nangbah instructed that all available foodstuff and grains from recent harvests be stored inside granaries. For the safe shelter of women and children during the war, Nangbah created secret places in the caves of Jaintia Hills where the British had no access. The Dalois were hesitant to join the war but they were forced to. U. Kiang Nangbah became the leader of all the groups ready for war. Other leaders in the group were Shan Lalu, Giri Daloi of Shangpung, Myllon Daloi of Mynso, Bang Daloi of Nartiang, Suwar Daloi of Sutnga, and the Dalois of Nongkhlieh and Rymbai.

Nangbah held siege of the Jowai British military post for nine days until the Commanding Officer, Lieutenant Colonel Richardson, relieved the garrison. Further to curb the rebellion and attacks in other places of Jaintia Hills, the British sent a force comprising of one Eurasian Battery, four battalions of Native Infantry, and one Battalion of Bengal Military Police. These soldiers were to march from Cherrapunji to the Jaintia Hills. When U. Kiang Nangbah heard about it, he entrusted a group of warriors armed with fire-bearing arrows and bows to resist the passage of the troops. He entrusted another group to attack another military post at Jowai. The British troops rested in military camps that had thatched roofs. The Khasi warriors showered several fire-bearing arrows into the thatched roofs of these camps. The camps caught fire. The alerted troops used water pumps to douse the fire. Khasi warriors continued with their attacks until Major Rowlatt and his contingent came to the rescue. And the troops from Cherrapunji reached Jowai. The British destroyed few monoliths, Khasi heritage structures, with elephants at Jowai.

The war continued for a year. Initially, 2,000 Khasis joined the war and the number increased to 50,000. Attacking British posts at different places and defiance against Government regulations in all interior areas of Jaintia Hills continued. Upon the appeal of Nangbah, the Khasis did not pay taxes to the British. The Khasis occupied many positions. In retaliation, the British under Colonel Richardson with an organized force stormed all the Khasi stockades, plundered the granaries, burnt houses, looted properties and wealth. Many villages turned desolate. During that period of a year, many freedom fighters were arrested and Giri Daloi of Shangpung was shot dead by the British. U. Kiang Nangbah resorted to guerrilla warfare, attacking the British every now and then. Nangbah's guerrillas burnt British properties. Additional troops of the British marched towards Jaintia Hills to suppress the rebellion.

Unable to contain the attacks by the Khasis and unable to quell the rebellion in Jaintia Hills, the British appointed Brigadier General Showers as the Commissioner of Jaintia Hills and Khossiah with an office at Jowai. The Act XVI of 1857 was enforced in Jaintia Hills. The Khasis were warned not to participate in the rebellion and stop supporting the Khasi leaders and threatened them with dire consequences citing the Act.

But the promulgation of the Act had little effect. The Khasis turned more rebellious. On 16th June 1862, the Khasis attempted to assassinate Commander Morton at the Nartiang market but in vain. They also surrounded another British officer Andrews and threatened him. To further quote from *The History and Culture of the Khasi People*: "The Jaintias resorted to archery. They concealed themselves inside almost invisible caves from where they shot their arrows. The guerrffectarfare conducted by the Khasis prolonged the battles. A large number of Khasi volunteers from the wesffected the Pnars in their heroic operations. The effect of inIion was great. Cultivation ceased in many areas... Much loss of life recorded on the GovernmI side. The Khasi-Pnars were not prepared to submit... While many members were inclined to accept the offers of Government, Kiang Nongbah and his assistants resorted to a more hostile and bellicose attitude. Operations were resumed by the Pnar camp. Rebel Dalois were appointed in place of those refusing to join the movement in its last stage."

Around the end of December 1862, U. Kiang Nangbah fell ill. He was at the Umkarai village in Nartiang Daloiship with his wife and children. The British were already on a hunt for Nangbah for several months and they also announced a reward to those who would inform them about his whereabouts. U. Long Sutnga and U. Bur, Daloi of Nartiang turned traitors. They informed the British about Nangbah. The British under Commander J.R. Sadlier and Assistant Commander E.Y. Walcott of Nartiang surrounded the house where Nangbah was taking rest. When Nangbah learned about the same and also who the traitors were, he aimed his pistol at the latter. But his deteriorating health failed him. He again tried to shoot with his double-barrel gun but by then the British forces captured him on the dawn of 27th December. They seized six guns and a pistol from his home and also imprisoned his wife and children. His family escaped during a night halt on the way.

Like a low criminal U. Kiang Nangbah was hanged near Iaw Musiang, the Jowai market. Before he died, U. Kiang Nangbah uttered aloud thus, quoted in the aforementioned reference: "…if his face turned to the west when he died, his country would remain forever captive, if to the east, the contrary." When Nangbah breathed his last, his face turned to the east.

Traitors U. Long Sutnga and U. Bur received rewards from the British. Traitors did more harm to the motherland compared to foreigners. If the two traitors remained loyal to the motherland, the history of Jaintia Hills in particular and India, in general, would have been different. U. Kiang Nangbah's last words turned true. The motherland, in less than a century, attained freedom from the British. Jai Hind!

52

Harphool Jat

Attacked Slaughterhouses, Released 1,000s of Cows during British Rule

Harphool Jat, also known as Harphul Jat Julani Aala was a *gau rakshak* (protector of cows) and freedom fighter. He was called the *Sawa Sher* and Robinhood of Haryana. During British colonial rule, there were scores of slaughterhouses built by Muslims under the patronage of the British in his region. Cows were killed for meat in those centers. Harphool, who considered the cow as a mother, attacked many of those butcher houses, killing butchers and released thousands of cows. Besides, he was witness to the exploitation of poor peasants and women by the British. He came to their rescue. Most of the time, Harphool remained in hiding and from his hideout, he continued with his exploits against the British. He succeeded in every attempt and was never caught. The British, who were on a hunt for him for several years, caught him through treachery. A traitor leaked about his whereabouts to the British. Harphool Jat was hanged to death on 27th July 1936 by the British.

Not much information is available about the childhood of Harphool Jat Julaniwala. He was born in 1892 at Barwas village in Bhiwani, Haryana. His father Chatru Ram was a farmer. Severe drought affected the region in 1899. Chatru Ram succumbed to plague during that drought, Harphool was then aged seven years. Due to poverty, Harphool left Barwas along with his maternal uncle and started living in Sandowa village in Bhiwani at the house of his relatives. Meanwhile, his mother was married to her brother-in-law. Harphool along with his family soon shifted base to Julani village in Jind, his ancestral home. Harphool belonged to a Jat family, his surname Julaniwala represented his hailing from the village of Julani. Harphool grew up in a stressful atmosphere at Julani village as his relatives did not want him to hold any share in the ancestral property. Meanwhile, he grew up to be a strong and well-built young man.

Harphool joined the British Army and even participated in World War I. Joining the army was his passion to learn the art of warfare. Noticing increased British oppression of natives of the motherland, he left the Army. While in service for only 10 years, he was very brilliant and also once saved the children of a British colonel. Hence, when he asked for a folding gun as an award during retirement, he was granted the same.

Harphool was a victim of bullying during his childhood. During his young days, he was falsely charged and arrested for a crime he did not commit. He was tortured by a police officer during his lock-up in Jind. After he got a gun, he decided to take revenge. He had not been to his village for many days while he was posted in the Army. He first went to the police station and shot dead the police officer. He then went home. His mother was already dead. Shocked at the news and unable to bear the grief, Harphool left home and went to the forest. There he met a Sadhu who also reared cows. The Sadhu consoled the grieving Harphool and explained to him how the cow was a mother too. Ever since Harphool considered the cow his mother.

Slaughterhouses were then a common sight and slaughtering of cows were very common in the region where Harphool Jat lived. Harphool started attacking and destroying slaughterhouses and killing the butchers. He released the cows from those sites. He also saved many cows from being smuggled.

During the British rule, hundreds and thousands of Hindus and Sikhs revolted against the slaughter of cows. The British allowed Muslims to build slaughterhouses across the country. During the 1870s, the Kuka movement gained momentum. Kuka members were mainly Namdhari Sikhs and were gau rakshaks. They were the disciples of Sat Guru Ram Singh. Their key objective was preventing the slaughter of cows, saving cows, fighting for the freedom of the motherland, following Swadeshi culture including wearing homespun cotton clothes.

According to the book *Kuka Movement: Freedom Struggle in Punjab* by Jaswinder Singh, in January 1872, 150 Kukas attacked butchers of Maler Kotla (Sangrur, Punjab). The butchers had the support of the British. The British Police immediately set to action. They arrested 66 Kukas, brought them to Maler Kotla ground, and without any trial, executed them with guns and cannons. The execution was ordered by Cowan, the Deputy Commissioner of Ludhiana, and Forsyth, the Commissioner of Ambala. Among the martyred freedom fighters and gau rakshaks were three children including 12-year-old Bishan Singh. This massacre of Kukas by the British doesn't find mention in history textbooks or mainstream narratives.

Harphool Jat continued with this legacy of gau rakshak activities in Haryana. Meanwhile, the British started searching for him. But they could not catch him as he remained underground for most of the time.

During that time, the British imposed heavy taxes on farmers. Many farmers became landless and homeless. Harphool Jat came to the rescue of poor villagers, especially peasants and women, from British oppression in his region.

One of the biggest attacks of a butcher house by Harphool was on 23rd July 1930 at village Tohana. Despite continuous opposition from the local Hindus, the butchers did not stop their activities. The Hindus then sought the help of Harphool. What did Harphool do as the butchers were alert about him and were well guarded? He disguised as a woman and entered the butcher house. He not only shot dead several butchers but also freed all the cows trapped there. The brave act earned him the title of *Sawa Sher* (meaning strength and aura of 100 lions) from local Hindus.

Harphool Jat continued attacking many slaughterhouses in several districts of Haryana and released cows. Meanwhile, the British, unable to catch him, announced an award for his arrest. A traitor from Pacheri, Jhunjhunu informed the British about Harphool's whereabouts. The British arrested him at night while in sleep. He was lodged at Firozpur jail. The British hanged him to death in Firozpur jail on 27th July 1936.

Harphool Jat's service for Dharma will always be remembered. Vande Mataram!

To be continued in Vol III of Saffron Swords, portraying another 52 episodes of valor of our warrior ancestors, who defended Dharma and the Motherland…

Bibliography

Chapter 1– Kurma Devi: Chittor Rani Who Defeated and Wounded Qutb al-Din Aibak

1. Lt. Col. James Tod, *Annals and Antiquities of Rajasthan: The Central and Western Rajpoot States of India*, Vol. I, The Society for the Resuscitation of Indian Literature, Printed by H.C. Das at Elysium Press, 1902.
2. Anant Sadashiv Altekar, *The Position of Women in Hindu Civilization, from Prehistoric Times to the Present Day*, Motilal Banarasidass Publishers, 1959.
3. Indira Mahindra, *The Rebellious Home-makers*, SNDT Women's University, 1980.

Chapter 2– Rani Durgavati

1. S.R. Sharma, *Mughal Empire in India: 1526-1761, Part I*, Karnatak Printing Press, Bombay, 1934.
2. Gordon Johnson, C.A. Bayly, John F. Richards, edt, *The New Cambridge History of India: The Mughal Empire*, Cambridge University Press, 1995.
3. Rai Bahadur, A.C. Mukherji, *Heroines of Indian History*, Oxford University Press, 1993.
4. Alice Thorner, Maithreyi Krishna Raj, edt, *Ideals, Images, and Real Lives: Women in Literature and History*, Orient BlackSwan, 2000.
5. Vincent A. Smith, *Akbar The Great Mogul: 1542-1605,* Oxford at the Clarendon Press, 1917.

Chapter 3– Gangu Mehtar

1. Crispin Bates, *Mutiny at the Margins: New Perspectives on the Indian Uprising of 1857: Muslim, Dalit and Subaltern Narratives*-Vol. 5, SAGE India, 2014.
2. Vinayak Damodar Savarkar, *The Indian War of Independence of 1857*, Publishers in London, 1909, Columbia University Library.
3. *'Identity and Narratives: Dalits and memories of 1857'*–a paper by Badri Narayan Tiwari Professor, Social History and Cultural Anthropology, whose narrative of Gangu Mehtar in the paper is based on his field trip to Kanpur as a part of the project *'Myth, Memory and Politics: A Study of the Language of Mobilization of Grassroots Dalits'*, sponsored by ICSSR, New Delhi, April 2004 and oral history on the freedom fighter narrated to him by 'an old woman Bhagwanti Devi of Duari located in the district Kanpur Dehat of North India on 10th January 2007'.

Chapter 4– Rani Bhavashankari

1. Binoy Ghosh, *Paschim Banger Sanskriti*, Pustak Prakashak, 1950.
2. Bidhubhusan Bhattacharya, *Raybaghini O Bhurishrestha Rajkahini*, Nababharati Prakashani, 2009.
3. Durga Prashad Pathak, *Palm Leaf Etchings of Orissa,* Abhinav Publications, 1989.
4. John R. McLane, *Land and Local Kingship in Eighteenth-Century Bengal*, Cambridge University Press, 2002.

Chapter 5– 10 Very Young Freedom Fighters of India

1. Manmatha Nath Das, *Medinipur Charitabhidhan*, Dey's Publishing, 2007.
2. Harvilas Gupta, *Balidani Balak*, Kshem Prakash, Balaji Offset, 2015.
3. Narendra Nath Das, *History of Midnapore Vol II*, Midnapur Samskriti Parishad, 1962.
4. Shyamapada Bhowmik, 'Militant Nationalism in India Midnapore, 1931-1933' in *Proceedings of the Indian History Congress*, Vol. 68, 2007.
5. Jaswinder Singh, *Kuka Movement: Freedom Struggle in Punjab (Documents, 1880-1903 A.D.)*, Atlantic Publishers & Distributors, 1985.

Chapter 6– Dahir's Resistance to Arabs; How His Daughters Ended Life of Mohd Bin Qasim

1. Manan Ahmed Asif, *A Book of Conquest*, Harvard University Press, 2016.
2. Thomas Postans, *Personal Observations on Sindh: The Manners and Customs of Its Inhabitants; and Its Productive Capabilities*, HardPress, 2018.
3. AI Akram, AB al-Mehri, *The Muslim Conquest of Persia*, Maktabah Publications, 2009.
4. R. Stephen Humphreys, *Between Memory and Desire*, University of California Press, 1999.
5. Andre Wink, *Al-Hind: The Making of the Indo-Islamic World*, Vol 1: Early Medieval India and the Expansion of Islam, BRILL, 1990, 1996.
6. Iqtidar Husain Siddiqi, *Indo-Persian Historiography up to the Thirteenth Century*, Primus Books, 2010.

Chapter 7– How Satnamis Drove away Aurangzeb's Forces from Narnaul in 1672

1. R.C. Mazumder, H.C. Raychaudhuri, Kalikinkar Datta, *An Advanced History of India*, Macmillan India, 3rd edition, 1967, 1970 (reprint).
2. Saqi Mustad Khan, translated by Sir Jadunath Sarkar, *Maasir-i-Alamgiri: A History of Emperor Aurangzib-Alamgir*, Royal Asiatic Society of Bengal, 1947.
3. James Hastings (ed), 'Sadhs' in *Encyclopedia of Religion and Ethics, Vol XI: Sacrifice-Sudra*, Morrison & Gibb Limited, 1920, ASI Library.
4. Waldemar Hansen, *The Peacock Throne: The Drama of Mogul India*, Motilal Banarsidass Publishers, 1986.

Chapter 8– Bhima Bai Holkar: Defeated British Col Malcolm in Guerrilla Warfare

1. *Madhya Pradesh District Gazetteers: Indore*, Government Central Press, 1965.
2. Ravindra Pratap Singh, *Geography and Politics in Central India: A Case Study of Erstwhile Indore State*, Concept Publishing Company, 1987.

3. Jadunath Sarkar, *Fall of the Mughal Empire: 1789-1803*, Orient Blackswan, 1988.
4. Maj. Gen. John Malcolm, *Memoir of Central India*, Vol II, Printed for Kingsbury, Parbury, & Allen, London, 1823; copy in Office of the Director-General of Archaeology, India.
5. Ghanshyam Holkar, *Maharaja Yashwant Rao Holkar: Bhartiya Swatantra Ke Mahanayak*, Notion Press, 2018.
6. Shrikrishna Saral, *Krantikari Kosh: Prathama Khanda*, Prabhat Prakashan, 1998.
7. Rashtrabandhu, *Prerak Prasang*, Prabhat Prakashan, 2012.
8. Govind Sakharam Sardesai, *New History of the Marathas, Vol III*, Phoenix Publications, First published 1948.

Chapter 9: Bibi Dalair Kaur: Led 100 Women Warriors in Battle against Mughals

1. W.H. McLeod, *The A to Z of Sikhism*, Scarecrow Press, 2009.
2. Harjit Singh, *The Warrior Princess 2: Sikh Women in Battle*, 2003.
3. Tony Jaques, *Dictionary of Battles and Sieges: A-E*, Greenwood Publishing, 2007.

Chapter 10– Haipou Jadonang: Built an Army of 500 Men/ Women against British; Hanged at 26

1. G.K. Ghosh, *Tribals and Their Culture in Assam, Meghalaya, and Mizoram*, Ashish Publishing House, 1992.
2. John Parratt, *Wounded Land: Politics and Identity in Modern Manipur*, Mittal Publications, 2005.
3. Jangkhomang Guite, 'Monuments, Memory and Forgetting in Postcolonial north-east India' in *Economic & Political Weekly* Journal, Vol. 46, Issue No. 08, 19 Feb 2011.
4. John Thomas, *Evangelising the Nation: Religion and the Formation of Naga Political Identity*, Taylor & Francis, 2015.
5. "The Constitution (Scheduled Tribes): Order, 1950", Ministry of Law and Justice (India).

6. Cachar District Record Room, Superintendent's Letter Book, 1837–38, No 130 (NMML Occasional Paper).

Chapter 11– How Pazhassi Raja Resisted Troops of Hyder Ali, Tipu Sultan, British

1. K. Rajayyan, *South Indian Rebellion*, Rao and Raghavan, 1971.
2. D.P. Ramachandran, *Empire's First Soldiers*, Lancer Publishers, 2008.
3. Harald Fischer-Tine, Michael Mann, *Colonialism as Civilizing Mission: Cultural Ideology in British India*, Anthem Press, 2004.

Chapter 12– How Samgramaraja of Kashmir Repulsed Attacks of Mahmud of Ghazni

1. Mark Aurel Stein, *Kalhana's Rajatarangini: A Chronicle of the Kings of Kashmir*, Volume 1, Volume 2, South Asia Books, 1987.
2. *India: Early History*, Publications Division, M/O Information & Broadcasting, Govt. of India, 2016.
3. Mohibbul Hasan, *Kashmir under the Sultans*, Aakar Books, 2005.
4. G.M.D. Sufi, *Kashīr: Being a History of Kashmir from the Earliest Times to Our Own*, University of the Panjab, 1949.
5. Firishta, John Briggs (translation), *History of the Rise of the Mohammedan Power in India*, Atlantic Publishers and Distributors (P) Ltd., 2016.

Chapter 13– Sanyasi Rebellion: How Jagannath Pilgrims Attacked British in 1770-75

1. Nares Chandra Sen-Gupta, *The Abbey of Bliss: A Translation of Bankim Chandra Chatterjee's Anandamath*, Padmini Mohan Neoci, 1906, Worldcat (source edition).
2. Fredrik Albritton Jonsson, *Enlightenment's Frontier: The Scottish Highlands and the Origins of Environmentalism*, Yale University Press, June 2013.

Chapter 14– Dantidurga II

1. Pandit Bisheshwar Nath Reu, *History of the Rashtrakutas (Rathodas)*, Jodhpur The Archaeological Department, 1933.

2. Dr. A.S. Atlekar, *The Rashtrakutas and Their Times,* Oriental Book Agency, 1967.

3. Khalid A. Blankinship, *The End of the Jihad State: The Reign of Hisham Ibn 'Abd al-Malik and the Collapse of the Umayyads*, Khalid Yahya Blankinship, SUNY Press, 1994.

4. R.C. Majumdar, *Ancient India*, Motilal Banarasidass Publishers, 1952.

5. M.A. Stein, *Kalhaṇa's Rājataraṅgiṇī: A Chronicle of the Kings of Kaśmīr*, Constable & Co., 1900.

6. Hermann Goetz, *Studies in the History and Art of Kashmir and the Indian Himalaya*, Harrassowitz, 1969.

Durga Prasad Dikshit, *Political History of the Chālukyas of Badami,* Abhinav Publications, 1980.

Chapter 15– Hambirrao Mohite: Defeated Mughals and Adilshahi Army Several Times

1. N.S. Takakhav, K.A. Keluskar, *The Life of Shivaji Maharaj: Founder of the Maratha Empire*, Manoranjan Press, 1921, digitized edition.

2. C.A. Kincaid, Rao Bahadur D.B. Parasnis, *A History of the Maratha People*, Vol. II, Oxford University Press, 1922, digitized edition.

3. Pandit Shankar Joshi, *Chhatrapati Sambhaji, 1657-1689 AD*, S. Chand, 1980.

Chapter 16– Jayi Rajaguru: Royal Priest Who Waged War against British in 1803-05

1. Prafulla Kumara Pattanayaka, *A Forgotten Chapter of Orissan History with Special Reference to the Rajas of Khurda and Puri, 1568-1828*; Punthi Pustak, 1979.

2. Krishna Chandra Panigrahi, *History of Orissa: Hindu Period*, Kitab Mahal, 1981.

3. Sir Hans Singer (editor), *History of the Jagannath Temple*, BR Publishing Corporation, 2019.

4. Prafulla Kumar Pattanaik, *The First Indian War of Independence: Freedom Movement in Orissa, 1804–1825*, APH Publishing, 2005.

5. Prasanna Kumar Mishra, *Political Unrest in Orissa in the 19th Century: Anti-British, Anti-Feudal, and Agrarian Risings*, Punthi Pustak, 1983.

Chapter 17– Chennabhairadevi: Protected Karnataka Coast from Portuguese

1. Prof P. Gururaja Bhatt, *Studies in Tuluva History and Culture*, published by the author at Manipal Power Press, 1975.

2. Jadunath Sarkar, *Shivaji and His Times*, Orient Longman, 1992.

3. Suryanath U. Kamath (chief editor), *Karnataka State Gazetteer Part II*, Government of Karnataka Publication, 1983.

4. Archaeological Survey of India excavations 2000-2005 report, Karnataka

5. Durga Prasad, *History of the Andhras till 1565 AD*, PG Publishers, 1988.

Chapter 18– Babu Kunwar Singh: Won Several Battles against British at Age 80

1. Dr. K.K. Datta, *Biography of Kunwar Singh and Amar Singh*, KP Jayaswal Research Institute–Patna, 1957.

2. Robert Montgomery Martin, Emma Roberts, *The Indian Empire*, London Print and Pub. Co., 1858, digitized version.

3. E. Jaiwant Paul, *The Greased Cartridge: The Heroes and Villains of 1857-58*, Roli Books Private Limited, 2011.

4. Dr. K.K. Datta (editor), *Unrest against British Rule in Bihar, 1831-1859*, Superintendent Secretariat Press Patna, 1957.

5. Badri Narayan, 'Popular Culture and 1857: A Memory against Forgetting', in *Social Scientist* journal, Vol. 26, No. 1/4 (Jan- Apr 1998), pp. 86-94.

6. E. Jaiwant Paul, *The Greased Cartridge: The Heroes and Villains of 1857-58*, Roli Books, 2011.

7. Isabel Giberne Sieveking, *A Turning Point in the Indian Mutiny*, D. Nutt, 1910, OCLC 13203015, University of California Libraries (digital archive).

8. John James Halls, *Two Months in Arrah in 1857*, London: Longman, Green, Longman and Roberts, 1860, OCLC 877907, University of California Libraries (digital archive).
9. Shrikrishan 'Saral', *Indian Revolutionaries: A Comprehensive Study, 1757-1961*, Volume 1, Prabhat Prakashan, 1999.

Chapter 19– Marthanda Varma: Defeated the Dutch in Battle, Crushed their Indian Expansion

1. Shungoonny Menon, *History of Travancore from the Earliest Times*, Asian Educational Services, 1997.
2. A. Sreedhara Menon, *A Survey of Kerala History*, DC Books, 2019.
3. Yogesh Sharma, *Coastal Histories: Society and Ecology in Pre-modern India*, Primus Books, 2010.
4. J.C. Heesterman, Albert W. Van den Hoek, Dirk H.A. Kolff, M. S. Oort. (edited), *Ritual, State, and History in South Asia: Essays in Honor of J.C. Heesterman*, Brill, 1992.

Chapter 20– How Naga Sadhus Defeated Aurangzeb's Forces Defending Kashi Vishwanath in 1664

1. Jadunath Sarkar, *A History of Dasnami Naga Sanyasis*, Sri Panchayati Akhara Mahanirvani, 1959, Digital Library of India Item 2015.32182.
2. James G. Lochtefeld, *The Illustrated Encyclopedia of Hinduism*, Volume 1, Rosen, 2002, opensource collection.
3. Baba Rampuri, *Autobiography of a Sadhu: A Journey into Mystic India*, Destiny Books, 2010.

Chapter 21– Chaitanya Mahaprabhu: Started Kirtan Movement in Bengal Defying Orders of Bengal Sultanate

1. R.C. Mazumder, *History and Culture of the Indian People: The Delhi Sultanate*, Vol. 6, Bharatiya Vidya Bhavan, 1960.
2. Nripendra Krishna Chattopadhyay, *Sri Sri Chaitanya Charitamrita*, Shri Krishna Chandra Gupta, Shri Madan Gopal Gupta, Jenabel Library, 1961.

3. Manmatha Nath Das, *Glimpses of Kalinga History*, Century Publishers, 1949.

Chapter 22– Baba Deep Singh: Defeated Afghans in the Battle of Amritsar in 1757

1. Singh Bhagat, *A History of the Sikh Misals*, Publication Bureau, Punjabi University, 1993.
2. Ajit Singh Aulakh, *Illustrated Stories of Baba Deep Singh Ji Shaheed*, B. Chattar Singh Jiwan Singh, Jeewan Printers, 2010.
3. Santokh Singh Jagdev, *Bedtime Stories – 7 (Sikh Martyrs)*, Sikh Missionary Resource Centre, 1995.
4. Joginder Singh Sahi, Naindeep Kaur, *An Encyclopaedia of Sikhism and Sikhs Abroad*, Common World, 1999.
5. Tom Lansford, *Afghanistan at War: From the 18th-Century Durrani Dynasty to the 21st Century*, ABC-CLIO, 2017.
6. August Friedrich Rudolf Hoernle, Herbert Alick Stark, *A History of India*, Orissa Mission Press, 1906; digitized by Google from the library of the University of California.
7. Khushwant Singh, *A History of the Sikhs (1469-1839)* - Vol. 1, Oxford, 2004.
8. Jaswant Lal Mehta, *Advanced Study in the History of Modern India 1707–1813*, Sterling Publishers, 2005.

Chapter 23– Dhan Singh Gurjar: His Role in the 1857 War of Independence in Meerut

1. Christopher Hibbert, *The Great Mutiny: India 1857*, Allen Lane, 1980.
2. Crispin Bates, *Mutiny at the Margins: New Perspectives on the Indian Uprising of 1857: Anticipations and Experiences in the Locality*, Vol. 1, SAGE Publications, 2013.
3. Kim A Wagner, *The Great Fear of 1857: Rumors, Conspiracies and the Making of the Indian Uprising*, Peter Lang, 2010.

Chapter 24– Krishnadeva Raya: Defeated the Sultans of the Deccan

1. William J. Jackson, *Vijayanagara Voices Exploring South Indian History and Hindu Literature*, Routledge, 2004.
2. Suryanath U. Kamath, *A Concise History of Karnataka*, MCC Publications, 2010.
3. K.A. Nilakanta Sastri, R. Champakalakshmi, *A History of South India*, Oxford, 1997.
4. Vincent A. Smith, edited by Percival Spear, *The Oxford History of India*, OUP India, 1997.
5. Krishnaji Nageshrao Chitnis, *Medieval Indian History*, Atlantic Publishers and Distributors, 2003.
6. Sindigi Rajasekhara, *The Map Approach to Vijayanagara History*, Sujatha Publications and University of Michigan, 2008.
7. Phillip B Wagoner, *Tidings of the King: A Translation and Ethnohistorical Analysis of the Rāyavācakamu*, University of Hawaii Press, 1993.
8. Kittu Reddy, *History of India: A New Approach*, Standard Publishers, 2003.
9. P. Raghunadha Rao, *Ancient and Medieval history of Andhra Pradesh*, Sterling Publishers, 1993.
10. M.H. Rama Sharma, *The History of the Vijayanagar Empire*, Popular Prakashan, 1956 (first published).
11. Pandurang Bhimarao Desai, *A History of Karnataka: From Pre-history to Unification*, Kannada Research Institute, Karnataka University, 1970.

Chapter 25– Krishna Bahadur Mukhia: Netaji Subhas Bose's Bodyguard in Burma Jungles

Note: Besides the below books, this chapter is also based on interviews done of INA veterans Lt. Rama Mehta, Lt. Asha Sahay Choudhry, Shri Jagram, Shri Parmanand Yadav, and Shri Bhagmal Yadav by the author including newspaper reports, and oral narrations.

1. Ian Sumner, *The Indian Army 1914-1947*, Osprey Publishing, 2001.
2. Maj. Gen. G.D. Bakshi, *BOSE or GANDHI: Who Got India Her Freedom*, KW Publishers, 2019.

3. Dr. Kalyan Kumar De, *NETAJI: India's Independence and British Archives*, Garuda Prakashan, 2020.
4. Bhuvan Lall, *The Man India Missed the Most: Subhas Chandra Bose*, Notion Press, 2017.

Chapter 26– Sangolli Rayanna: Mobilized Masses and Attacked British from 1824-1830

1. Gopalakrishnan Subramanian, edited *The South Indian Rebellions: Before and After 1800*, Palaniappa Brothers, 2007.
2. Lewis Sydney Steward O'Malley, *Indian Civil Service, 1601–1930*, Frank Cass, 1985.
3. Amaresh Datta, edited, *Encyclopedia of Indian Literature: Devraj to Jyoti*, Volume 2, Sahitya Akademi, 1988.

Chapter 27– Velu Nachiyar: 1st Queen in the History of India to Win a Battle against the British

1. Madhan Kumar, *Thamizh Is Not Just a Language: The Valour*, Educreation Publishing, 2017.
2. Z. Madhur, *Legendary Leaders*, Book 3, Aakar Books, 2018.
1. K.R. Venkatarama Ayyar, *A Manual of the Pudukkóttai State*, Sri Brihadamba State Press, 1938.

Chapter 28– How Khen Rulers of Assam Defeated Islamic Invaders in 13th-14th Century

1. Dimbeshwar Neog, *Introduction to Assam*, Vera, 1947, Digital Library of India.
2. Minhaj-ud-Din Maulana, Abu-'Umar-I-'Usman, edited by Maj H.G. Raverty, *Tabakat-i-Nasiri, A General History of the Muhammadan Dynasties of Asia, including Hindustan*, Vol 1, Oriental Books, 1970, Digital Library of India collection.
3. Minhaj-i-Siraj, edited by H.G. Raverty, *Tabakat-i-Nasiri*, Gilbert & Rivington, 1873, Digital Library of India.

4. M. Neog, 'Origin of the Baro-Bhuyans', in *The Comprehensive History of Assam*, 2, edited by HK Barpujari, Assam Publication Board, 1992.

Chapter 29– Raja Ganesha: Re-established Hindu Supremacy in Bengal in the 15th Century

1. Richard M. Eaton, *The Rise of Islam and the Bengal Frontier, 1204-1760*, University of California Press, 1996.
2. R.C. Mazumder, *The Delhi Sultanate*, Bharatiya Vidya Bhavan, 1960, Digital Library of India.
3. Mohammad Mohar Ali, *History of the Muslims of Bengal*, Vol. 1, Imam Muhammad Ibn Sa'ud Islamic University, 1985.

Chapter 30– Lalitaditya Muktapida: Defeated Arabs and Subjugated Turks in Eighth Century

1. P.N.K. Bamzai, *Culture and Political History of Kashmir*, Volume 1, MD Publications, 1994.
2. M.A. Stein, *Kalhaṇa's Rājataraṅgiṇi: A Chronicle of the Kings of Kaśmīr*, Motilal Banarsidass, 2017.
3. Hermann Goetz, *Studies in the History and Art of Kashmir and the Indian Himalaya*, Jay Kay Books, 2017.
4. André Wink, *Al-Hind, the Making of the Indo-Islamic World: Early Medieval India and the Expansion of Islam 7th-11th Centuries*, Brill, 2002.

Chapter 31– Uyyalawada Narasimha Reddy: Led 5000+ Farmers against British in 1846; Hanged

1. Narahari Gopalakristnamah Chetty, *A Manual of the Kurnool District in the Presidency of Madras*, Palala Press, 2016.
2. R.C. Dutt, *The Economic History of India Under Early British Rule. Vol. I: From the Rise of the British Power in 1757 to the Accession of Queen Victoria in 1837*, Routledge, 2000.
3. K. Venugopal Reddy, *'Dominance and Resistance: A Study of Narasimha Reddy's Revolt in Andhra against the Injustice and towards India's Freedom Movement (1846–47)'* in *Social Scientist*, Vol. 38, No. 1/2 (Jan.-Feb., 2010).

Chapter 32– Bhama Shah: Funded Rana Pratap Restore Army, Regain Mewari Area from Mughals

1. G.N. Sharma, *Mewar and the Mughal Emperors: 1526-1707 AD*, Shiva Lal Agarwala, 1962.
2. Shri Ram Sharma, *Maharana Pratap*, Hope India Publications, January 2002.
3. Gopi Nath Sharma and MN Mathur, *Maharana Pratap and His Times*, Maharana Pratap Smarak Samiti, 1989.
4. Bhawan Singh Rana, *Maharana Pratap*, Diamond Pocket Books, 2013.

Chapter 33– Rani Abbakka Chowta: Successfully Resisted Portuguese Attacks for 40+ Years

1. Venkataraya Narayan Kudva, *History of the Dakshinatya Saraswats*, Samyukta Gowda Saraswata Sabha, 1972.
2. Kailash Kumar Mishra, *Abbakka Rani: The Unsung Warrior Queen*, Indira Gandhi National Centre for the Arts, 2002.
3. Gayathri Ponvannan, *Unstoppable: 75 Stories of Trailblazing Indian Women*, Hachette Book Publishing India, 2019.
4. Sarojini Shintri, Kurukundi Raghavendra Rao, *Women Freedom Fighters in Karnataka*, Prasaranga, Karnatak University, 1983.
5. 'Queen Abbakka's Triumph over Western Colonisers', Press Information Bureau, Govt., of India, 2007.
6. Kailash Kr. Mishra, *Vihangama*, Vol. I (January-February), 2002; digital record in ignca.gov.in.

Chapter 34– Shivappa Nayaka: Defeated the Portuguese and the Bijapur Sultanate

1. M.N. Pearson, *The New Cambridge History of India*, Cambridge University Press, 2008.
2. Suryanath U. Kamat, *A Concise History of Karnataka from Pre-Historic Times to the Present*, Jupiter Books, 2001.

3. *Portuguese Studies Review*, Baywolf Press, ISSN 1057-1515
4. Basavaraj S. Naika, *Keladi Nayakas: The Rebellious Rani of Belavadi and Other Stories*, Atlantic Publishers, 2001.

Chapter 35– Vigraharaja IV: Defeated Ghaznavid Rulers Bahram Shah, Khusrau Malik in 12th Century

1. Dasharatha Sharma, *Early Chauhan Dynasties,* Motilal Banarsidass, 1975.
2. Cynthia Talbot, *The Last Hindu Emperor: Prithviraj Chauhan and the Indian Past, 1200–2000*, Cambridge University Press, 2015.
3. R.B. Singh, *History of the Chahamanas*, N. Kishore, 1964.
4. Peter Jackson, *The Delhi Sultanate: A Political and Military History*, Cambridge University Press, 2003.

Chapter 36– Govindachandra: Defeated Ghaznavid Forces of Mas'ud III in Early 12th Century

1. Pandit Bisheshwar Nath Reu, *History of the Rashtrakutas*, Jodhpur Archaeological Department, Marwar State Press, 1933, Digital Library of India.
2. Roma Niyogi, *The History of the Gāhaḍavāla Dynasty*, Oriental, 1959, Digital Library of India.
3. Sanu Kainiraka, *From Indus to Independence: A Trek Through Indian History*, Volume 3, Vij Books 2016.
4. P.C. Roy, *The Coinage of Northern India*, Abhinav Publications, 1980.

Chapter 37– Kalyani Das and Nameless Women Freedom Fighters in Jail in the 1930s

Key Reference:

1. Kalyani Das Bhattacharjee, *Jeebon Adhyayan,* translated from the Bengali Original by Dhira Dhar titled *A Study of Life*, Jayabrata Bhattacharjee, 1952 (Bengali Edition, published by Abhinash Mazumdar, eldest brother of freedom fighter Dinesh, who was executed by the British in 1931), 2016.

Other References:

1. Meghna Guhathakurta, Willem van Schendel, *The Bangladesh Reader: History, Culture, Politics*, Duke University Press, 2013.
2. Geraldine Hancock Forbes, *Indian Women and the Freedom Movement: A Historian's Perspective*, Research Centre for Women's Studies, S.N.D.T. Women's University, 1997.
3. Bonnie G. Smith, *The Oxford Encyclopedia of Women in World History*, Volume 1, OUP, 2003.

Chapter 38– Avanijanashraya Pulakeshin: Defeated Arabs in Gujarat in 737 CE

1. Sharada Srinivasan, '*Satem copper plates of Avanijanasraya Pulakesiraja*' in *Journal of the Epigraphical Society of India*, Volume 14, The Society, 1987.
2. Durga Prasad Dikshit, *Political History of the Chālukyas of Badami*, Abhinav Publications, 1980.
3. Dr. A.S. Atlekar, *The Rashtrakutas and Their Times,* Oriental Book Agency, 1967.

Chapter 40– Hadi Rani: Gifted Head to Husband to Motivate Him to Go to War against Mughals

1. Dina Nath Dube, *Folk Tales of Rajasthan*, Publications Division, GOI, 2017.
2. Lindsey Harlan, *Religion and Rajput Women*, University of California Press, 2020.
3. Lindsey Harlan, *The Goddesses' Henchmen: Gender in Indian Hero Worship*, OUP, 2003.
4. K. Satchidanandan, *Indian Poetry: Modernism and After: A Seminar*, Sahitya Akademi, 2016.
5. Gopi Nath Sharma, *Mewar & the Mughal Emperors (1526-1707 A.D.)*, Shiva Lal Agarwala & Co Ltd, 1954.

Chapter 41– How Naga Sadhus Defended Gokul from Abdali's Afghan Army in 1757

1. Jadunath Sarkar, *A History Of Dasnami Naga Sanyasis*, Sri Panchayati Akhara Mahanirvani, 1959.
2. Ganda Singh, *Ahmad Shah Durrani: Father Of Modern Afghanistan*, Asia Publishing House, 1959.
3. Baba Rampuri, *Autobiography of a Sadhu: A Journey into Mystic India*, Destiny Books, 2010.

Chapter 42– Onake Obavva: A Guard's Wife Who Fought against Hyder Ali's Forces

1. Sarojini Shintri, Kurukundi Raghavendra Rao, *Women Freedom Fighters in Karnataka*, Prasaranga, Karnatak University, 1983.
2. G. Ramakrishna, N. Gayathri, Debiprasad Chattopadhyaya, *An Encyclopaedia of South Indian Culture*, KP Bagchi, 1983.
3. Cathy Spagnoli, Paramasivam Samanna, *Jasmine and Coconuts: South Indian Tales*, Greenwood Publishing Group, 1999.
4. Conjeevaram Hayavadana Rao, *History of Mysore (1399-1799 AD) 1766-1799*, Vol 3, Govt. of Mysore, 1943.

Chapter 43– Prafulla Kumari Devi: Maharani of Bastar Who Challenged the British

Note: Besides the below-mentioned literary references, this story is also based on an oral narration by Rachna Naidu from Chhattisgarh. A lawyer by profession with a keen interest in history, Rachna has collected information from local historical folklore and ballads, references from local writers besides meeting the descendant of Maharani Prafulla Kumari Devi in person and gaining further information.

Other References:

1. Rajiv Ranjan Prasad, *Bastar ke Jananayak*, Yash Publishers and Distributors, 2015.

2. Rajiv Ranjan Prasad, *Dantakshetra*, Yash Publishers and Distributors, 2018.
3. Dr. Hiralal Shukla, *Bastar ka Mukti Sangram (1774-1910)*, Madhya Pradesh Hindi Granth Academy, 2009.
4. Lala Jagdalpuri, *Bastar: Itihas Evam Sanskriti*, Madhya Pradesh Hindi Granth Academy, 2016.
5. Wilfred Grigson, *Maria Gonds of Bastar*, Oxford University Press, 1936, 1992.
6. Hugh Chisholm, 'Bastar' in *Encyclopædia Britannica*, Cambridge University Press, 1911.
7. Angma Dey Jhala, 'Courtly Indian Women in Late Imperial India' in *Journal of the Royal Asiatic Society* Third Series, Vol. 19, No. 4 (Oct. 2009), ed John McLeod, Cambridge University Press.

Chapter 44– Rajachakravarty Pratapaditya of Jessore: Defeated Mughals in Several Battles

1. Alauddin Isfahani, translator Dr. M.I. Borah, *Baharistan-i-Ghaibi* Vol. I, Government of Assam, 1936, Digital Library of India.
2. Lewis Sydney Steward O'Malley, *Jessore*, Bengal Secretariat Book Depot, 1912, Wellcome Library, the UK (digital).
3. James Westland, *Report on District of Jessore: Its Antiquities, Its History, and Its Commerce*, Bengal Secretariat Office, 1871, Digital Library of India.
4. Nagendra Kr. Singh, *Encyclopedia of Bangladesh*, Anmol Publications, 2003.
5. Jogendra Nath Bhattacharya, *Hindu Castes and Sects*, Thacker, Spink and Co., 1896, Digitized by Google from the library of the University of Michigan.
6. Jos J.L. Gommans, *Mughal Warfare: Indian Frontiers and Highroads to Empire, 1500–1700*, Routledge, 2002.

Chapter 45– Kapilendra Deva: Defeated Sultans of Bengal, Jaunpur, Malwa, Bahmani Kingdom

1. R.D. Banerji, *History of Orissa: From the Earliest Times to the British Period*, S.K. Das, Prabasi Press, 1930, Digital Library of India.

2. R.C. Mazumdar, *History and Culture of the Indian People, The Delhi Sultanate*, Volume 6, Bharatiya Vidya Bhavan, 1967.

3. Krishna Chandra Panigrahi, *Sarala Dasa*, Sahitya Akademi, 1975, Digital Library of India.

Chapter 46– Role of Bishnupriya Manipuris in Early Phase of Freedom Struggle

1. Pandit Nabakhendra Singh, Translated by Nabadweep Singha, *Khumal Purana*, De Quality Printers, Agartala.
2. Braja Gopal Sinha, *Bishnupriya Manipuris in Freedom and other Movements*, Puspa Publications, 2020.
3. Dr. Kali Prasad Sinha, *The Bishnupriya Manipuri Language*, Firma KLM Pvt Ltd, 1960.
4. George A. Grierson, *Linguistic Survey of India* Vol V, 1903, Motilal Banarsidass, 1967-68, Digital Library of India.
5. Raj Mohan Nath, *The Background of Assamese Culture*, A.K. Nath, 1948, Digitized by The University of Michigan, 2008.

Chapter 47– Chhatrasal: Defeated Mughals in Many Battles; Reclaimed Bundelkhand

1. Mata Din Trivedi, *Outline of the History of Charkhari State*, Allahabad Law Journal Press, 1927, Digital Library of India
2. Jaswant Lal Mehta, *Advanced Study in the History of Modern India 1707-1813*, Sterling Publishers, 2005.
3. K.K. Kusuman, *A Panorama of Indian Culture: Professor A. Sreedhara Menon Felicitation Volume*, Mittal Publications, 1990.
4. James Grant Duff, *The History of the Mahrattas*, Normanby Press, 2014.
5. Ravindra K. Jain, *Between History and Legend: Status and Power in Bundelkhand*, 2002, Orient Blackswan.

Chapter 48– Bhoja Paramara: Resisted Attacks of Ghaznavid Forces in 11th Century

1. Mahesh Singh, *Bhoja Paramara and His Times*, Bharatiya Vidya Prakashan, 1984, Digital Library of India.
2. P.T. Srinivasa Iyengar, *Bhoja Raja*, J. Jetley, Asian Educational Services, 1931,
3. K.N. Seth, *The Growth of the Paramara Power in Malwa*, Progress Publishers, 1978
4. S.N. Sen, *Ancient Indian History and Civilization*, New Age International, 1999.
5. Pranab Kumar Bhattacharyya, *Historical Geography of Madhya Pradesh from Early Records*, Motilal Banarsidass, 1977.
6. Sheldon Pollock, *The Language of the Gods in the World of Men: Sanskrit, Culture, and Power in Premodern India*, University of California Press, 2003.

Chapter 49– Birsa Munda: Spearheaded Revolt against British in Tribal Regions; Martyred at 24

1. R.R. Prasad, *Encyclopaedic Profile of Indian Tribes*, Volume 1, Discovery Publishing House, 1996.
2. Aditi Chanchani, Kavita Kanan, Mamata Dash, Rosemary Viswanath, Sinduja Ananthkrishnan, Vidya Rangan, *This is Our Homeland,* Equations, 2007.
3. Neeraj, *Birsa Munda*, Ocean Books, 2006.
4. A.K. Dhan, *Birsa Munda*, Publications Division, Ministry of Information & Broadcasting, 2017.
5. Piyush Kamal Sinha, 'The Sardari Larai of the Mundas of Chhotanagpur' in *Proceedings of the Indian History Congress,* Vol. 71 (2010-2011), Indian History Congress.

Chapter 50– Rash Behari Bose: Founded INA in Foreign Lands for the Freedom of India

1. Radhanath Rath, Savitri Prasanna Chatterjee, Rash Behari Basu: *His Struggle*

for India's Independence, Biplabi Mahanayak Rash Behari Basu Smarak Samity, 1959, Digital Library of India.

2. J.G. Ohsawa, *The Two Great Indians in Japan: Sri Rash Behari Bose and Netaji Subhas Chandra Bose*, Sri K.C. Das for Kusa Publications, 1954, Digital Library of India.
3. K.K. Ghosh, *The Indian National Army: Second Front of the Indian Independence Movement*, Meenakshi Prakashan, 1969, Digital Library of India.
4. Uma Mukherjee, *Two Great Indian Revolutionaries: Rash Behari Bose & Jyotindra Nath Mukherjee*, Firma KL Mukhopadhyay, 1966, Digital Library of India.

Chapter 51– U. Kiang Nangbah: Organized military-style attacks on the British in 1861-62

1. Hamlet Bareh, *The History and Culture of the Khasi People*, 1964, Spectrum Publications, 1985, Digital Library of India
2. Rajiv Gandhi University-Arunachal Pradesh, *History of Northeast India (1228-1947)*, Vikas Publishing House, 2016.
3. Suryya Kumar Bhuyan, *Studies in the History of Assam*, Laksheswari Bhuyan, 1965.

Chapter 52– Harphool Jat: Attacked Slaughterhouses, Released 1,000s of Cows during British Rule

Note: Besides the below-mentioned references, this story of valor is also based on an oral narration by Manoj Mor from Jind where Harphool Jat lived. Manoj Mor has given a detailed narration based on the oral historical folklore on Harphool, passed on from one generation to another.

1. Bhaleram Beniwal, *Jat Yaudhaon Ka Itihas*, Beniwal Publication, 2008.
2. Jaswinder Singh, *Kuka Movement: Freedom Struggle in Punjab*, Atlantic, 1985.

GARUDA PRAKASHAN BOOKS

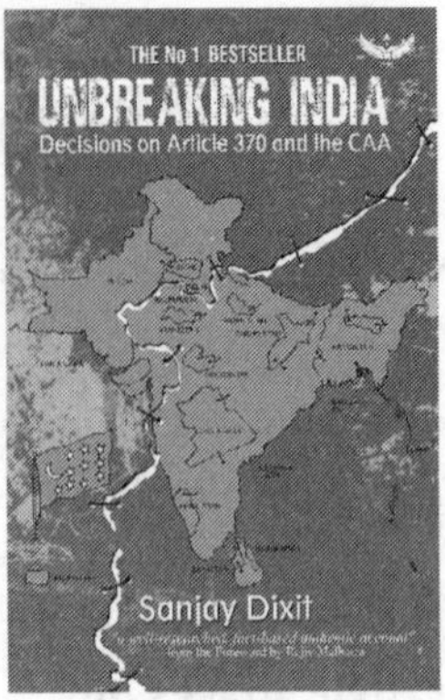

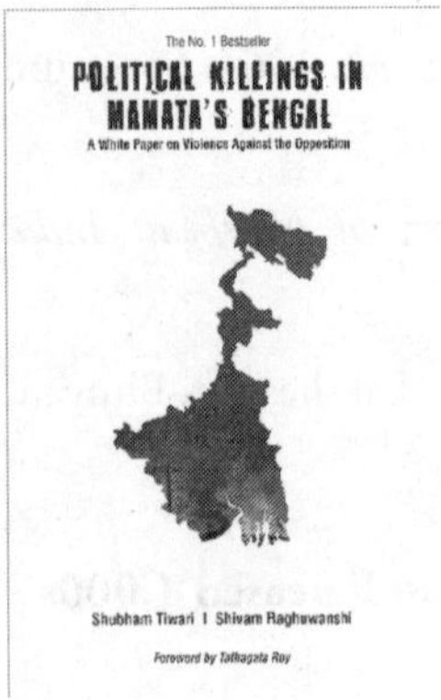

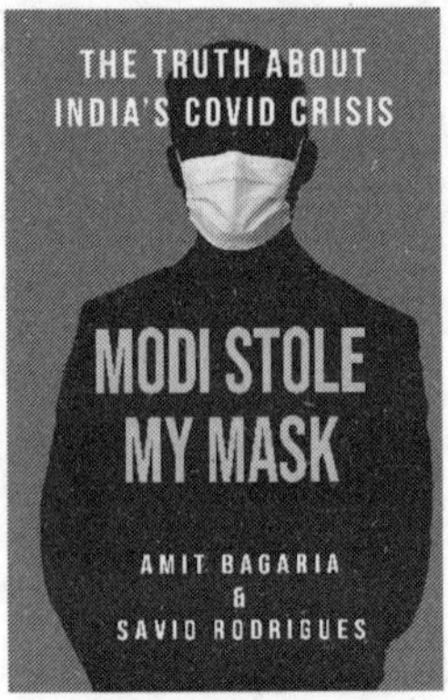

GARUDA PRAKASHAN BOOKS

GARUDA PRAKASHAN BOOKS

गरुड

Register:

Please register your book purchase at **grpr.in/register** to stay in touch and get informed about future books!

To order:

www.garudabooks.com

Follow us:

WEBSITE : **www.garudabooks.com**

FACEBOOK : **www.facebook.com/garudaprakashan/**

TWITTER : **@garudaprakashan**

INSTAGRAM : **@garudabooks**

YOUTUBE : **/garudabooks**

Contact:

EMAIL : **contact@garudabooks.com**

International queries:

EMAIL : **international@garudabooks.com**

About the Author

Manoshi Sinha is the author of several books, including *Saffron Swords I* (co-authored by Yogaditya Singh Rawal). She is the founder of www.myindiamyglory.com, an emagazine that describes Bharat from ancient to present with special focus on Indic history, culture and heritage. Also a blogger, she has interviewed a few freedom fighters.

Together, along with her husband Yogaditya Singh Rawal, a history and fitness blogger, Mr. India 2016 (Federation Cup Body building), an ancient martial art learner and practitioner, Manoshi Sinha has been exploring historical places, ancient and medieval temples, forts and fortresses to unearth information about India's glorious past. Most of the episodes of *Saffron Swords* series are based on the husband-wife duo's research visits across India.